MOSCOW '41

Alexander Werth

Simon Publications
2003

Library of Congress Card Number: 43001139

ISBN: 0-9725189-6-7

Published by Simon Publications, Inc. P. O. Box 910455,
San Diego, CA 92191-0455

Let us earn the gratitude of foreign nations,
and may Europe exclaim in astonishment:
"The Russian warriors are invincible in battle
and exemplary in their generosity and their
peace-time virtues!"

That is a noble aim, worthy of you; let us
achieve it, my brave Russian soldiers.

Kutuzov's Order to the Army,

December 1812

CONTENTS

Moscow War Diary

Introduction

The German invasion of Russia stirred me perhaps more deeply than any event since the war began. June 22nd! Exactly a year had passed since the evening when I landed at Falmouth on board the *Madura*, at the end of that melancholy voyage from Bordeaux. Since then I had lived through the Battle of Britain, and through the grim nights but exhilarating days of the London blitz; but when we learned on June 22nd that Russia had been invaded, it was clear that, for a time, at least, the centre of the world war had shifted to the East. It also became apparent, almost at once, that there was going to be no walk-over for the Germans. (I did not think there would be, and, for that reason, doubted till the last moment that Hitler would attack Russia.) Obviously, a successful, long and extensive Russian resistance would enormously increase our chances to win the war quickly, and, from what one heard, the mood of the Russian people for such a resistance was admirable. The "Second Fatherland War," the "Second 1812"—such were the slogans; and they were more inspiring to the Russian people than any other slogans could be. "For country, honour and freedom," was the official slogan put out by Molotov in his broadcast of June 22nd. The Stalin régime and, with it, the whole Russian people, were rising to fight *our* enemy.

I felt I had to go to Russia. I had spent my childhood and

boyhood years in St. Petersburg; the Russian half of me was clamouring to "go home"—after twenty-four years. I had always kept up my Russian, especially during my years in Paris; I had continued to read Russian books and papers, and had followed as closely as possible the political events of the Soviet Union and whatever was new in Russian thought and literature. Not always with approval, but always with interest. To see Russia again—and in her hour of supreme national trial; how could such a chance be missed?

My personal antecedents—that is, the Liberal bourgeois background of my boyhood in Russia—were none too good from the point of view prevalent in the U.S.S.R. before the adoption of the Stalin Constitution (which, in principle, put an end to discrimination on social grounds); but that was ancient history now, and as a journalist I was not undesirable. Since the Nazi menace had appeared over Europe I had always advocated the closest military collaboration with the Soviet Union. I had never made the mistake of saying that there was "nothing to choose between Hitler and Stalin." I was convinced that if the Litvinov policy failed, it was not the fault of Litvinov, but the fault of Chamberlain and Bonnet. I was not at all convinced that the Molotov policy that superseded it was a pro-German policy. It was merely the *faute de mieux* of the Litvinov policy. I believe to this day that, of all the great Powers, the U.S.S.R. was, during those years, the only wholehearted supporter of the League of Nations, and that if Litvinov had not been let down by Britain and France this war would probably have been averted.

In 1939 Russia was not able to resist Germany single-handed, and if, after overrunning Poland, the Germans had attacked Russia, is there any reason to believe that the French would have advanced beyond the Warndt Forest, or that the R.A.F. would have dropped anything other than leaflets over Berlin? A large part of France would have been so delighted with the invasion of Russia that it would have exalted the virtues of the "phony" war in the West even more than it did. And we know how certain politicians and business-men in this country would have reacted. Strategically, Russia was justified in occupying Eastern Poland and the Baltic States; by doing so, she merely prevented Germany from taking them over, or using them as a springboard against Russia, as she was going to use Finland in 1941. Nor did I get hysterical over the Russian attack on Finland; and Sir Walter Citrine's raptures over Field-Marshal Mannerheim (who, I knew, had always been a German agent, at least in the wider sense of the word) I found as silly then as I do now. On the other hand, Russia's failure to react more vigorously to the German invasion of the Balkans struck me as a much more shortsighted piece of policy than the pact of August 1939; and the shilly-shallying in which the half-hearted overtures to Yugoslavia were followed, soon after the Balkan collapse, by the expulsion of the Yugoslav and other Allied legations from Moscow and the virtual recognition by Moscow of the Rashid Ali Government of Iraq, savoured of a timid opportunism suggesting the continued existence of a strong appeasement current in the Soviet Union.

At the same time, there is little doubt that, despite Sir Stafford Cripps's efforts, the Soviet Government did not greatly believe in the friendly disposition of the British Government; and so deep were their suspicions that it took a very long time to convince Moscow that the British Government had *not* fallen for Rudolf Hess's offer. The Russians, of course, had their own idea of what that offer contained.

On June 23rd I began to take steps to go to Russia. At first I was not quite sure in what capacity I would go. I tried the War Office and the Foreign Office. Then, out of the blue, came an inquiry from the Foreign Office News Department whether I would go to Russia as Reuter's "special correspondent" (whatever exactly that meant). I had never worked for an agency before, and should have preferred to go out for a newspaper—but I was told that that was impossible. The transport possibilities, I was told, were so restricted that it would have to be Reuter's or nothing. Perhaps, if I had had more patience, I would have got out to Russia a week or so later, as the correspondent of one, or both, of the papers with which I had been connected for years—just as Philip Jordan did for the *News Chronicle*. However, I got Reuter's to agree that I continue to work from Moscow for the *Sunday Times*. I wish to record my deep appreciation to Lord Kemsley and the *Sunday Times* for their continuously helpful and encouraging attitude.

Some days after my acceptance of the Reuter offer Mr. Maisky handed me my passport with a Soviet visa freshly stamped on it and signed in his own hand. It was July 1st, a lovely summer evening. I walked down Kensington Palace Gardens feeling strangely elated, and just slightly wondering what I was letting myself in for.

At this fatal hour of Russia's history I wanted to see Russian faces, and hear Russian speech. A grim tragedy, affecting the lives of millions and millions of Russian people, had begun. I had seen the effects of the *Blitzkrieg* in France; I knew what it meant to individual human beings. This war brought me emotionally nearer to Russia than I had been for years. The moment was too grave for sentimental boyhood reminiscences; the important thing was to see how, for their own sakes, and for the sake of the world in general, the Russian people would resist Hitler.

And yet, during those last days in London, there were moments when I could think of nothing but my boyhood in St. Petersburg. . . . It was strange that my very earliest childhood memory should have related to war—to the Russo-Japanese War. I was three and a half when I saw a large troop train, crowded with shouting soldiers with shaved heads, steam out of the railway station at Peterhof. . . .

Another, almost equally early childhood memory was this:

One winter day, when I was four, I was in the Panteleimonskaya Street with Miss Kelly, my old, fat, English nurse, who had been taking care of me since my mother's death, when I saw people running and shouting and several Cossacks galloping past; an old lady, who was just then driving past in an old-fashioned shiny black *kareta*, told the coachman to stop, and Miss Kelly lifted me into the carriage, which, I suppose, took us home. Miss Kelly, of course, told me that the first lot of people who ran and shouted were nasty people, and that the Cossacks were nice people. That is all I remember of the 1905 Revolution.

My boyhood was that of any child of the small but increasingly important liberal, industrial bourgeoisie of Russia. My father was a *kadet*, a member of the Liberal Party, which had emerged from the 1905 Revolution, and so also was his brother, the St. Petersburg barrister. My father's people, who had moved from the Baltic provinces to St. Petersburg in the early years of last century and had become completely Russified, though they still nominally belonged to the Lutheran Church, did not, however, rise to economic prosperity until the Russian industrial revolution of the '80's and '90's. In the eyes of my father, Witte was a very great man, the man who was going to turn Russia into a second America. He was also personally indebted to Witte. For it was Witte who in 1895 sent him on a special job to China. He stayed there for five years, with cosmopolitan Shanghai as his headquarters, working on the building of the famous Chinese Eastern Railway. Later, when he returned to Russia, he concentrated his energies on the development of the Donbass coal industry. For years he worked in close co-operation with his chairman, the famous Nikolai Stepanovich Avdakov, the leading mining engineer of the Donetz Basin. Later still, he extended his activities to the development of the almost untapped industrial resources of the Urals, and became a director of the Bogoslovsky Engineering Works. Looking back, it has often given me some satisfaction to think that, although my father was a *burzhui*, he was at least a constructive *burzhui* and one who could rank as one of the pioneers of Russia's great industrial development. . . . Had he not, after all, contributed something to laying the foundations of Russia's present industrial strength?

When I was fourteen, my father took me with him on one of his frequent trips to the Donbass. I was taken down a coalpit in a large lift that travelled very fast and very far down. It was all very modern and efficient and impressive. I did not like the look on the miners' faces, though. They were not friendly. They were getting reasonable wages, for skilled labour was at a premium in war-time, but they already had their own ideas about capitalism. . . .

But I think I can honestly say that I have never borne the Soviets a grudge for having taken away from me those collieries, which I, at any rate, had done nothing to build up. They had, however, helped to provide me with a pleasant boyhood. And I also remember that night in May 1915 when we stayed in a small country house, a mile or two from the collieries—it was the manager's house. The manager was a sly-faced little ginger-haired man called Login Ignatievich, a self-made man, who had started life as a miner. There was a garden round the house, and the nightingales sang as I have never heard them sing either before or since. . . .

But life in St. Petersburg is what I remember best, and also the country life in summer on the big *datcha* on the hill overlooking the Gulf of Finland and the naval base of Kronstadt. In the summer of 1914 I saw a British squadron, and later a French squadron, with M. Poincaré on board, steaming into Kronstadt. There were eighty acres of forest behind the *datcha*, mostly birches and fir trees, and we had two or three cows and a large number of hens; an old man and his wife looked after this livestock. In winter we would go shooting hares in the wood behind the *datcha,* and those winter week-ends in the country were very pleasant. What could be more satisfying than to go skiing through the woods on a sunny winter day, and to come back to the *datcha* and get warm in front of a huge log fire? And it only took an hour by train and another hour by sleigh to get there from St. Petersburg. . . .

I loved St. Petersburg, and the Summer Garden with its centenarian lime trees, and the little house of Peter the Great, and the alley of Greek gods and goddesses with their chipped noses (in winter they used to build little wooden huts round the gods and goddesses), and the majestic sweep of the Neva, with the lofty, graceful spire of the Fortress silhouetted against the "white" summer night. I remember the smells and the sounds of St. Petersburg; the clatter of trotting hoofs on the wooden pavements of the Mokhovaia; it was the first sound you heard when you woke in the morning; the jam of horse traffic in the Simeonovskaya, with the carters—the *lomovyie*— swearing obscenely at their horses and at their fellow carters; and I can still smell the hot tar of the road-mending squads in midsummer. The town was then half-deserted, and in the houses pictures and furniture were covered, and carpets were rolled up, and everything smelt of camphor.

When I was nine I began to read the Russian poets; Lermontov first, then Pushkin; and then there came years of intensive reading—Gogol and Tolstoy—I was thirteen, and was in bed with measles, when I first read through *War and Peace*—and Turgeniev, and Goncharov, and Dostoevsky, and Nekrasov, and Leskov, and a little later Gorki and the other moderns; and, of course, a quantity of French and English books as well. There was a good library in the house. Petersburg became like a living illustration to these Russian books. After school I would walk along the Neva Embankment and go up to Peter's great equestrian statue, and recite to myself those Pushkin lines from *The Bronze Horseman,* which to this day I find so thrilling:

> Bezhít, i slýshet za soboí
> Kak búdto gróma grokhotánie,
> Tyazhélo-zvónkoie skakánie
> Po potresénnoi mostovoí. . . .
> I ozaryón lunóyu blédnoi,
> Prostérshi rúku v' vyshynié
> Za ním nesétsa vsádnik médnyi
> Na zvónko skáchustchem koné.

Every bit of St. Petersburg had its literary associations. For instance, on my way to the Yussupov Garden, with its skating pond, I would pass in a tram through the noisy, busy, vociferous Sennaya—the scene of *Crime and Punishment.* In an attic, in one of these dismal side-streets, Raskolnikov might still be brooding; or in one of the crowded *traktiry* (barrooms), with the drunks round the billiard-table, strange conversations might still be going on between Raskolnikov and the immortal Marmeladov, the drunken, dignified down-and-out.

In all this reading, Uncle Petya was my mentor. He was an enthusiast, a real Russian intellectual, and Left-wing in his ideas, though easy-going in his life. As an undergraduate he had had some trouble with the police, and was very proud of it. He had taken part in some political demonstration against the Government and had been locked up for two days. Uncle Petya did ten times more for my literary education than my school did. It was rather a dreary school, and all it taught me fairly well was French. The Greek and Latin I learned there I soon forgot; though I shall always think kindly of my Greek teacher, Erich Feodorovich von Voss, who had a sense of beauty and made his lessons on the *Odyssey* truly inspiring. He is one of the few Germans I have met in my life who was really a civilized human being. In commenting on Homer, he would read out bits of Schopenhauer: *"Die meerumrauschten Seiten der Odyssee . . .* a wonderful phrase," he would say, and pause dramatically.

It was strange, when I come to think of it, to have devoted so much time to reading, grinding over Latin and Greek, and going to theatres and concerts, and practising the piano, while the Great War was in full progress, and millions of Russian soldiers were losing their lives, or rotting away in trenches. But the war affected the life of the capital very little. The front was far away; and although there were many refugees in the town, and many military hospitals—including one in the building of my school—it had little effect on ordinary life. We were, of course, upset by the disaster of the Masurian Lakes, and we rejoiced over the great Brussilov offensive, and towards the middle of 1916 my father's Liberal friends who came to the house talked grimly of Rasputin and Stürmer and Protopopov and the other Fifth Columnists, as we should call them now. And Naum, a young chauffeur of ours (for we owned one of the two thousand cars of St. Petersburg), who had been called up at the beginning of the war, kept writing me, in an illiterate hand, increasingly plaintive and angry letters, first from the trenches, then from a hospital, and then again from the trenches; and he wrote openly about the lack of ammunition, the bad food, and the general mismanagement. One day he came to Petrograd on leave, and he talked even more angrily about it all than he had written.

But Petrograd continued to be a city of light and glamour, the theatre-goer's and the music-lover's paradise. It was the city of the Alexandrinka and of the Mariinsky Theatre. When I was twelve I started going regularly to the Alexandrinka matinées. Those were no longer its greatest days: Varlamov and Savina and Kommisarzhevskaya were dead; but I still had the luck to see the great Davydov as Gogol's Revisor and as Famusov in *Gore ot Uma* (*The Misfortune of Being Clever*). And Yuryev, the new rising star, played Chadsky in that great play. I also saw there one or two of the Shaw plays. At the Mariinsky and at the newly-built Musykalnaya Drama I saw many operas, but more particularly the great Russian operas of Rimsky-Korsakov and Mussorgsky and Borodin and Tchaikovsky. *Onegin* and the *Queen of Spades* I must have seen half a dozen times. The war had saved me from Wagner, and all the Wagner I had seen was a *Lohengrin* just before the war. However, we got some Wagner thrown in at symphony concerts.

But the real craze of the Petrograd musical world during the war was Scriabin. We young people used to regard him as a super-super Beethoven; and when we heard Koussevitzky conduct the *Poème de l'Extase*, we thought we had been present at one of the greatest events in the musical history of all time. I used to dash to concerts with young Volodya Evdokimov and his father, Vassili Petrovich, who was himself a highly accomplished musician and had studied the 'cello under Verzhbilovich. He was a Bach-worshipper, and was also a great connoisseur of Russian music. He was very proud of his acquaintance with Rimsky-Korsakov during the last years of the composer's life. And he used to say: "Rimsky-Korsakov was like Bach: he was a very hard worker, and very methodical. He looked upon music as a job of work. There was no romantic nonsense about him—no muses and mistresses and moments of 'inspiration.' " In his house on the Moika Embankment he had delightful evenings of chamber music, which I was allowed to attend. It was a proud moment in my life when in that select company I was once allowed to perform a few Grieg pieces I had practised for weeks.

Before the war my father had taken me abroad on several occasions. Twice I had gone to England and Scotland; and another time to Germany, France, Switzerland, and Italy. I

was also taken to Finland, Sweden, and Norway. Travelling
in Europe was considered an essential part of a young lad's
education. When the war came, it was no longer easy to get
abroad; but it was a blessing in disguise, for I was able to see
parts of Russia which I should probably otherwise have missed.
I was taken to the Donbass, and on the way there we stopped
for a couple of days in Moscow (I had already been in Moscow
for two days the year before); and part of the summer of 1915
I spent in the Ukraine, in a small country house in the Gogol
country, near Sorochintsy.

The place belonged to a cousin of my father's. She was
married to an unsuccessful littérateur, Valentin Valentinych
Yakovenko, with a large grey beard and a gentle smile. He
believed in popular education, and had specialized in writing
little scientific pamphlets for popular consumption, and he
had also published an edition of the works of Belinsky. He was
mixed up in some way with the 1905 Revolution. I still remember little Valya, their youngest daughter, aged fourteen;
she was a very pretty little dark-eyed thing, and sang Ukrainian folk-songs most amusingly. That summer I also saw the
Crimea and the Caucasus. Ever since I had opened Lermontov
at the age of nine, I had longed to see the Caucasus. To us
Petersburgers, it was the great land of romance. The Crimea
I found disappointing; but the Caucasus lived up to all my
expectations. At Kislovodsk—it just *would* be Kislovodsk, the
scene of *A Hero of Our Time*!—I fell violently in love with
Murochka Chernova; she was fifteen, with long blond curls,
and very lovely. This first calf-love, with the Caucasian mountains around us, and our minds full of Lermontov, was very
poetic. Absence, however, did not make the heart grow fonder,
and in the winter of 1916 Gassya Nazaryeva took the place of
Murochka. She was fifteen, and played the piano much better
than I did. She and I and a cousin of hers would go for walks
along the Neva at night, and we'd all feel romantic and recite
Pushkin. Murochka, in the meantime, had got engaged to an

army officer; much later I learned that it had all ended very sadly. He fought on the side of the Whites and got killed at Perekop, and Murochka escaped to Yugoslavia with the remnants of the Wrangel Army, and there she married a boorish elderly colonel—the kind of chap who, for all I know, may now be doing little quisling jobs for Hitler. . . .

One night shortly before Christmas 1916 my father came home from his office and said to me: "They have killed him." "Killed whom?—Nicholas?" "No, not Nicholas, but Rasputin." He looked pleased and phoned the news to several friends. And then, after two uneasy months, the Revolution started in the streets of Petrograd. The Rasputin business had turned us young Liberals into great revolutionaries. We shared in the joy and elation of the crowds in the streets. We lived opposite the house of Goremykin, the gaga Prime Minister of the last Tsarist Government. One day in early March—the melting ice was dripping from the water-pipes—a crowd gathered outside Goremykin's house and proceeded to ram the heavy oak door with a large plank. I joined in the battering process, and the door finally gave way. The people were, so they said, in search of sharpshooters on the roof of the house. None were found, however, and the crowd withdrew, without any looting. . . . I read, and, with a certain historical sense of perspective, even collected, as many as possible of the hundred and one newspapers that were published in Petrograd during those days of "perfect democracy." If anybody still has my newspaper file of 1917 he will find there the first issues of *Pravda* and *Izvestia.*

One day I learned that Lenin had arrived "in a sealed German railway car." We were prejudiced against Lenin, chiefly for that reason. But that did not prevent me from going to hear him. I went with Gassya and somebody else—I forget who. We didn't get very near the Kshesinsky Palace, but we saw somebody who looked like Lenin talking from a platform.

There was much shouting and cheering.

In the summer of 1917 my father decided to go to England, with which he had had many contacts since the China days. He decided to take me with him—to that *other* country of mine which I knew so little. I thought I was going away for only a few months. I stayed away for twenty-four years. Sometimes, in later years, I wondered if I would have gone had the decision rested with me. . . .

With my Liberal upbringing I was anti-Bolshevik at first, but in the early '20's I became increasingly interested in what was happening in Russia. I began to subscribe to Soviet magazines and newspapers. I was stirred by the revolutionary romanticism of Babel's *Konarmia* and of Vsevolod Ivanov's *Armoured Train, No. 26.* I translated into English some of the new works of Soviet fiction. I was revolted by the cruelties of the régime, but tried to understand the whys and wherefores. I felt that the end of Trotskyism in Russia was a healthy sign, and the complete changes made by Stalin in the teaching of Russian history in schools struck me as something profoundly significant. I disliked ignorant pro-Bolsheviks as much as I disliked uncritical anti-Bolsheviks.

I fully supported the Litvinov policy of collective security; and although I found the Stalin-Ribbentrop agreement of August 1939 disturbing, I could not help feeling some satisfaction at the thought of "the Russians on the Carpathians," and saw no serious objection to their occupation of the Baltic States and none at all to their occupation of Bessarabia.

So I went to Russia with an open mind, but, at heart, rejoicing at the thought that my first country and my second country were allies.

The diary form of this book calls for a few words of explanation. It is not the verbatim text of my diary as I wrote it in Moscow. But those seven little notebooks contain all the gist of this book. The conversations, the political reflections, the reactions in Moscow to this or that piece of war news, and the ordinary everyday experiences were usually jotted down briefly and untidily, and no publisher in his senses would have accepted the book in that form.

In rewriting the diary I, naturally, refrained from such easy tricks as the insertion of "true prophecies" which weren't made at the time; and the reactions (sometimes quite erroneous) which I record are those which I felt or observed in Moscow on the particular date at the head of the entry. Several of the entries which I was able to make at leisure—for instance, on the flight out, or during those long hours in air-raid shelters —are printed here just as they appeared in the diary. For the rest, it was a case of giving a more coherent and, I hope, readable form to my day-to-day notes.

I preserved the diary form because I believe it gives a more direct impression of Moscow at different moments of the war and makes the book correspond more accurately than it would in any other form with what I actually saw, heard, felt, and noted down. A few names have been changed; one or two conversations—but only one or two—have been "synthetized"; and a number of descriptive passages, which I did not have time to write just then, have been added. Does it matter if one describes a road or a piece of country a few hours or a few weeks later?

For obvious reasons, I omitted all private conversations with public men in high authority, whether Russian or British, notably with Sir Stafford Cripps. This I regret, for Sir Stafford's constant faith in Russia, even at dark moments, and his proper appreciation of her great role in this war, rendered his conversations stimulating and encouraging; and his reasoned optimism has been justified by the events of this winter.

I hope my American friends will bear me no ill will for a few references to what appeared to us, last summer, as the insufficient share the United States was taking in the common war effort. Those lines were written in Moscow, at a time when the outlook for the anti-Axis powers was none too bright; and it was natural to complain that America was not yet taking the war sufficiently seriously, to note (from what many Americans themselves said) that "only half America was in this war"; and to resent the "aren't-we-neutrals" attitude of a few individual American citizens. These people were just what, in the past, the "appeasers" were in this country; people who had to be taught by events that Roosevelt was right—just as in this country many had to learn from experience that Churchill was right—and had been right for years.

I am returning to Russia shortly.

A. W.

LONDON, *January* 1942.

PART I

JULY

Thursday, *July 3. On the plane going north*

Off at last. These last two days in London were very trying. I could hardly sleep the night before last, and was feeling rather demoralized all yesterday. The thought of leaving London had suddenly become hateful to me, and people were irritating me with the same wisecracks: "You'd better hurry up, or Hitler will get there first." Or, "You'll be able to write *The Last Days of Moscow*." Actually, the Germans seem already to have overrun most of the Russian "reconquered" territories—Lithuania, Latvia, eastern Poland—and are getting near Minsk, inside Russia proper. But Moscow—that's still some way to go.

What made matters worse was yesterday morning's false start. When I got to the Home Office, where the party were starting from, I learned that there was a hitch. Two elderly colonels were there, one of them carrying a stirrup-pump. They are members of the Military Mission. One is going out as a fire-fighting expert, the other as an expert on shelters. We were told to come back at ten o'clock, but learned, on doing so, that the flight had been cancelled; no reason given. A bit of me rejoiced at the thought that the whole thing might be called off; though it could, obviously, be completely called off only if the Russians were already about to collapse. What a price to pay for the pleasure of staying on in London!

Looking at St. Paul's from the top floor of the Reuter building, and at the shell of St. Bride's, just at the back of it, gave me a pang of regret. And in the afternoon I walked along the Thames Embankment and through the ruins of the Temple, which I had seen disintegrate and go up in flames during all those blitz nights. I went to bed early, but couldn't sleep at first, and then, when I did, I was wakened at three in the morning by a phone call. "This is Squadron Leader X speaking. Will you please be at the Home Office at ten o'clock this morning? You aren't *cross* being wakened at this hour, are you? I am most frightfully sorry." He sounded an unusually pleasant person. . . . In the morning I was no longer looking back, but ahead. It was a sunny morning in Fleet Street. The platinum-blonde lift girl—old Rutter's daughter—was standing outside the *Guardian* building. I remembered old Rutter; what a grand old boy he was on the *Guardian* roof that night of the big blitz on May 10th! Little Johnnie, to whom I had given two bob yesterday as a farewell gift, wasn't sitting outside Mitre Court yet with his *Evening Standards*; too early. The buses, bright red in the morning sun, were running along Fleet Street. I took a taxi outside St. Dunstan's and went down the Strand to the Home Office. My two colonels were already there, luggage, stirrup-pump and all. The stirrup-pump colonel, Symonds by name, turned out to be a Home Office official; he was actually the inventor of the stirrup-pump, and the pump he was carrying was the *millionth* pump manufactured. He was taking it to Moscow to demonstrate it to the Russians. I wondered if the Russians, who through the Ossoaviakhim had practised A.R.P. and anti-gas precautions for years, had not invented something on the same lines already. But, after all, we had the *real* experience. In fact, it makes one quite proud to go out there as one who's gone through a year of London blitz! Outside the Home Office I ran into Ellen Wilkinson, the Labour M.P., who thought my trip a good idea. She offered to give me a complete collection of A.R.P. pamphlets to take to Moscow, but with luggage limited to fifty pounds, including typewriter, I said I'd rather not, and, anyway, there were these two A.R.P. experts going. The second one, round and cheery, is called Colonel Croad, and is an expert on shelters.

There wasn't enough room in the R.A.F. car, so I had to follow it to the airfield in a taxi. The driver, who must have been about seventy, and was a typical London cabby to look at, raced behind the swift R.A.F. car with great gusto. Up Regent Street, and then farther north. There were few formalities at the airfield. What an enormous place it is! No wonder it's difficult to knock out an aerodrome. . . . Only I hope we've taken all the necessary precautions against parachutists and glider troops.

The luggage was weighed, and they weren't as fussy about my four or five pounds excess as I thought they might be. . . .

And now we are flying due north. The other passengers are members of the Military Mission—second batch. The first, with General McFarlane, left for Russia a few days ago. Three hours flying to X, I'm told.

First, a stretch of monotonous fields. We are flying at about 2,000 ft.; then, as it gets bumpier, we go up higher. 1½ hours away from London, we fly over an industrial area; it must be Yorkshire. And then, with the clouds gathering, we climb up to 7,000 ft. It is sunny here, and no longer bumpy.

Now the great adventure has started. Gone the drudgery of daily visits to the M. of I. and of messing about with diplomatic and second-hand French news. Instead, Russia! At the *Guardian* office I yesterday saw old Sir Bernard Pares. He thought my going to Russia was a grand idea. "It's a genuine *national* war," he said enthusiastically. "Watch out for the German eyewitnesses' accounts of the war in Russia; very interesting is the implication of those I have already seen, that this is the first *real* war the German Army has yet had to face."

We flew over a large stretch of water; I thought for a moment it was the Firth of Forth, but of course it couldn't be. Somebody said it was the Humber. After a while we were back over land again. And then once more it became very cloudy, and through the gaps in the clouds I could see a rugged coast, with wide stretches of sand, and then, suddenly, I caught a glimpse of the Tay Bridge! Then more clouds. It was odd to think that, at this very moment, I might be flying 7,000 ft. above B., and that my daughter was playing in the garden, completely unaware of my presence in the "airyplane" whose engines she was perhaps able to hear! And then, with the clouds clearing, we flew over the Grampians, and the colour of the landscape was a sterile, dark brown, slightly greenish. We flew over a deep glen, with a river, but no signs of human habitation. And then it was all faded out again by the milky clouds. . . .

SATURDAY, *July 5. Somewhere over the sea*

I have never before been as far north as this. We are flying low. Nothing to be seen except water and clouds. It is very cold, but I haven't seen any icebergs. For some minutes now I've been watching two of the R.A.F. lads. There's a crew of five, and five or six passengers. I find these boys fascinating. What is that little wrinkle between their eyes—even in the youngest of faces? They can't be more than twenty or twenty-two. They would look so ordinary in ordinary life. One might, for all one knows, do well as an office boy in a bank; the other, with his pink cheeks and slightly prominent teeth, might be a sort of suburban beau. But there is something unusual about their faces. I can't explain it; but I am sure artists have noticed it. The nearness of death—is that it?—transfigures the most ordinary faces. They looked quite ordinary while on land. Leather helmet, earphones, round the little suburbanite's head. He is tired, and dozes. . . . It is 12.30. We've been flying for nearly ten hours. There are only four bunks in the plane, and one is crammed with luggage. I slept for five hours —more than my share, I fear. Why did nobody waken me? And why should the R.A.F. boys have the trouble of having to cook breakfast for me on a little electric heater, or for the colonels, or for anybody else, for that matter?

It's grey, grey, grey, this northern seascape. I wish I could see a polar bear. It's all rather fantastic. Yesterday afternoon we were still having a Scottish tea at the Royal Hotel at Z, with scones and pancakes, and with a lot of elderly buddies at the other tables. Rather an anticlimax to have had to wait there for several hours till the plane got ready to take off. Or, rather, we were waiting for somebody from Glasgow to join the party. At one o'clock this morning it was like early evening, almost like daylight. . . .

The plumbing arrangements on this plane are odd. A rubber tube—inevitably for gentlemen only. And then a kind of tub with a green lid, with, beside it, a roll of toilet paper, and that in the midst of wireless apparatus and Bren guns and the other elaborate scientific contraptions in the "bubble." Before we started on this big hop, we were given teddy-bear coats, and leather caps, and high fur-lined snow boots and huge fur gloves. A dinghy took us to the plane. It was choppy, and a cold wind was blowing.

At least two members of the party can talk Russian. One is a Wing Commander, who had spent part of his boyhood in St. Petersburg. We reminisced about various streets in the place. He revisited Leningrad in some official capacity a couple of years ago. The other Russian-speaking member is a young N.C.O., who told me (in Russian) that he spoke Russian "absolutely perfectly," though he had never been in Russia, and had learned it from a governess. It was, in fact, surprisingly good, though not perhaps as perfect as the governess had told him it was.

My hands are numb with cold. Wish I had brought my warm

overcoat with me; but it was so hot in London yesterday morning, it seemed silly.

Pity the plane is making such a noise; it's difficult to talk to anybody.

One of the bunks was empty and I fell asleep again. I was wakened by the giant pilot—six feet six, and a former London cop—who told me we were over land, and that he'd just caught sight of a herd of reindeer. . . . I looked out. We were flying over a vast country, with small fir trees and birches and lakes and stretches of marshes. For two hours or more we have been flying over this vast expanse of uninhabited country; marshes, and still more marshes, and thousands and thousands of little birches and meagre fir trees. Before long, we shall see men, but so far we have only seen trees. . . . At last two log cabins on the shore of a lake. . . .

Now that I've got here, I feel much better. Before me is the vast expanse of the Soviet Union. We must fight the filthy Germans. We and the Russians are two immense forces which, between us, ought to crush Hitler and all that scum. What does it matter what I liked or disliked about the Soviet régime? . . . It has become warm; I have taken off my teddy-bear suit. In about an hour we shall be there.

Moscow, *July* 6

That evening, as we flew over Archangel, a violent rainstorm battered against the mica bubble. Down below we could see miles of timber yards. Colonel Symonds, the A.R.P. expert, remarked that the timber was well stacked, according to all the A.R.P. rules; that is, with wide spaces in between. Through sheets of rain we could see the wide stretch of Archangel harbour, with its timber yards. Impressive; but was the harbour really well equipped for anything else? And where, if anywhere, could the timber be exported now, and had it

been exported since the German occupation of Norway? In
the town, near the waterfront, was one large but obviously
derelict church, and a number of large new Government buildings. But there were very few ships in the harbour. Was the
timber being stacked here with nowhere to go? . . . At
length, three small Russian seaplanes piloted us several miles
up the river. The trees, on the high sandy banks of the river,
looked much larger than farther north. At last we came down;
a motor-launch came up to us, and I heard the first Russian
speech. It was odd. They took us, not ashore, but to a kind of
large houseboat, the *Krasnaya Zvezda*. The steward, a kindly
little muzhik, showed us to the cabins. "This way, please; just
make yourselves at home, *pozhálte, pozhálte, gde ugodno.*"
He was exuberant, as though his dearest friends had arrived.
We were then conducted to the dining-room, where a sumptuous table had been laid. Here was an array of *zakuski*—caviar
and smoked salmon, and jellied fish, and cucumber and tomato
salads, and large dishes of butter with a big flower of butter
on top. And bottles, all the way down the table. . . . Two
pretty waitresses, both with alluring figures under their thin
white cotton blouses. . . . Our hosts were a colonel and two
majors, and as the meal progressed, other army men continued to arrive. Later a mysterious brunette arrived; she talked
moderately good English. The colonel and the two majors,
who knew none, were however very genuine fellows, exuberant in their manner, especially towards the end of the evening
(by this, I mean two or three a.m.), and eagerly interested in
Britain. I had to do a lot of interpreting. After the *zakuski*
came a variety of cooked dishes—which I cannot even remember—and sweets and fruit and coffee; and the vodka and the
brandy were followed by Soviet champagne. The conversation is hard to remember, except that both the colonel and one
of the majors showed an extraordinary interest in Rudolf
Hess's visit to England. They seemed, in fact, rather worried
about it. Now, they said, was I really *absolutely* sure he had

been "turned down"? They also inquired about America's intentions; perhaps I was a little indiscreet in suggesting America wasn't doing nearly enough for winning this war. Clearly, they were not quite sure yet of Britain's disposition towards the Soviet Union. We must work hard to break this ice. . . .

One of the majors assured me that Moscow's defences were such that it would probably *never* be bombed, and the same was true of Leningrad.

Outside, it had been a "white night" throughout, almost as bright as daylight. The fir trees on the steep sandy bank of the river looked so calm. . . . There were lots of mosquitoes about, and they kept on biting my feet mercilessly. At three, we decided to turn in, to snatch just a couple of hours' sleep. At six, we were taken in motor-boats some distance up the river, and then by car to the aerodrome. And so, for the first time, as somebody remarked, we stepped on to Russian soil. The sun was already high in the sky. Blades of grass and wild flowers were swept by the wind as we walked along to the plane.

It was a luxurious giant Douglas, with armchairs and settees and a large table in the middle, and bottles of *narzan* [1]— very thoughtful of them, after the night's entertainment! And then, for three or four hours, we flew over what was one big, interminable forest. There were one or two small towns on the way; then, at Rybinsk, we crossed the Volga; and finally, after flying over some more thickly populated country, we reached the outskirts of Moscow. Colonel Grier, the Military Attaché, had come out to meet the party. The Mission members were going to the "Yugoslavsky"—that is, the Yugoslav Legation, which had been vacant since the expulsion of the Minister and his staff; while Colonel Grier, the Military Attaché, obligingly dropped me at the Metropole. I wasn't really taking anything in. The whole journey, with the vodka night at Archangel on

[1] The famous Caucasian mineral water, rather like Perrier.

top of it, did not make for good perception or vivid reactions, and Moscow made little impression on me that first day. At the Metropole, with its hideous "style moderne," reminiscent of some of the worst architectural atrocities of 1900 Paris (the place, I later learned, had been built by a French chef), struck me as a gloomy and dismal haunt. "Intourist" was written all over it, above the bookstall, with works of Lenin in English, and on the doors of the inquiry office; and when I talked Russian to the thin, dark, tight-lipped dame behind the reception desk, and produced my passport, she immediately turned to page 2, and said: "Hm . . . born St. Petersburg, February 4, 1901." I immediately felt a suspect; and then the dark dame had a consultation with a plump blonde, and they said they would keep my passport for registration, and I was taken down a gloomy passage and shown into a room with a rather shabby bathroom attached. The plush furniture was old-fashioned, and must have been there long before the Revolution, and the bath-plug didn't fit. However, unlike Sir Walter Citrine, I decided not to attach any great symbolic significance to that fact. Later I went downstairs, to the Intourist Inquiry Office, with the busts of Lenin and Stalin, and with large photographs of Moscow and Leningrad and the Crimea, still with German captions, and I was glad to get my passport back. I hadn't a penny of Russian money, and, finding that the British Embassy was not too far away, I decided to walk there. It turned out to be a good half-hour's walk—the first stretch along the north side of the Kremlin—and it was infernally hot in the sun. When I asked the way, I was told to take the subway to the Arbat, or a tram-car, but I said I was going to walk, which puzzled at least one young fellow in a white shirt and canvas *kartuz*, who said: "Well, it's your lookout." He may also have been puzzled by my tweed jacket, especially in that weather; though there was nothing to show I was being taken for a foreigner. So my Russian was still O.K.! I saw Cripps, who did not sound too hopeful about an improvement

in the conditions for newspaper work in Moscow; but he
seemed fairly optimistic otherwise. I phoned Lovell, Reuter's
resident correspondent, telling him I was in a fix about money,
and he soon came down in the car, and we drove to the Reuter
flat, in the Khokhlovsky Lane, off the famous "A" Ring of
Moscow boulevards. The streets were very crowded, and the
pedestrians seemed careless about cars; we passed several lots
of soldiers marching along and singing. At the far end of the
Khokhlovsky was a dilapidated old church, with the cross on
top of it untidily broken off; and outside was a crowd of people—mostly middle-aged men—carrying bundles. Lovell said
they were enlisting for the *opolchenie* (roughly, the Russian
Home Guard). The maid was a rather grumpy-looking old
Volga German woman, who did not seem in the least pleased
to see a new arrival. Just before we sat down to lunch there
was an air-raid warning, and women and children and also
men were seen running to the shelters; in no time the street
was completely empty except for one or two soldiers and militiamen in their blue and red caps. Lovell said that when the
warning sounded, everybody was driven into shelters, though
not a single bomb had yet been dropped on Moscow. He
thought some of the warnings were merely intended for A.R.P.
practice—so that people should know what to do when there
really was a raid. After lunch Lucien P. came in, a tall, jovial,
baby-faced Frenchman with goggles. He had been one of the
Havas men in Moscow for some years, but had now joined
the Free French after some conscientious scruples. He said the
Vichy Embassy, with Gaston Bergery, the Ambassador, were
being turned out of Russia. Lovell very kindly suggested that
I move my things from the Metropole to this flat—even at the
risk of giving Katya, the Volga German maid, a fit. At night
we went to see Cholerton, of the *Daily Telegraph*. With his
little black beard and exuberant manner he looks like an old-
fashioned Russian intellectual; and though, that evening, he
abused everybody and everything, he obviously loves this

country dearly. I gave him my note of introduction from Hadley, of the *Sunday Times*. His flat, at the top of an old five-storey building, was so severely blacked out, and so poorly lighted, that I could get only a faint idea of what the place looked like. But it had a lot of books, and seemed to have been inhabited for a long time.

Along the dark streets, in the absolute black-out of Moscow, we drove back, and Lovell dropped me at the Metropole. There I discovered that three of the British N.C.O.'s who had arrived this morning—including the "perfect-Russian-speaking" little fellow (Nares is his name, I think)—had been dumped at the Metropole. I went up to their room. They were still excited over their unfortunate adventure this morning. From the aerodrome they went into Moscow in a lorry, together with the Mission's luggage. But at a street corner they were stopped by the police, and, puzzled by the unfamiliar British uniforms, a crowd had gathered round them, and somebody said "parachutists," and the crowd grew angry and vociferous, and the three N.C.O.'s were taken off to a police station. In the end somebody from the Embassy had to come and rescue them. Clearly, with hardly any foreign contacts for years, the Russians are morbidly suspicious of anything foreign. And little Nares said that the fact that he talked Russian fairly well (he no longer said "perfectly") had only made matters worse. . . .

This story wasn't exactly a happy ending to my first day in Moscow. However, that wasn't quite the ending yet. I went to bed feeling tired and in a bad humour; and no sooner had I put out the dim light on the bed-table than an air-raid warning sounded. A few minutes later, the old *korridornyi* banged on all the doors, including mine, shouting: "*Trevoga, trevoga*"— "You've got to go down to the shelter." I answered something inarticulate, and he went away and didn't bother me any more. I could hear no noises except some hurried steps in the corridor and a few cars dashing past at break-neck speed. I turned over a corner of the black-out curtain and looked out on to the big square in front of the hotel. It seemed completely deserted. Nothing happened, and I went to sleep.

SUNDAY, *July* 6

My second day in Moscow was a distinct improvement on the first. For one thing, I was glad to get out of the Metropole. Lovell had said he would send the car for me at ten o'clock. Before that and after settling my hotel bill, which came to fifty roubles, I went for a stroll down the Theatralny Proyezd, the wide avenue running east from the Sverdlov Square. On the other side of this square, facing the Metropole, is the Opera House, the Bolshoi Theatre. I looked at the bookstalls outside the Metropole, and bought some cigarettes for 3 roubles 15 for 25—not dear, but not very good either. Will I have to get used to them? These long cardboard tubes seem an awful waste of cardboard and space.

Misha, Lovell's ape-like chauffeur, took me down to the office. There were no messages for me except an invitation to dinner from Cripps. There was really nothing to do, and I went out to have a look at the Moscow streets. Moscow is a most confusing town, with its river and its semicircular lines of boulevards as the only guidance. All the other streets seem just a tangle. I walked down the Maroseika, a shabby street composed mostly of old two- and three-storey stucco houses— built around 1860 or so, I should think. I walked into a big food shop, and was surprised at the enormous display of sweets and *pastila* and *marmelad*—*pâtes de fruit* they used to call them in France. I bought half a pound of pink *pastila* (schoolday memories!) for four roubles.[1] There seems no food shortage of any kind in Moscow; it's very much better than I had

[1] In the old days the same would probably have cost 30 or 40 kopeks; but wages and prices have all changed; and many other factors have to be considered, such as privileges and payments in kind to certain classes of workers and officials. Roughly speaking, it seems that a rouble now is worth about one-tenth of its pre-last-war value; but some things are correspondingly

expected, and in the food shop people were buying everything freely, and without any coupons. But they've got an odd system of paying; they pay first, after finding out what their purchase costs, and then hand the receipt over the counter. The cash register was an old contraption, obviously pre-last-war, with the name of the makers spelt according to the pre-1917 spelling. In the Maroseika I took a crowded tram-car down to the Skvoretsky Bridge—the one opposite the St. Basil Church, a riot of colour on that sunny morning. Crossing the bridge, I walked down the Ordynka, one of the old streets of the Zamoskvorechie—the part of Moscow on the other side of the Moscow River, immortalized by Ostrovsky in his 1850 comedies about the old Moscow merchants. In their summer clothes the young people of Moscow looked anything but shabby. Most of the girls wore white blouses, and the men yellow, or white or blue "sport" shirts with open necks, or buttoned-up shirts with embroidered collars. Although there was little talking going on about the war, there was a confident, determined look on all faces. The posters on the walls were being eagerly read—and there were certainly plenty of posters! A Russian tank crushing a giant crab with a Hitler moustache, a Red soldier ramming his bayonet down the throat of a giant Hitler-faced rat; "*Razdavit' Fascistskuyu gadinu*" ("Crush the Fascist reptile"); appeals to women: "Women, go and work on the collective farms, replace the men now in

dearer, and others cheaper. For instance, a drive on a tram-car still costs only 10 kopeks, which is only twice, and not ten times, the nominal charge in 1914. A less favourable estimate is made by an English economist, who holds that to get £1's worth of goods in Moscow, it is necessary to spend 130 to 140 roubles. Allowing for the depreciation of the pound since 1914, this is putting the value of the rouble extremely low. In 1914 the pound was worth about 9½ roubles. The difficulty for a foreigner of making ends meet in Russia may be appreciated from the fact that the official rate of the pound is only 21 roubles. Diplomats are allowed 100 roubles to the pound, and certain privileged residents such as journalists 48 to the pound. Until some time before the war there was a black bourse in Moscow which foreigners used freely. The authorities more or less tolerated it. It made it possible for foreign residents to live fairly comfortably in Moscow, without spending more than twice what they would spend at home.

the army!" There were crowds of people round an open book-stall. The old woman was selling a new edition of Lermontov, whose centenary falls due at the end of this month, and a large tome of Sholokhov's *Don*—fourteen roubles; and piles of pamphlets about the war, all very cheap, five or ten kopeks, among them Emelian Yaroslavsky's pamphlet on the *Second Fatherland War*. On several houses the front page of *Pravda* or *Izvestia* of July 3rd, with the full text of Stalin's speech, complete with portrait, was stuck up on the walls; and everywhere people were rereading it. It is certainly an immensely important speech, telling people exactly what's what. On this hot summer day the lemonade stalls were having a busy time. Soda water with natural fruit syrup costs twenty kopeks, and with artificial syrup thirty-five kopeks. There are some who still prefer the latter. A tribute to science and progress, no doubt. I remembered a lemonade bottle I saw in Warsaw some years ago with "guaranteed artificial fruit juice" printed on the label.

Funny things are happening about religion in Russia. Most of the churches I passed yesterday seemed to be used as warehouses; and there are no signs of much Sunday churchgoing. However, Lovell tells me there are twenty-five or thirty churches open in Moscow, only one has to look for them; they don't hit you in the eye.

But in the office yesterday I looked at the latest copy of the *Bezbozhnik*, the anti-God paper, and the whole of it was devoted to indignant denunciations of the Nazi persecutions of the Protestant and Catholic churches in Germany! There were several long articles on the subject. Clearly, Stalin is working for the greatest unity among the Russian people, and anti-religious propaganda is one of the things which has completely vanished since this war began. However, the *volte-face* of the *Bezbozhnik* is just a trifle blatant.

One of the Americans told me today about his recent inter-

view with the Metropolitan of the New Church. He looked a
sly old fox, but talked very eloquently and, apparently, sincerely of the Russian Fatherland, Alexander Nevsky, and
Russia's great national tradition, and of the general acceptance of the Soviet régime. The man has a large income from
the faithful, pays heavy taxes, lives in a luxurious flat, with
"Prof. So-and-So" written on the name-plate, and owns several admirable Murillos, of whose value he is perhaps unaware,
for they are hung side by side with some trashy nudes of 1900
or so.

I decided to take it easy this first Sunday in Moscow, and to
postpone my official visits till today. Lovell, Lucien, and I
went out in Henry Shapiro's car to Khimki. Shapiro is the
U.P. man here, a clever little fellow, and apparently a tre-
mendously hard worker.

We drove along a wide avenue where enormous new blocks
alternated with the remains of a pre-war village with tiny
gabled log huts. This is the Leningrad Chaussée. Khimki is a
favourite bathing-place some miles out. But yesterday it was
deserted, or almost so. It has an incongruous-looking tower
with two storeys of colonnades, and looks rather like a wedding
cake. It was built in '37 to mark the opening of the Moscow-
Volga canal, which begins just here. There are cabins, but you
can use them only for dressing and undressing, and it says on
the doors "5 minutes only"; they have no keys, and while you
bathe you have to keep an eye on your clothes, which you dump
on the bank. The men and women are separated, and pants are
compulsory. The water was pleasantly warm. There were lots
of little proletarian boys swimming about. One had a wrist-
watch on while in the water. I told him he should take it off;
the others laughed, and said it was only a toy watch. No sooner
had we dressed than a militiaman came and told us all to go to
the police commissar. We obeyed meekly, and found him inside an office on the ground floor of the wedding cake. Some-

body had heard us talking French or English and must have reported us. The man was quite polite, and was impressed by my passport, signed by Mr. Maisky. We were told we could go. I don't like this kind of thing generally, but it was quite welcome as a sign of vigilance in a place like this; for the Volga-Moscow canal is no doubt of military importance, and it's better to see that no undesirables hang around.

MONDAY, *July* 7

I started the day by paying my first visit to the Narkomindel—the Russian Foreign Office. As I hadn't a press card yet, there was a lot of fuss about getting in. I had already heard from Lovell that Palgunov was the head of the Press Department, which pleased me greatly; for I had known Palgunov quite well when he was the Tass correspondent in Paris. He looked much the same, his baby face a little fatter, though, and his golliwog hair a little longer, and he was still as short-sighted as ever, putting papers right in front of his nose to read them. He was, all together, quite friendly, and we reminisced about the old days in Paris. He also said: "When you lived in St. Petersburg before the Revolution, you went to the Reformatskoie School—didn't you tell me so in Paris?" "I may have done so; but, anyway, you've got an excellent memory, Nikolai Grigorievich." At which he laughed. All together, I don't think Palgunov is a bad chap. I was also presented to the censors. One of them is a jovial-looking fellow called Anurov—not at all the stiff bureaucrat I had expected to meet; the other, Kozhemiakov, is one of the most handsome youths I've ever seen—but as hard as nails, I imagine. Wonder how I'll get on with him.

The Narkomindel occupies a large pre-war block of flats, with a courtyard in the centre. Here they've put up a statue of Vorovsky, "Murdered at Lausanne by White Guards in 1923." The whole place looks a bit dusty and grimy; and there's a lift up to the Press Department on the fifth floor, but you can't use it for coming down, and the soldier at the door scrutinizes your papers very carefully before you're allowed into the building at all—or out of it. The headquarters of the Ogpu—now called the N.K.V.D.—are just across the street—the Dzerzhinski Street, formerly the Lubianka—in a huge new building, built rather in the style of Mendelssohn's Columbus House in the Potsdamer Platz in Berlin.

Now that I am settled in the Reuter flat—or rather in Lovell's sitting-room, with a settee to sleep on—we have usually lunch at home. Katya produced an excellent chicken and fruit salad. Lovell says she was very pleased to hear the other day that a German plane had been brought down near Moscow by the Russians; I wonder if she really is. These Volga Germans talk the oddest German; but it's just because they talk an allegedly European language that Volga Germans have almost monopolized the domestic jobs in foreigners' houses in Moscow.

Later we went to Lozovsky's press conference. There are three a week, and the press attaches great importance to them. He is Vice-Commissar for Foreign Affairs and assistant chief of the Soviet Informbureau, and he holds his meetings in a small, old-fashioned *osobniak*—a sort of private little manor-house—which the rich Moscow merchants used to build for themselves in the past. It is built in Empire style, and has a large room with windows looking out on a garden. The place was, until recently, used as the Greek Legation, but now the Greeks, like the Yugoslavs, are no longer represented in Moscow, though they may soon come back. They were turned out as a gesture of goodwill to Germany. Lozovsky, who, with his white goatee, looks rather like old Charles Martin, the French professor in Glasgow, was very friendly; he had lived in France for many years, he told me, and loved Paris and admired the French people immensely for their intelligence.

"But they were betrayed!" he said. There certainly was something of the man about town about Lozovsky; I could just see him sipping his Pernot or his *café crème* on the terrace of the Napolitain around 1900 or so, discussing the world revolution. At the press conference, which took place round a long table with a green cloth—and on it stood glasses and bottles of *narzan* and a yellow kind of lemonade—Lozovsky spoke with great confidence of everything, stressing the 700,000 German casualties in the past fortnight, but declining to say how great the Russian casualties were: "It's hard to make an exact count."

Later I went to the press room at the Narkomindel, on the same floor as Palgunov's office. It's a small room with odd bits of old-fashioned furniture which must have belonged to the bourgeois flats of which the building was once composed. The hideous alabaster inkstand must also have come from the same source. There was, on the wall, a map of the U.S.A. (with place-names almost unrecognizably transliterated into Russian), and another of Europe. The accommodation for typing is somewhat restricted; it is surprising, though, how few foreign journalists there are in Moscow. Maurice Lovell and Cholerton and I are the only British correspondents here, while the Americans only have, as regulars, three or four agency men. Henry Cassidy, the A.P. man, I had met in Paris. He knows no Russian, but that never seems to worry Americans, or handicap them. There is also a Jap here called Hatanaka; and at the Lozovsky conference there were a few foreign correspondents "of the Comintern variety," as somebody described them, and they don't mix with us. One is a young American woman, Janet Weaver, I think, is her name; an old boy called Epstein, with a fabulous nose, who works for the Jewish press in New York; a tall Negro; and a Spaniard, who writes for South American papers, and whose face was at once familiar to me. He turned out to be Jesus Hernandez, the Minister of Education in the Negrin Government, whom I had

met in Madrid in '37. I must talk to him some time. I remember
how, on that occasion, in welcoming Attlee and Noel Baker,
leading members of the Labour Party, to Madrid, he spoke
with just a slight point of irony about "the active sympathy
shown for the Spanish Republic by the British Labour Party."

I was interested to learn from Cassidy that he had left Paris
long after the German occupation. We also reminisced about
Paris and, in the process, naturally got on to the question of
the Fifth Column elements among the foreign journalists in
Paris. Cassidy thought I was "slightly exaggerating." Dog
doesn't eat dog.

Dinner at the British Embassy tonight. What a beautiful
building it is, especially inside, with its panelled dining-room
and tapestries and parquet floors, and what a glorious view of
the river from the balcony, and of the Kremlin right opposite!
The place once belonged to Kharitonenko, one of the sugar or
dry-goods kings of Moscow—sugar, I think. Some of these
Moscow merchants had good taste even in matters like furniture. General Mason McFarlane was there, a little disgruntled
because he had not yet been invited to visit the front; and also
Laurence Cadbury, of the British Mission, pink and jovial,
and wearing a cream-coloured canvas suit. He talked about
the revision of our navicerts policy in relation to Russia, and
of the use that could be made of Iran as a transport route. He
said he had visited several Moscow chocolate and biscuit factories, but had found them old-fashioned, with pre-last-war
machinery. He is here as head of the Economic Mission and has
lengthy negotiations with Mikoyan, the Foreign Trade Commissar, to whom he refers as "old Mick."

The party broke up early, about ten thirty. There was an
amazing view of the domes and towers and battlements of the
Kremlin with the full moon shining on them.

I turned on the radio last night and, oddly enough, got on
to the Russian propaganda from Germany. What absurd

tripe the rusty old White colonels, with their alcoholic voices (I wonder if any of those I once knew in Paris are on this Hitler racket), are dishing out. They are already talking about the "desperate plight of the Red Army," of "Stalin and his Jews," and about "their fat bank deposits at Buenos Aires." And, of course, "the quickest plane is ready to take Stalin abroad when the German Army gets a little nearer Moscow." This sort of thing, I am sure, could have no effect here, even if the Soviets hadn't, at the beginning of the war, requisitioned all the radio sets, other than the "local" ones, on which only the Soviet programs can be heard.

TUESDAY, *July* 8

After a rather futile day Lovell thought I had better see something of Moscow "night life." He and Lucien and I took the 22 tram at the Pokrovka to go into town. It was crowded, as usual, and at each stop more people kept barging in. An old man of about sixty, with a wrinkled face and wearing a black *kartuz*, had been watching the three of us for some time. "A Frenchman?" he said to me, pointing at Lucien. "Yes, quite right." "I knew it. One can always spot a Frenchman by his delicate behaviour. Fine, delicate people the French! Not like our chaps," he said, pointing to a bunch of citizens who were vociferously pushing their way into the tram-car. "Just listen to them! Awful! . . . And just look at our students—our university students of today. Why, they're no better than the commonest of muzhiks; such *coarse* manners"; but before we had time to argue it out, we had to get off.

We walked across the Sverdlov Square to the café of the Hotel National. The place was rather dark, but there were cosy little orange-shaded lamps on each of the small tables. At one of them sat a bunch of Czechs—one a journalist, another an old boy with a huge white beard, almost like Karl Marx's. He had been a manager at the Skoda works; but when the Germans took charge and suggested he work for them, he told them to go and kick themselves. These Czechs had, until lately, been interned by the Russians, but now they were celebrating their release with beer and *narzan*. The beer, rather like French bock, tasted a bit mouldy, but was not bad otherwise. There were many couples sitting in corners. I noticed one young army officer with a pretty young girl—very like little Gassya. Wonder where *she* is now. Aged nearly forty. . . . An awful thought. Looking at the girl with the officer, Lucien remarked: "A decent young girl, but—I wonder." He says, however, that there are lots of floozies in Moscow, though none of them official. The whole atmosphere at the National seemed more friendly than at the Metropole.

We walked from the National across the wide square, and along a wide street with vast new blocks—one of them was the newly built Sovnarkom—alternating with small old houses. A lovely evening, with a bright moon. There were many couples in the streets, most of them in white. Some of the new Soviet buildings are monstrosities, others not so bad, while some are very impressive. The churches and old gates east of the Kremlin look very dilapidated, though. But there's a certain grandeur about Moscow; one felt it in the air that night, in the wide spaces, in the tall silhouettes of new buildings. The Tverskaya, now known as Gorki Street, is entirely new, with a certain unity of planning in the new buildings on both sides, and the street is now about three times wider than it used to be. Suddenly, as we were walking along in silence (one is rather reluctant in the streets, especially at night, to talk French or English), a woman came up and said gruffly: "Why are you smoking?" It was Lucien smoking a pipe. People are morbidly air-raid conscious, though I'm not so sure that they'll know how to go about the job when—. No question of "if"; it is "when."

WEDNESDAY, *July* 9

Moscow is preparing for air-raids. Trucks are running along the tram-lines, distributing sand all over the place. A big pile of sand was dumped outside our house this morning. It caused a row. A young fellow and girl proceeded to fill up big sandbags—and an elderly fellow with some kind of official badge on his cap came along yelling that people had no right to take the sand; it belonged to the State, and he'd call the militia. Others on the pavement encouraged the young man and the girl to take no notice of him. I don't know how the row ended.

I sent a message to London on the gas danger to Moscow, and urged that the British Government make it plain that it will use gas as reprisals against the Germans if people here are gassed.

This morning I went with Lucien to the place beside the Metropole to get my passport photos taken. There was some mistake about the car, and I waited for it in vain, standing in the blazing sun for an hour or more. But I was not bored as I watched the crowd in this great central square of Moscow. These people did not look unhappy; and since ordinary living-conditions have improved so much in the last two or three years, they felt that they were owing a great deal to the régime. No wonder they hate the Germans, who have smashed up this normal life, the result of so many years' labour, privations, and hardships. They are not unhappy, I'm sure. The shoe-shine girl rubbing the white shoes of a citizen was joking and laughing. There were crowds round the lemonade stall, and queues for newspapers, but none for cigarettes, which are plentiful. I wanted to buy a map of Moscow, and walked down the Petrovka to the Kuznetsky Mosst. It was a famous shopping street in the '20's and '30's of last century—Griboyedov in *Gore ot Uma* talks about the beaux of Moscow parading down it, and the smart shops and horses and carriages—but it looks just a mess now, with a lot of large bookshops as the only redeeming feature. Some of them even sell books in Braille. There are also many second-hand bookshops; one of them was selling, cheaply, a complete leather-bound set of White-Russian Merezhkovsky, and the *Odessa Almanac*, and other prettily printed books of 1840 or thereabout. In another bookshop I noticed a luxurious edition—Vol. XLIV—of the *Complete Works of Tchaikovsky*. (By the way, I was struck this morning by the remarkably high standard of the piano music on the Russian wireless.) But I had no luck with my map of Moscow; in fact, one or two of the bookshop clerks I asked for it looked rather startled.

I walked back along the Petrovka, and across to the Red Square, which is certainly one of the most magnificent things in the world.

I tried to enter the Lenin mausoleum, but was waved away by two uniformed, bayoneted guards. "When will it be open?" No answer. Then a civilian on the pavement outside said: "It doesn't open at all." They haven't really evacuated Lenin, have they? I went on to St. Basil's Church and walked in. The church is treated as a museum, with an entrance fee of one rouble. In an ascending spiral, I walked through several little chapels, one under each of the domes, and searched in vain for the *church*. There was really no church, but only another chapel, slightly larger than the others, under the central dome. What a fantastic and yet beautiful building, with its pastel-painted domes—each different in shape and design and colour! Inside, there were some old women in charge, very old-fashioned with the scarves round their heads, but nothing in their behaviour to suggest a religious attitude. Outside, I looked in vain for the Giant Bell and the Giant Gun—which were among the few things I remembered from my last visit to Moscow in 1915. However, the famous statue of Minin and Pozharsky, who chased the Poles out of Moscow in 1612, was still there.

Pity I know so little about Moscow. I was here only twice,

and only for a day or two at that. The first time I was here was just at the beginning of the last war. I remember how through the window of a hotel opposite the Kremlin—it must have been the National, now that I come to think of it—I saw an enormous crowd of people watching the Tsar and his Fifth Column Tsarina—she was wearing a long white summer dress and large white hat—enter the Iversky Chapel at the north end of the Kremlin. It was a sort of Day of National Prayer. The chapel has since been pulled down. The other time I was in Moscow was on my way from St. Petersburg to the Donbass, where my father was going to inspect some newly completed coal mines. It must have been in May 1915, for I remember the newsboys shouting in the Tverskaya, near the equestrian statue of General Skobelev: "Italy has declared war on Austria! Italy has declared war on Austria!" The Tverskaya (now called Gorki Street) is quite unrecognizable now, and the Skobelev statue is gone; pity, it must have gone in the days of the internationalists and anti-nationalists; Stalin wouldn't have scrapped it, I'm sure. It must have been that day, too, that I was shown the Red Square, and taken to Testov's for a big feed. And that night in Moscow my father took me to a kind of restaurant-garden called the Ermitage. On an open-air stage, an opera company was performing Glinka's opera *A Life for the Tsar*, which has now been renamed *Ivan Susanin*. Old Susanin that night sang his stuff in a particularly ventriloquist bass, and the scenery, I remember, was very shoddy. And that's about all I can remember of Moscow.

Even so, it's odd to be here *again*.

When I told Maurice about my failure to get a map of Moscow, he said I was quite crazy, at a time like this, to have tried to buy one: "They have spy mania, and it's a wonder they didn't take you for a *diversant*. Just as well you can talk Russian properly. Remember that Stalin specially warned people against *diversants*!"

We had an excellent roast *teterka* (a kind of woodcock) for lunch; then I went back into town to collect my passport photographs (they made me look like an old Negress) and thence to the Stary Dom. The "old house" which used to be the Embassy before the new house on the Sofiskaya Embankment was bought, is now a sort of annex of the Embassy, though the Ambassador and his terrier seem to spend much of their time there. It is a pleasant little *osobniak*, with a garden and tennis-court behind it, and it is in the Vorovsky Street, running north from the Arbat Square. It used to be called the Povarskaya Street, and in pre-Revolution Moscow Povarskaya was what Park Lane is (or, rather, used to be) to London. Several of the rich merchants' *osobniaks* are now used as embassies; the famous Morozov *osobniak*—wasn't Morozov the textile magnate who financed the revolutionaries?—is owned by the Japs. I gave my passport and the photos to McAdoo, an old Scotsman, to whom I had to explain who I was and what it was all about. Apparently he presides over Burns Nights in Moscow, and gets very lively on these occasions.

I walked down the Vorovsky Street, lined with trees, to the lively, noisy Arbat Square with its spectacular subway entrance. Funny how a lot of Soviet buildings look like exhibition pavilions, with wedding-cake effects. Some are good, others less so. Through the open windows of a cheap beer-house or restaurant in the Arbat Square, I heard a scolding going on. An elderly man was shouting something to the effect that he was "a Bolshevik, do you understand, an old Bolshevik, who fought in the Civil War," and that he had a right to speak his mind—not that anybody seemed to be contradicting him in anything. It was pleasant, in this hot weather, to go in a fairly empty tram along the so-called "inner ring" of the Moscow boulevards with their continuous gardens. At the end of the Tverskoi Boulevard we passed the Pushkin statue, at the unveiling of which, in '81, Dostoevsky made his famous speech. The boulevard, with the statue, is, I remembered, the scene of

Leonid Andreyev's charming play about Moscow University
students, *Days of Our Life*, or rather, Act I of the play is.

In the evening Maurice and I went to a cocktail party at
Henry Cassidy's. It was a good long way away, in an old,
rather shabby house in the Arbat district, and with "Associ-
ated Press of America, Moscow Bureau" written on the door-
plate. It was quite a large party, with gin fizzes, and whisky,
and olives and caviar *tartines*, and cheese straws, and Camels
and Chesterfields. I talked to the charming Russian wife of H.,
an American business-man here. He had tried for years to get
her nationalized as an American, but it is only now—a good
sign of improved Russo-American relations—that the Russians have agreed to it and are allowing her to go to America.
She was told, however, that she would probably not be allowed
to return to Russia; and though Mr. H. doesn't seem to care
about that, the idea that she may never see Russia again is
upsetting her.

Other straws in the wind. Several British war prisoners, who
had escaped from Germany, and who have since been kept in
Russian internment camps, have just been released by the
Russians.

Mr. Nierstone, an American living here, was at Henry's
party. He said he couldn't take the Soviet figures of German
losses seriously. "Why doesn't England invade France? My
God, don't you *realize* that it's the only thing that'll keep the
show here really *going*? Can't you at least start *preparing*
something, so that the Germans are kept guessing, and must
keep at least part of their troops in the west?" Now Stalin, he
said, was a great man; but with the Germans pushing right
ahead towards Moscow, it was *very important indeed* that the
evacuation of Moscow shouldn't be left till the last moment.
"It would just be chaos, my *God!* If they didn't worry so much
about *prestige*, they could move the Government to Kazan

right now, and in that case they could go on putting up a *darned* good show."

Mr. Nierstone admitted that, in view of the unhappy memories of the last war, the American people had no desire to come into this one. "In 1917 a college boy wasn't considered a man unless he was going over to France to fight. Nobody's got any such ideas in America now. And what's the good, anyway? *Jesus*, you don't want *troops*?"

"Of course we do. And we also want your navy."

"Well," said Mr. Nierstone, "you see, the best part of our navy is in the Pacific. *You've* got enough ships in the Atlantic."

"What, for landing an expeditionary force in France, and keeping it supplied, in addition to all its present jobs?"

Mr. Nierstone changed the subject. "That was a lousy show you put up in Libya. And although your airplane production is pretty good now, your production of tanks just *isn't good enough*. Now, we in America decided last November to produce tanks on a big scale, and, by God, in three months from now—in September '41—it'll be spectacular."

I said I was glad to hear it.

I wrote a long article in Russian last night about the London blitz and London's A.R.P. and fire-fighting experiences. I shall take it along to Palgunov and see what he can do with it.

THURSDAY, *July* 10

This morning I had a long talk with a bunch of children—four of them—who kept looking into my window out of the yard. Nice, these Russian kids; full of human freshness. They were interested in a nickel sail-boat on Maurice's mantelpiece and wanted to know how much it cost. They told me all about a rubber boat they had wanted to buy at the Resintrust shop (funny to hear such a composite Soviet word come quite naturally from a child's lips!) but Mamma said it was too expensive. They said they wouldn't go to school any more; the two girls (eight and six) and the baby were going to be evacuated tomorrow to Ryazan, or maybe it was Kazan, they weren't quite sure; and they wouldn't go to school any more; and Mamma would come with them, and they would all live on a kolkhoz, where Mamma was going to work. "And are you going to work on the kolkhoz, too?" And they said no, they were much too little, but they would play on the river, and bathe; and they would help to gather berries and mushrooms in the woods. The older girl, who did most of the talking, was eight, with dark hair and bright shining eyes and teeth and delicate features; the boy—who apparently belonged to another family—was a chubby little fellow with a "Tatar" cap. He said his mamma also would work on the kolkhoz, but Papa, who was "working for the war," would stay on in Moscow. I gathered he was a munitions worker. Papa and Mamma and he and his little brother, he said, were all living in one room—"but it's a big room, much bigger than yours." They were interested to see on Maurice's table the elementary reading book with pictures they were using at school. I showed them a page with some political stuff about "our Soviet State," but they weren't interested and said they would read to me instead the page about cherries and strawberries.

At the press conference today Lozovsky ridiculed the Finnish attempts to persuade Britain and America that the U.S.S.R. had attacked Finland a fortnight ago. Lozovsky said the Russians were only too well aware long before the Finnish war of 1939 of the constant military co-operation between Germany and the Finnish General Staff. Since then this co-operation had continued increasingly, with troop "transits" and all that. In 1939 Russia had to do something about it. She couldn't tolerate this German springboard twenty-six miles from Leningrad.

The news tonight is still fairly good, except for the fighting against "superior German forces" in the area of Ostrov, which the Germans claim to have occupied. Lozovsky emphasized the much soberer tone of the German press, and quoted the *Frankfurter Zeitung* article admitting that the Russians are far tougher than the French, and do not get demoralized by tank wedges and try continuously to cut the tails of these wedges and pincers. The Germans admit that for the first time they are faced with an army equipped much the same way as their own.

I think it's highly significant of a better disposition on the part of the Russians that they should have published my article on the London blitz, without delay, and not just in some rag, but prominently, in *Izvestia*. I talked in it a lot about the spirit of the British people during the blitz. It is something that is almost new to the Russians; for during their "appeasement" period they paid us very few compliments in their press. Nor did the Russians fully realize the difference between Chamberlain's England and Churchill's England. The fact that I am allowed to explain all this in *Izvestia* is a very healthy sign. Cripps is very pleased about it.

People tell me that on June 22nd many of the Russians believed that we had given leave to the Germans to attack Russia. This was absurd, and could only have arisen from a complete ignorance of Churchill England.

And yet—if they still distrust some of our people (which is quite different from distrusting the *whole* of England), one can hardly blame them.

I had a phone call from Leonards, who is on a special mission here. He had just come from Egypt, and had interesting things to say about the Near and Middle East. He says that Wavell was rushed into the Syrian campaign by the urgent political and strategic necessities of the moment. There was no time to lose, but there wasn't enough heavy stuff (tanks) available for a *Blitzkrieg*, which would have settled Syria in a few days. The Free French hadn't been very helpful—though that wasn't their fault, really. Only their presence somehow encouraged the Vichyites to put up a real fight. However, the Syrian business was now fortunately over; and the Vichyites had at last asked for an armistice. Leonards thought we would have a crack at Rommel as soon as the weather got a little cooler. It was very important from the Russian point of view that we should. Leonards says the German campaign against Russia shows that Hitler has accepted the necessity of a long war. Taking a long view of it, this campaign will not be to our advantage if the Germans smash the Russians in a short time. (He doesn't think, though, that they will. Only, does he mean it will be "to our advantage" if they take a *long* time to smash the Russians!?)

We were sitting upstairs in Leonards's room at the National, drinking whisky and iced water, when in came young Binkley. I had already seen him some nights ago. He has lived here for some years, is unsympathetic to the people here, and likes to tell stories about Poland, Latvia, Estonia, where, he claims, the population is more anti-Russian than anti-German. He thoroughly dislikes Moscow, though he likes rubbing shoulders with diplomats, and he keeps himself amused collecting ikons, and gypsy gramophone records. He has obviously come here with a strong prejudice and has made no attempt to judge people or the régime intelligently. We had a bit of an argument. I argued, roughly, on these lines:

I've had no particular reason until now to like Stalin; but he *does* represent the Government; most of the people here regard him as a very great man, and the normality of life in the last two years at least is put down to his credit. Now that I am seeing Stalin's Russia in the flesh, there is one thing that strikes me very forcibly. *What, in western Europe, have been our sources of information on Stalin?* Practically all the well-known books about Stalin are hostile: Trotsky, in the first place; and behind him comes a whole army of supporters, imitators, or sympathizers—Max Eastman and Souvarine, with his monumental tome, being the most important. Clearly, Stalin has been severely handicapped by the absence of effective propaganda on his behalf. His propaganda was non-existent. Perhaps he did not bother how much the Trotsky-ites barked. Or else the subtle game he was playing just did not lend itself to propaganda—without giving too much away.

The foreign Communists—British, French, and the rest—confused the issues hopelessly. Partly because they were try-·ing to prove something that could not be proved—namely, that Stalin was just as much an internationalist as Trotsky. André Gide's book, *Return from the U.S.S.R.*, was perhaps the first foreign book of any weight which vaguely guessed the essence of Stalinism and of the nationalist basis of Stalin's Russia. But it was written in a hostile tone; what offended Gide was Stalin's loss of "internationalism"; he thought the support given by Russia to the Spanish Government the only redeeming feature in Stalin's policy. Gide said so, because he thought the motives behind this aid were internationalist. If he had realized that they were primarily nationalist, he might not have approved even of that. Actually, did not Russia support the Spanish Government because this seemed a good way of making common cause with England and France? But, scared of "Bolshevism," they wouldn't have it. It was, of course, unfortunate that France should have been infested with strikes just at *that* moment. . . .

Whatever may have been my feelings about Russia's internal affairs, it became clear to me in 1933 that the real menace to Western civilization was not Russia, but Germany. I knew that the chance of enlisting Russia on the side of the angels must not be missed. Those were my *Manchester Guardian* years in Paris. I supported Barthou's policy of rapprochement with Russia; and considered the death of Barthou, and his replacement by Laval, a far greater European disaster than the death of Alexander of Yugoslavia.

Russia—Stalin's Russia—had clearly scented the danger. Russia's entry into the League, the Litvinov policy of collective security, were a godsend to Britain and France. If our statesmen had had any vision, any foresight, they could have averted the war by grasping firmly Russia's hand. But the Communist bogy, and the hope that Germany could be bought off at Russia's expense—a hope firmly entertained by people like Bonnet and a good many people in England—proved an insuperable obstacle. German propaganda played continuously on the anti-Communist string, and half of France and a good part of England listened rapturously.

The Comintern was clumsy in countering this propaganda. True, it got the French Communists, in the 1936 election, to suggest as clearly as possible that they weren't *really* out for a Communist revolution, and that they were only anti-Fascists, and patriots in the best tradition of the Paris working class; but nobody quite believed them. The truth perhaps is that Stalin had no control over the French Communists; he approved French rearmament, and welcomed the use of patriotic and anti-Hitler slogans in the election; but local rank-and-file Communists and Trotskyites in disguise, and people suffering from anarcho-syndicalist hangovers, and the Marceau Pivert "pacifists" and anti-Stalinites, and plain German agents and anarchists inside the C.G.T., and others, including Communists, who just didn't understand what Stalin wanted, misapplied the policy which Stalin would have liked to see carried through. The election victory of the Communists led, industrially and militarily, to results which were in flat contradiction with the foreign policy of Litvinov—a policy one of the foundations of which was a strong France.

Who was running the show—Stalin or the Comintern? And if the Comintern's instructions were in conflict with Stalin's plans, why did not Stalin do something about it? The only explanation for this must perhaps be sought in the internal situation in Russia. The internationalist doctrine—as distinct from "Socialism in one country"—had still a vast number of supporters in Russia—including some who sincerely believed it was the right thing, though, heaven knows, the chances of international Communism were not looking bright anywhere since the rise of the Nazi tide. I am pretty well convinced, now that I look back on it, that Stalin had, throughout these years, felt the war coming; and he knew that an internationalist Russia could stand up to it less well than a national Russia. It was hard going, for many old shibboleths had to be respected. But, on vital issues, Stalin got things done, however unpopular they might be. For instance, on the question of piece-work. The introduction of Stakhanovism, which shocked the Marxist purists so profoundly, was essential if heavy industry was to be built up and armament production raised to an adequate level for purposes of national defence. Then there were the old Bolsheviks. To show them up as traitors to Russia, before liquidating them, was essential if their liquidation was to be accepted by the mass of the Russian people. And even if they had not committed the crimes with which they were charged, would not these old Bolsheviks have undermined or delayed the growth of Russia's military strength had they continued to play an important part in Russian affairs? Probably Stalin knew from the outset that his job was to prepare Russia for a German invasion. That the purge of 1937-8 involved thousands of probably innocent people (many of whom were later released) was, clearly, less the work of Stalin than of Yezhov, head of the secret police, and his gang, who had gone "giddy with success." The "purge of the purgers" followed; not that that in itself put an end to spying, victimization, and other practices which were bound to take some time to eradicate. To treat Stalin as an enemy of all Yezhov had stood for would be going too far; but Stalin had the instinct to realize that "Yezhovism" had become something detestable to the Russian people. In this, as in other respects, *Stalin took account of Russian public opinion.* The Yezhov "régime" had to be eliminated if national solidarity was to be cemented on a solid basis.

Even in the brutal process of dekulakization the war danger may have played a certain part, though the process actually was started before Hitler came into power. Collectivization was, in fact, the necessary first step towards a long-term political education and "conditioning" of the peasantry. Here, also, to meet public opinion, certain important concessions, modifying collectivization, were, in 1935, made to the disgruntled peasantry. But had there been no collectivization at all, would not certain peasant elements today be acting as a Fifth Column? The absence of a real Fifth Column in Russia has, so far, been very striking; and it is by preparing for this war and by putting this war from the outset on a national basis that Stalin has achieved this result. If he had called upon the Russian people to "defend Marxism," the response might have been much less unanimous.

I am also pretty sure that the purge in the Red Army had a great deal to do with Stalin's belief in an imminent war with Germany. What did Tukhachevsky stand for? People of the French *Deuxième Bureau* told me long ago that Tukhachevsky was pro-German. And the Czechs told me the extraordinary story of Tukhachevsky's visit to Prague, when towards the end of a banquet—he had got rather drunk—he blurted out that an agreement with Hitler was the only hope for both Czechoslovakia and Russia. And he then proceeded to abuse Stalin. The Czechs did not fail to report this to the Kremlin, and that was the end of Tukhachevsky—and of so many of his followers. Here again, however, the purge went "giddy with success," and probably became more extensive than was at first considered necessary.

What made it all very awkward for Stalin—just as the Communist purge was awkward, though for other reasons—

was, no doubt, the necessity of giving all sorts of reasons—or none at all—rather than the deep reason for so many of the "liquidations." He could not very well say: "Tukhachevsky was going to sell out to Hitler." The purge in the army unquestionably weakened the army in a technical sense; and that, in turn, made the longest possible period necessary, and desirable, for a policy of appeasement towards Nazi Germany, and of active military preparations. The progress made between 1938 and now seems to be enormous; if Hitler waited another year, he wouldn't have a chance at all. And that also is why the Russians tried to the last to put off the evil hour—for instance, by expelling the Yugoslav and Greek and other legations, and by trying to be pleasant to the Germans as late as June. Another year without war meant invincibility.

I talked roughly on these lines to Leonards and Binkley. Binkley got rather annoyed, and said I hadn't lived in this country long enough; while Leonards merely said: "Very interesting, very interesting." Binkley, however, raised at least one objection which needs thinking out: "If," he said, "national defence was Stalin's primary motive, why did he have to turn Estonia and Latvia into Soviet Republics, instead of leaving them their old régime?" Perhaps because there were too many Ulmanises and other pro-German Fascists around. Or perhaps because Estonia and Latvia aren't really *countries*.

Outside, tram 22 to the Ilyinka was incredibly crowded. It was the rush hour. There was much pushing and shoving, but nobody seems to mind that. The passengers in front hand their ten or fifteen kopeks backwards, so that they eventually reach the conductress. Everybody was wearing summer clothes. But, unlike Paris, there is no unwashed smell in the Moscow trams —or not much. And most of the girls have nice figures showing through the thin summer dresses. I didn't see many people looking particularly worried about the war.

Lucien tells me a lot of selling of personal belongings is going on in the "commission shops." Actually, I had noticed something of a queue outside one, in the Petrovka. Probably it's because people have spent what loose cash they had on buying things for their departing soldiers and are now temporarily hard up.

FRIDAY, *July* 11

The big offensive against Moscow is awaited at any moment. The Germans are getting near Smolensk and seem to have overrun pretty well the whole of the annexed areas except Estonia, and to be pushing on to the Ukraine. But their main job is still to try to push in different directions, in order to find the weakest point. It doesn't seem, though, that the Russian command has so far made any serious mistakes. The Russian Air Force is still a very big force, despite serious losses and despite extravagant German claims. The Germans, too, have suffered great losses. Our military experts are all pleasantly astonished at the comparative lack of transport disorganization and other forms of confusion. Rather disturbing, on the other hand, is the speed with which the Germans are managing to change the gear of the railways; this, of course, they are doing by using slave gangs made up from civilian "war prisoners," in addition to their formidable Todt organization with its 100,000 workers and engineers. They are careful, in anticipation of new advances, not to wreck the railways behind the Russian lines, and are only trying to cause confusion, with the minimum of damage, by dropping small bombs. The Russian command seem well aware of the obvious German move to reach the upper reaches of the Volga in a great enveloping movement round Moscow, and they have taken their precautions. The Russians estimate that the Germans have 10,000 tanks. I shouldn't be surprised if they had more. How many tanks the Russians have is hard to say; I have heard one estimate, though—6,000. If so, they are likely to be seriously outnumbered by the Germans before long. However, the heavy Russian tanks are said to have proved very good indeed; and there seems little doubt that the Germans have already suffered hundreds of thousands of casualties.

The Russians tend to underestimate the importance of our big blitzes on western Germany, at least if I am to believe the British story that the Germans are getting very rattled by them, and no longer enjoying this war at all. It seems that for some days past the Russians have been urging our people to invade France. Our people here don't seem to think it likely to happen. A huge shipping problem, they say; not only a question of getting troops there, but also of keeping them supplied. "The troops," one of our people said, "are trained for island defence, not for big *Blitzkrieg* stuff, and," he added, "if things were to go wrong over here, the Germans would invade us in September."

The Russians greatly resent any mention of a possible evacuation of Moscow. They are quite right to resent it.

I find that some anxiety is already felt for Leningrad. It has important industries, and the Baltic Fleet would be hard to get out—even the submarines and the destroyers. The locks on the White Sea canal could easily be smashed up by dive bombers.

The Russians are showing ever-increasing willingness to cooperate; and I have the impression that the British are anxious to maintain an eastern front at any price—short of landing troops in France!

Why have we had no blitz yet? The German Air Force seems much too busy at the front to have time for spectacular bombings of Moscow, four hundred miles away, and the nights are very short. . . . Leonards today said we might have five or six nights of super-blitz once they get nearer to Moscow. Personally, I doubt if they can do it on such a vast scale; they never kept it up on London.

This evening Maurice and I went to see Mrs. Duranty off to the railway station. I had heard a lot about "Katya," and was interested to see her. She lives in a tiny wooden house, very old, in the Zamoskvorechie, beyond the river. There was an Intourist car in front of the house, packed with bundles and other luggage. With her was a little Russian boy—about ten, Duranty's Russian son. Katya was about forty, white-haired, and speaking rather poor English. The boy was dressed like a Russian child, and Russian was his only language. Very like his mother. Katya looked very upset at leaving Moscow. She kissed two old women good-bye; the old women, one a fat one, the other an old scraggy one with a black shawl over her head, cried. "God bless you, my dears, God bless you!" they kept on saying; and when the car was about to move, the old scraggy one made the sign of the cross over Katya. "It's the evacuation of Moscow," Katya said, as we drove along the Ilyinka. "I must take the boy away. We are going to Gorki; from there to the country. I shall work on a kolkhoz." "You'll be back in Moscow in two months," said Maurice, cheeringly. "Yes, in October." She shook her head doubtfully. "Do you think so?" She thought the bombing of Moscow was frightening. Did she think the Germans would ever get here? She didn't say.

We went in the car along the usual mixture of old and new streets towards the Kursk Station. At one of the entrances of this old but freshly painted station, was a bas-relief of Lenin: from this station Lenin had travelled into exile in Siberia. There were a large number of people at the station, but it was nothing like a panic exodus. The large, clean waiting-room was crowded with women and children and a few old men. Katya got two porters to carry the stuff. She had to wait for the 10.30 train, that is, for an hour and a half. It seems that only people with permits are able to leave Moscow. It's a good enough system for avoiding the infernal Paris-like stampedes; but the danger is that not enough people are being allowed to leave Moscow while there is no danger yet. . . . Women, it is true, are being urged to go off to the kolkhozes, but I don't know how many are actually going, or have gone, and many children are still about.

From the station buffet there came an appetizing smell of cooking. We entrusted Katya and her brat to the care of an elderly porter with a walrus moustache, and left them in the buffet having tea and sugar-buns.

I've just been listening to the French news from London. It is strange to think of them still going on with their same old job in their basement in the Strand. A little way down is Fleet Street, past the shell of St. Clement Dane's, and Weingott's tobacco shop, and the entrance into the Temple; and Middle Temple lane, and poor old Pump Court, most of it burned on that fantastic night of May 10th. Will I regret having left London?

This evening, as we drove past the Chisty Prud, and then again near the Sretenka, we saw two large lots of recruits marching along the street, both singing lustily. And it's good, the music of their marching songs.

It is one a.m. I am sitting in the office waiting for Maurice to return. The wireless is on. Around me are books left over by ex-Reuter correspondents here—a mixed bag, including a lot of Left Book Club stuff, and works of Trotsky and other forbidden fruit. Volume V of Kluchevsky's *History of Russia* is about the only thing in the whole lot that interests me.

SATURDAY, *July* 12

Great progress is being made towards a regular Anglo-Russian alliance, and Cripps's two visits to Stalin this week seem to have been very important. Cripps had a difficult time during the "appeasement" period; but he has managed to keep up at least a minimum of goodwill towards Britain, and now he is reaping the fruits of his policy. There is a certain

breeziness about Cripps which the Russians—or some of them
—like. An agreement was signed tonight at the Kremlin; but
I'll have to find out more about it.

Today Leonards introduced me to a really good Moscow
restaurant. It looks bogus, but the food is good. It's a Caucasian place called the Aragvi, and is in one of the new white
blocks off Gorki Street. It's a dive, and pleasantly cool. There
are absurd murals of galloping Circassians; the band wasn't
playing—either because of the war, or simply because it was
lunch-time. The whole atmosphere was not unpleasant. Leonards, who was recently in Cairo, talked about the awful
blunders that had led to the fall of Benghazi. I said: "In London people were in a foul stew, and thought the Germans might
be in Cairo in a week." "Well, the trouble is that a lot of people
in Cairo thought so, too," Leonards said. "It was a very unpleasant moment. Fortunately, the Germans pushed on much
farther than they'd ever expected—and they exhausted themselves. The state of the German soldiers, without food or drink,
was lamentable." We had excellent caviar. Also *salade olivier*,
then *shashliks* and salad. The *shashlik* was made of very good
pork, not mutton, as it really should be. Vodka and a rather
harsh Caucasian red wine; later coffee.

I don't think spies and parachutists would have much of a
chance in Moscow—judging from tonight's experience.

Tonight Maurice and I walked home from the Embassy
along the Moscow River and the boulevards. I had, earlier in
the day, got my press card, and my pass for going out after
midnight. It was a glorious night. How wonderful it must be in
the Russian countryside! We walked along the Sofiskaya Embankment. The moon was shining on the weird, majestic outline of the Kremlin, on Ivan Veliki's golden domes, the great
palaces, and St. Basil's Church. But we felt uneasy. We passed
a power station. Every two or three minutes we were stopped
by sentries telling us to produce "*dokumenty.*" They couldn't

really see much in merely the moonlight, but they seemed satisfied. We walked on along the embankment, and at last crossed a bridge—I forget which. Anyway, the bridge produced three more inspections. Then we walked along the boulevards in silence, for we somehow preferred not to talk English. Again and again we were stopped—once by a couple of fat girls— "voluntary sentries." "Can't see anything; bring along a lamp." So somebody went for a lamp. We waited. "Get along!" one of them cried angrily. Rather inconsistent, I thought. We went on. Then there was a large building—a barracks, it turned out to be, with numerous lorries outside. Here the military got hold of us and very distrustfully took us along the boulevard "to the next corner," two soldiers with fixed bayonets following. Damned undignified! We were handed over to a bunch of militiamen, who immediately took us off to a shed inside a yard. It was infernally hot inside. They were suspicious and wanted to know this and that. They also objected to our being out after midnight, since our night passes, they said, were valid only *till* 24 o'clock. We pointed out that these said "after 24 o'clock," at which the Dogberry at the desk grunted. However, in the end a soldier was ordered to escort us home, which was just round a corner, and when we got there he asked for the "office." We said that *this* was our office. "No," said he, "I mean the office of the house committee." We said we didn't know. However, he seemed impressed by our having the key, and also by the size of the rooms. So he went away; but I thought he'd go to the *domkom* and expected more complications—with possibly a whole night at the police station, till the Narkomindel fished me out in the morning. However, we waited for half an hour and nothing happened. Except—a siren; and then somebody knocked on the front door, shouting: *"Trevoga!"* Maurice wondered if he should waken Katya. But despite the distant droning of planes, nothing happened, and we got to bed eventually. People outside, on the stairs, were meantime hastily going off to their shelters.

Maurice said my dispatch to the *Sunday Times* had safely gone off this evening. It had taken the censors from one o'clock to seven to get the thing done.

At the Narkomindel today I met a Chinese. He seemed an intelligent little fellow, and spoke excellent Russian. He confessed that the Russians were very fussy just now about not hurting the feelings of the Japs in any way. He also thought they would have to reduce their arms shipments to China still further, though these no longer amounted to anything much as it was.

Having a car—especially with a rush job like this—is an absolute necessity in Moscow. Trams are all very well for local colour, but the time one would waste waiting for trams would be terrible. And taxis—well, there just aren't any, except "Intourist" cars, which have to be specially ordered, and which cost about £1 for a short run. Misha, Lovell's chauffeur, looks like an ape—"*tête de dégénéré*," Lucien calls him—but I like talking to him. Maurice says he is a great Don Juan and has a very complicated sex life. He certainly always looks a bit washed-out—especially after his day off. He fought in the Finnish war and told me how he and his fellow soldiers had entered Kuokkala and Terijoki at the very beginning of the war. (Funny to hear of Kuokkala, only some thirty miles from St. Petersburg; an aunt of mine had a *datcha* there, among the sand dunes. I must have been seven or eight when, on the beach at Kuokkala, I first learned to ride a bicycle.) The fact that he fought in the Finnish war seems the chief reason why he has not yet been called up this time. He's a good chap; he probably reports occasionally on his foreign employers to the authorities, but he has to do it, anyway. He has lived in Moscow since '24, and says it has changed a lot since then; conditions were very difficult in '31-'33, but are not at all bad now; there are plenty of manufactured goods, and any amount of food—it may be a little expensive but you can get it; and life is very normal, and now these bloody Germans have started this infernal war. Incidentally, I've noticed there's no swearing in the streets, and no kissing and pawing of any kind; the behaviour of the Soviet citizens is very proper. Not like the Paris Métro. Lucien finds it rather bewildering. At the same time, they must go in for quite a lot of love-making, for there's a large number of pregnant women in the streets; I am told it's because the abortion laws weren't abolished until fairly recently, and the people haven't yet learned how to "regulate their fun." And contraceptives are rationed and hard to get.

Most of the Americans here are appreciating the vital importance to their own country of this gigantic struggle the Russians are putting up; but one or two of the newspaper men still regard it primarily as "a big story." I find this rather irritating. Even more irritating, for its cold-hearted non-belligerent "objectivity," is this sort of thing. There's a more or less young American damsel here called Angelina who hangs about embassies and legations and newspaper men. She asked me for a drink in her room at the National. "Isn't this a swell room?" she said. "Well, yes; very sumptuous, though I don't much like the mantelpiece ornaments." One of these was an outrageously large china clock, all the colours of the rainbow, composed of Neptune with a broken trident, and a lot of nymphs and dolphins and fishes floating in a great big pale-blue wave round the dial. "I don't mean that," said Angelina. "But look at the swell view from the window. Why, my God, I'll be able to see the Germans march right across the Red Square." "So you are going to stay on here—if the Germans come to Moscow?" "You bet I'll stay here; don't you think it'll be a swell story? Who's to stop me? Aren't we nootrals?"

It's been so hot that Maurice and I decided to go native and to buy white embroidered shirts and white canvas trousers, which a lot of the Russians wear in this weather. However, we found that the Gorki Street shops were already closing down when we got there. Lucien was with us, and I suggested we go to the Malyi Theatre, where they were showing a play, *In the Ukrainian Steppes,* by one Gribenuk or Korneichuk, or some such Ukrainian name. It had been highly praised in the Soviet papers. We got three stalls at fifteen roubles. Its theme was the conflict between a good and a bad collective farm. The propaganda was rather obvious, but the acting so excellent that one almost forgot it was a propaganda play. Particularly good was the lazy and useless chairman of the bad kolkhoz, "The Quiet Life"—an amiable old duffer, very different from the enterprising chairman of the good kolkhoz, "Death to Capitalism." The author had made the lazy old duffer a thoroughly sympathetic character. A good piece of slapstick was the scene of the two veteran imbecile peasants, one of whom keeps telling the other that you can keep away devils and ghosts by smoking cigarettes wrapped in the writings of Yaroslavsky, the anti-God propagandist; they thereupon proceed to fumigate each other with this magic smoke. The joke cuts both ways; the old peasants are absurd, but "anti-God" propaganda is also being treated as a bit of a joke. The audience applauded the lake and willow scenery of the second act. The scenery of the first act, suggesting the richness of the Ukrainian soil, with gigantic sunflowers and pumpkins and other plants and flowers, was a trifle muddled.

The audience was composed almost entirely of young people; many soldiers among them, and many pretty girls; and the theatre itself was nicely done up in white, with orange curtains on the side boxes, and with the hammer and sickle painted above the stage. The people reacted to all the propaganda passages with loud cheering, but nothing went down so well as old Chesnok's remark to his wife: "There is nothing more maddening than when you're interrupted just as you are completing the roof of your hut. If only we had five more years! But if war comes, then we shall fight with a fierceness and anger the like of which the world has never seen." The audience brought the house down. It was certainly an excellent summing-up of the Russian's attitude to the war. These people had struggled and worked hard, and suffered hardships, and just when things were beginning to look well, everything was upset by the Germans. But the loud cheering was not confined to the propaganda passages. These Soviet audiences have a sense of beauty, and they cheered almost as loudly the lovely lines from *Romeo and Juliet* which the peasant girl was rehearsing for some amateur show at the kolkhoz. Shakespeare sounds very good in Russian.

The final scene of *The Ukrainian Steppes* was perhaps the feeblest of all, with Marshal Budenny, rather like a grand duke —whiskers and all—entering the play at the last moment as a *deus ex machina* and fixing up all the troubles of the two kolkhozes and of the warring families and the enamoured young people.

In the foyer there are many portraits of famous actors of the past—a Repin portrait of the great Stchepkin, and photographs of Prov Sadovsky and the other Sadovsky and Davydov, and of other 1860-70 and even earlier celebrities. This place must have looked much the same then. The Revolution has carried on the great theatrical tradition, and has, moreover, made the theatre accessible to a great many more people than before.

Sunday, *July* 13

Started the day late. Breakfast—coffee, cream, black bread, and toast; and old Katya also brought out from somewhere a pot of Dundee marmalade. We got a call from the Stary Dom to hear Baggaley, the first Secretary of the Embassy, announce the terms of the new Russo-British Pact. Baggaley told us that the agreement was signed yesterday, at 5.15, in

Molotov's office in the Kremlin. Among those present were Stalin, Molotov, Admiral Kuznetsov, General Shaposhnikov; and on the British side there were Cripps, General Mason Mc-Farlane, and other senior members of the Military Mission, as well as Laurence Cadbury. Stalin, through an interpreter, talked at some length to McFarlane, and they served chocolates and Soviet champagne.

The Russians are increasingly amiable with us: it's a good omen for the future. Cripps seems a lot happier, too. The whole agreement seems to have been negotiated in the course of the two Cripps-Stalin meetings. I suppose some of our people were as afraid of another Brest-Litovsk as the Russians were afraid of a separate British peace with Hitler. What astonished me, at the Lozovsky meeting this afternoon, was the *surprise* the Russians were still showing at the signing of the agreement. Lozovsky said it was the biggest blow for Hitler, and smashed his plan for fighting east and west separately. Asked whether the U.S.A. could be considered a silent partner in the agreement, he said, gallantly: "The U.S.A. is too great a country to be silent."

Cripps is doing a good job of work. His "idealism" is much more sensible and practical and realistic than so many of the "realistic" views which one hears about Russia—and which would get us nowhere.

At home Maurice received a visit from two Englishmen who have just arrived from Persia. They crossed a corner of the Caspian in a paddle-steamer built (according to them) in 1860, and they had travelled for four days from Baku, which isn't so bad, considering. There was no dining-car, and they had some difficulty about food, as several of the hard-boiled eggs they had brought with them had proved rotten; so also had some of the tinned fish. However, they had been able to buy bread on the way. They complained of the bugs biting them, and also of the dirt in the lavatory. They saw trainloads of soldiers and equipment continually passing, and were impressed by this tremendous traffic.

Moscow is still very quiet. The Germans haven't bombed it yet. We are waiting for the next big German offensive, which may decide the fate of this campaign. Not that the situation on this central front looks too pretty with the Huns already at Vitebsk. They are, clearly, concentrating on this central front—always their infernal "one thing at a time"!—and going easy in the Ukrainian and northern sectors. Do they want the Russians to concentrate all their main forces in front of Moscow—so that they may have an easier time in the Ukraine? At the same time, there's no doubt that they want to have a big crack at Moscow first; and a lot of people here—especially among the foreigners—are getting nervous and are talking about moving to Kazan.

The world is beginning to take an extraordinary interest in the Russian Army. The Russian wireless keeps on reciting a little poem by Marshak, I think, in which a Red soldier talks about his father who fought under Chapaiev, the Red guerrilla leader in the Civil War, and of his grandfather who fought under the great Suvorov. When one comes to think of it, this grandfather must have been a hundred or more before he conceived the Civil War hero: a real old he-man! But never mind. . . . Anyway, everybody is going crazy about the Russian Army. Henry received a cable from his agency today asking urgently for two articles—one on Kutuzov, the other on Suvorov. I found him at the Nark, phoning agitatedly to the War Office in order to find out the Christian names and patronymics of these distinguished generals. "What? Mikhail Illarionovich. Two l's in Illarionovich? Thank you; now for Suvorov. . . ."

I listened to the German wireless last night. They were squealing about the *Verbrechen der englischen Flieger* (crimes of the English fliers) who had bombed churches in Münster, and machine-gunned a hospital ship marked with the Red Cross, off Tripoli. I like the Germans to squeal about British breaches of international law and British atrocities. It's a healthy sign that they are feeling uneasy.

MONDAY, *July* 14

According to the B.B.C., July 13th was the day when the Germans said they would march into Moscow. They aren't anywhere near it yet; though, if one looks at the map, the territory they have occupied in the last three weeks is pretty impressive. Not that they have occupied any vitally important centres yet; and the loss of Lithuania and Latvia and eastern Poland, which received the first big blows, was to be expected. The Russians don't seem to have openly admitted the loss of Riga, which is the most important industrial centre they've lost so far (tires and galoshes are among the things made there); but there seems little doubt that the Germans are there. The Germans, however, also claimed to have captured Murmansk early this month, and Murmansk is definitely still in Russian hands. In view of the co-operation foreshadowed by the Anglo-Russian agreement, it seems essential that Murmansk should be held. I wonder, though, how the Lithuanians and Latvians and Estonians are reacting to the German invasion. The Lithuanians were always on moderately friendly terms with the Soviets; Latvia is rotten with Fascist elements; while the Estonians have always looked to the Finns for spiritual guidance.

Some of the people here who are strongly prejudiced against the Soviets say that the Germans are sure to have been received with open arms by the people of the Baltic States, and that they consider the Germans a far lesser evil than the Russians. I don't quite believe all that; both Latvia and Estonia have a strong anti-Baltic-baron tradition; and I can well believe that in both countries there are strong elements to whom the Russians are distinctly the lesser evil, and that there must at least be some truth in the stories in the Soviet press of Lettish and Estonian guerrilla activity against the Germans. However, the Riga bourgeoisie, all those Riga shopkeepers (except the Jews, of course), must be very pleased to see the Germans. The "incorporation" of the Baltic States in the Soviet Union was followed by a great shopping boom in Riga and Tallinn; large numbers of Soviet citizenesses found some good reason for visiting these towns, and, in the process, they bought up in the Riga shops a lot of dresses and shoes and handbags. And, at least since the war has started, the "scorched-earth policy" has taken a peculiar form in the Baltic States; nearly all the matches on sale in Moscow are Estonian; and a good proportion of the confectionery—and there is plenty of it, including some excellent boxes of chocolate—is "made in Riga, Latvian S.S.R." It's quite a consolation to think that when the Huns got to Riga, ready to stuff their bellies with chocolate truffles, they found the cupboard bare. . . .

It seems clear that the Russians suffered very severe losses during the surprise attack of June 22nd. (Why it should have been quite such a surprise I can't imagine, but apparently it was.) They seem to have had about a thousand planes destroyed on the ground; but although this greatly helped the first phase of the German advance, it wasn't really of any decisive importance, as it was, for instance, in Belgium, where they knocked out the complete Belgian Air Force and a good part of the French one on the very first morning. Anyway, the first blow was struck at the newly incorporated border states; and if Stalin hadn't incorporated them, and the attack had started against Minsk and Kiev, I probably shouldn't be here in Moscow today to write this. . . .

Meantime, we don't know exactly where the Germans are, but they must be getting fairly near Smolensk. The other day

Lozovsky was asked whether the German claim was true that Minsk had fallen; and he replied evasively that the fall of this or that town wasn't of the slightest importance to the final outcome of the war. But he added that the Germans had "standardized minds," and that they had a way of imagining that if a certain war technique succeeded in France it was also bound to succeed in Russia. They would soon be undeceived, if they weren't so already. Anyway, it seems clear that the German advance, since they got as far as Minsk, has slowed down considerably, and that the Russians are concentrating large tank forces west of Smolensk. I can't help wondering, though, whether they've got anything like the 10,000 tanks used by the Germans (Lozovsky's estimate). According to all accounts, terrific tank battles are going on behind Smolensk.

I don't much like this German drive towards Ostrov; it is clearly aimed at Leningrad.

Very curious that business about the Litvinov broadcast the other day. We were given to understand that Litvinov would speak on all the Russian radio stations; when it came to the point, he only talked on the foreign wave-length, and in English. And the next morning the Russian press only gave a few scraps of his broadcast; none of his friendly references to Britain, nor his "let bygones be bygones," and "we've all made mistakes"; instead, the Russian papers picked on the phrase to the effect that the Germans were the common enemy of Britain and the Soviet Union, and that there must be "no *de facto* armistice in the west," which Hitler was counting on. . . . And when Lozovsky was asked what part Litvinov was going to play, he replied, very reluctantly, that he supposed Mr. Litvinov would broadcast again. All this, however, happened before the actual signing of the Anglo-Soviet agreement; so maybe the Litvinov policy, or its equivalent, will no longer be reserved for foreign consumption only. It will still take some time before the Russians trust us a little more; it

may require long, patient work; and this work will not be easy
if the Russians really get the idea that there is a *"de facto
armistice"* in the west. . . .

Regarding the average Russian's distrust of foreigners, the
little incident that happened to me today—with the papers
full of the Anglo-Soviet agreement—is typical. I couldn't be
bothered going, as all foreigners do, to the National or the
Metropole for a haircut; and I went instead to a plebeian place
in the Maroseika. The barbers were all women, in clean over-
alls, and the place looked perfectly decent, at about one-third
the Metropole price. I was attended to by a good-looking
young woman, who talked about the warm weather in Moscow,
and told me that she had trained for nine months to become a
hairdresser, and that it was a much more skilled job to be a
men's hairdresser than a ladies' (in the Soviet Union hair-
dressers' and lavatories are the only places where the word
"lady"—*damsky*—is used); and she made a few cracks about
my being "thin on top"—"but not bad enough to put off the
girls"; and then, expecting her to be keenly interested, I said:
"You know, I have only just come from London." Her reac-
tion was astonishing; she pretended not to hear what I had
said, and did not say another word until I again returned to
the question of the weather. And even then she was no longer
talkative, preferring not to have any further dealings with
anyone who had just come from abroad.

Today Erenburg had a sentimental piece in the papers
about Paris, this being the 14th of July. The Russian press is
showing an increasing tenderness for the sufferings of the op-
pressed people of Europe, and Erenburg, who loved his Paris,
and especially his Montparnasse, wrote a very moving piece
about it. He was actually in Paris during the early days of the
occupation, and described how filthy it was. He wouldn't have
been allowed to write all this a month ago.

Today, for the first time, I went on the Moscow subway. Its trains, escalators, and platforms are almost exactly like the London tube, but, in addition, the platforms are panelled with marble, or some kind of polished granite, and at one of the stations there are long rows of life-size bronze statues, all of ideal and handsome proletarians—different kinds of industrial workers—men and women—and fishermen, and peasants, and soldiers and sailors and airmen, and railwaymen, and what not. . . . It's a pity they didn't spend the money on an extra subway line, for there are only two for the present. But the Soviets have certainly a sense of the monumental—one sees it in so many things in this new Moscow—and must have thought it worth while. The subway is deep down, and will do well as an air-raid shelter. In the booking-halls there are little shops—a sort of Moscow Boots, and tobacco stalls, and sweet shops. I bought some excellent Latvian sweets. A young fellow came up and said he wanted to buy *one* sweet, but the girl behind the counter said one hundred grammes was the minimum; so he bought his hundred grammes. I got out at the Krasnyie Vorota, on the "B" ring of boulevards, and had to walk back to our "A" ring along the Kirovskaya. I passed a very beautiful modern building of the Commissariat of Light Industry. It had a lot of windows, and its lines were harmonious, very like some of the new houses in Amsterdam. Not that glass houses stand up to the blitz too well. Lovell later told me that Corbusier had built it, as he had built a number of other Government buildings in Moscow some years ago.

Thursday, *July* 17

The news isn't so hot today. Last night's communiqué talked of fighting in the Smolensk area. That's about 220 miles from Moscow. The Germans claim they've also got into the province of Leningrad, apparently round the south end of Lake Peipus. Does that mean the old Russian city of Pskov is gone? The offensive the Germans started on Saturday didn't, for the first four days, seem to have made much headway, despite the very heavy losses on both sides, which the Russians admitted. It's horrible to try to visualize all that the phrase implies. The Huns have got to Vitebsk, but there was nothing new in the Novograd-Volynsk area in the south. Vitebsk is already very much inside Russia proper.

Actually, it's pretty maddening to be in Moscow just now. The truth is we don't really know what's happening. The Red Army is fighting magnificently according to all accounts, but we have absolutely no direct contact and only very few indirect contacts with anybody at the front.

I've been listening to the Russian radio. They've been reciting patriotic poems of Denis Davydov, the "partisan" of 1812 and of *War and Peace* fame (isn't he the original of the hairy fellow who falls in love with fifteen-year-old Natasha?)—and a poem by Marshak about Stalin's speech—"The blast-furnace will respond to this speech," was the refrain. The propaganda is rather on the monotonous side. But its growing confidence, its treatment of victory as a certainty, is striking, as compared with the undercurrent of anxiety a week ago. The talks in Polish on the German atrocities against the Polish people are a significant war development. I could understand enough to make out that the roads leading out of Lwow were "lined with gallows." And throughout the program there was the constant refrain that "the war is in full swing throughout the enemy's rear." The Soviet communiqué today said that the Germans were killing wounded war prisoners. A terrific fury is being whipped up against the Huns. Interesting as a parallel was the B.B.C. talk saying that "Stay put" in case of invasion wasn't good enough. "Finish them off," the talk suggested, was a more inspiring slogan than "Stay put." That's all very well, but are civilians in England going to be *armed*?

If not, "finish them off" doesn't mean a thing. However, as long as the Russians last, I don't think we need to worry about invasion!

The Russians are also talking a lot about German deserters. No doubt to encourage such desertions the Soviets continue to discriminate between the Nazis and the German people. It is also the ideologically correct thing to say; but I am not sure that their real views on the subject are so very different from Winston's.

Another theme of Soviet propaganda is Hitler's failure to "unite Europe against the Bolsheviks." Last night Moscow radio produced a comic sketch in which Hitler was carrying out in practice his "United Europe." "How many United Europeans have volunteered to fight the Soviets, Goebbels? Is there an army corps?" "No, Adolf, just a platoon." Then, as a fact, the radio reported a story from Stockholm about the European volunteers who had gone to Finland—a party of ten quislings, to whom was later added one plane-load of passengers!

Our chauffeur is a bit of a loafer. He and the other journalists' chauffeurs are a peculiar crowd of loafers. They make more money than most people here (1,000 to 1,200 roubles a month), and they go in for wild orgies. He has been causing us a lot of trouble by being so unpunctual. And there's also been some trouble about old Katya. She is scared of a purge among the Volga Germans if their fellow Germans get a little closer to Moscow. Or, maybe, she's afraid of serving British journalists —in case the Germans come. Anyway, she is in a panic, terribly bad-tempered, and may quit at any moment and escape to the Volga.

Lucien today said: "There are a great many people in Russia who think that Stalin is a very great man." That in reply to my question whether he thought Stalin, who is seldom seen in public, was really popular. And a Russian woman, of whom I asked the same question, said he wasn't exactly "our dear beloved Joseph Vissarionovich"—the form of address frequent in letters sent by official organizations—but that everybody regarded him as the real chief, and a *bashka*, a great organizing brain. She thought the sloppy, "dear beloved" verbiage in the press rather irritated him, but he had to submit to his propaganda experts. Actually, Stalin is a man who has avoided direct, intimate contact with the masses, and is too much the mystery man of the Kremlin to be "dear" or "beloved" in the ordinary sense.

FRIDAY, *July* 18

The other night I went with Maurice and Lucien to the Park of Rest and Culture, now known as the Gorki Park— partly to distinguish it from the other Park of Rest and Culture at Sokolniki, in the north end of Moscow. We drove there in an incredibly dilapidated old taxi, which we discovered by accident in the Pokrovka. The fare was seven roubles. It was the first taxi I had yet seen in Moscow; there seem to have been a few more before the war, but not very many. It was driven by a dishevelled blonde with a business-like and completely non-committal expression. The Park of Rest and Culture, on the banks of the Moscow River, roughly opposite the site where the gigantic Palace of the Soviets is still at its preliminary steel-frame stage (it's been like that for some years, I am told), is a pleasant enough place, except for the continuous blaring of war propaganda by the radio loudspeakers. On the river young men were showing off their skill in diving. Near by, there was the parachute tower, but it did not seem to be in action at that hour. Then we got to some merry-go-rounds and swings, and these were well patronized by some very young people. The "culture" was represented by a very good theatrical exhibition, with miniature models of outstanding stage productions, not only of the Russian theatres, but particularly of the non-Russian theatres—of the National Theatre of Armenia at Erivan, of the National Georgian Theatre at Tiflis (now invariably spelt Tbilisi), and of the various national theatres of central Asia. There was a brilliant miniature model of some production of the Polovetz Camp in *Prince Igor*: and there were photographs of famous Moscow Art Theatre productions of *Gore ot Uma*, the *Revisor*, *The Three Sisters*, portraits of Stanislavsky, Nemirovich-Danchenko, and other great men, and of actors made up as Lenin and Stalin in some play about the October Revolution.

The question of nationalities, with cultural home rule, has certainly been well settled in Russia, and is one of the outstanding successes of the régime; it is remarkable that Stalin was the first Commissar of Nationalities in the first Lenin Government in 1917, and he always continued to take an interest in the question. In that first Lenin Government, it seemed a relatively unimportant job; it was actually one of far-reaching importance, not least at that difficult moment, and one that needed handling with a great deal of practical sense. Couldn't our experts on India learn a few lessons from the nationalities system in Russia? The question of a higher or lower level of culture is neither here nor there; it isn't equal among the nationalities of the U.S.S.R. either.

It was a lovely evening, with a rosy sunset and a clear blue sky. The Moscow River had an almost Mediterranean colour. We walked through the alleys of the park in search of food. An odd hangover from the appeasement days was still there—a war trophy of the Polish campaign—a Polish gun-turret. The thing was guarded by a marine, fixed bayonet and all. On the sports grounds, athletic youths, stripped to the waist, were playing volley-ball. At length we found two restaurants, both very crowded, mostly with soldiers and junior officers with their girls. Vodka is practically unobtainable in Moscow now, and its sale, though not completely prohibited, is not encouraged; so all we could get to drink was a clammy kind of cherry liqueur, and a bottle of "dessert drink," in reality a pink kind of lemonade. The waitress, in a pretty blue embroidered blouse, and rather Oriental-looking, was very slow and dilatory; and Maurice couldn't eat the *okroshka*, the sour iced cucumber and onion soup (an acquired taste, I admit, but once acquired, very good in hot weather), and then, instead of the schnitzels we had ordered, we were given some very ill-cooked stewed mutton, with a take-it-or-leave-it look on the Oriental damsel's face. This part of the rest and culture was disappointing. But it may have been just bad luck.

SATURDAY, *July* 19

There is quite a controversy raging in Moscow about the best way of putting out incendiary bombs. The trouble really started with that *Izvestia* article I wrote about the London blitz, in which I said, among other things, that in putting out incendiaries you must use either sand or a spray; but you must not pour water over them. A day later I noticed that new posters had been displayed all over Moscow showing how incendiaries should be put out: one drawing showed a fellow pouring a bucket of water over an incendiary, and another showed him taking it with a pair of pincers and throwing it into a tub of water. Two or three days after my article, there appeared in *Izvestia* an article by *voentekhnik* (military technician) Zuyev, who, while congratulating me on my "most valuable contribution," said I was talking nonsense about incendiaries. He said that the experiments which had been made had shown conclusively, etc., etc. . . .

Pravda, in the meantime, was going for some writer in *Komsomolskaya Pravda* who had put forward the same idea as mine. And Colonel Symonds, our Home Office expert, was having heated arguments with the Russians, who wouldn't agree with the official London "theory." . . . Nor would they adopt his stirrup-pump. Well, I suppose we shall just have to wait and see. Maybe they'll change their ideas if there's a blitz and somebody gets hurt through following the present instructions.

It's rather remarkable, all the same, that such controversies should be possible at all in the Soviet press. Rather a good sign, I think. . . .

Perhaps time and experience will also convince them that the Moscow black-out is as exaggerated as ours was at the beginning of the war. It doesn't matter so much in summer; but if the present system is adhered to, winter will be hell.

Yesterday I was asked to a pre-view at the Soviet Film Institute of the latest Russian news-reels. It started with a news-reel of the signing of the Russo-British agreement of last Saturday. At the Embassy somebody called it the Trent-Stalin pact; and I could now well see why. Right through the news-reel, fat, enormous old Trent (who is a former Consul or something) seemed to dominate the whole scene. I was interested to see Stalin. He was rather different from what I had expected, and from what the official portraits lead one to believe. He isn't a great big, powerfully built man, but quite a wee man, rather grey and wrinkled, though full of liveliness.

They were very fine, the faces of the Soviet airmen in the news-reel from the front; and the Soviet treatment of the German war prisoners was interesting. There was something snivelling and grovelling in their attitude, as they were being herded into a lorry; nothing defiant. Very German that; as soon as a German is underdog, he begins to grovel, just as his whole infernal country did after the Armistice in '18. I quite believe the Russian stories that many, though not all, the Germans, as soon as they fall into Russian hands, proceed to bleat about their Communist past, or their little home in Austria, and their dislike of Hitler and the Nazis. . . . One of the English people at the show said he did not like what he called "this snarling treatment" of the German war prisoners. I don't see his point; or, rather, I can see it perfectly well, and still disagree with it. To the Russians this is a peculiarly tangible life-and-death struggle; and hatred of the Germans is an essential aim of Russian propaganda; the more Germans are killed, the better, and you wouldn't kill them so cheerfully if they were nice fellows.

To conclude, we were shown a very exciting "Wild West" film of the Finnish war, with the hair-raising adventures of a Russian party of ski troops. The Finnish troops did their ski tricks as well as the Russians; and the real villain of the piece was a German officer in command of them. He was grotesque, and Hitler-like, with a large swastika on his helmet, and with sadistic glee he kept on shouting: *"Feuer!"*—"Fire!" The Soviet hero, trapped in the attic of a burning house, had a hair-breadth escape, after throwing his last three hand-grenades at the Finns; "this one for my country," he shouted; "this one for my party; and this one for my Stalin." The bit about the villainous German officer, who in the end gets his swastika helmet pushed over his face by a Russian rifle-butt, must have been added quite recently, for the film seems to have been made some time ago. . . .

The alcoholic colonel on the German Belgrade radio was again spouting in Russian: "The hopeless, desperate position of the Red Army. . . . The German Army is invincible. . . . We are bringing you real Socialism." He also said something about the high standard of living of the German workers, and the happiness which Hitler's generous labour laws would bring to the Russian workers. The Russians know enough about the German treatment of the other Slav peoples not to be taken in by that sort of thing—even if they had the radio-sets to listen to it. No doubt to show that the quislings were great believers in Russian culture, they ended the program with gramophone records of Tchaikovsky's Fourth. Gangsters.

SUNDAY, *July* 20

I must try to get out of this rut, for this routine of Moscow is very tiresome at times. Contacts are difficult to make outside the immediate circle of officials and Embassy people, and other journalists. The Narkomindel (or "Nark" as we call it for short), and the Hotel National, and the Embassy, and the Hotel Metropole, and then back again to the Reuter office, and then the Nark again, with trips to the Central Telegraph thrown in—such is an agency man's daily routine. And to think I was sent out here "to report the Russo-German war." . . . However, with Anglo-Soviet relations improving, the opportunities for work may also improve. It's important I should get out of Moscow, get to the front, get to Leningrad; but so far there's not much prospect.

Today I fixed up my residence permit; it took several hours to get it done. At the passport office one of the girls was quite amiable, but the other studiously ferocious-looking, and she terrified the life out of an old dame—don't know what her nationality was—who had failed to renew her permit in time. However, after bullying the old dame for about five minutes, she fined her five roubles, and that seems to have been the end of it.

I hate all passport offices; this, and the Polizeipräsidium, and the Préfecture de Police are all much of a muchness.

On my way to the passport place in the Upper Petrovka, I noticed a queue outside a "commission shop" where they buy up silver, gold, and other valuables. People no doubt want a little spare cash "just in case." (Things aren't looking quite so good round Smolensk just now.) A lot of the people were old. I noticed a couple of enamel spoons in the window; a nice present to take home. But what's the good of buying that sort of thing now? When I told Lucien about the commission-shop queue, he said: "The Russians love to buy and sell." I laughed, and said it reminded me of the story by some French journalist who, on discovering in 1921 a train which had taken twenty-four days to get from Sebastopol to Moscow, consoled his readers with the reflection that "The Russians love to travel."

JULY 21

Last night Henry Shapiro gave a sumptuous farewell party to the two Russian girls—both married to Americans here—who are leaving Moscow for America by Trans-Siberian tonight. As I believe I have already said, the Russians only recently allowed them to adopt American citizenship—since the war started. Now that they've got it, they don't seem too happy; in fact, they are both very upset at leaving Russia, perhaps for good. Nice women, both of them. Although one of them seems to have had a little trouble with the authorities —a few months in jail, to be precise—she is quite cheerful about it and doesn't seem to bear them any grudge, and is just as upset as the other one at the thought of leaving "dear, friendly *uyutny* Moscow." There's no English equivalent of *uyutny*—only the German *gemütlich*. One of the girls said she had just had direct news from the front; she had visited a wounded soldier in a hospital; he had just come from the Smolensk front. He said the roads running to Moscow from Smolensk and other places in the west were pretty well cluttered up with quite fantastic quantities of Russian vehicles, tanks and what not; the Russian troops had some difficulty in getting about these roads, and the Germans would find it just impossible. She had heard the same story from a Jewish doctor at the hospital, who had heard it from several other patients. The doctor seemed greatly reassured; for he was, naturally, greatly scared at the thought of the Huns getting to Moscow.

Then, very characteristically, the girl said: "Now, we know all about the Anglo-Soviet agreement; but tell me, what are the British really doing in the west to help us? We know, of course, that the British Air Force is doing a bit of bombing over Germany, but can't it do something *really very big?*"

And all that despite the much greater prominence given by the Soviet press in the last few days to these bombings. Not that it is big front-page news yet; but still, it's a great deal compared with what it used to be. . . .

The party was, on the whole, a rather gloomy one. There was a sense of foreboding—as though clearing out of Moscow was now a matter of days. That—or a big blitz on Moscow. Already on Saturday morning, when I went to the Stary Dom, I saw old Trent packing up crockery and two silver samovars in a large trunk. . . . Just in case? Or are they really going to move, at least some of the stuff, to the Volga?

For several days now we have had air-raid warnings—were they caused by reconnaissance planes?

10.30 p.m.

Looks as if the big blitz on Moscow has started. Is it, or isn't it, the blitz? I can't make head or tail of it. The guns are firing like mad; and the fireworks I can see from our kitchen window are fantastic. (It's the only window that isn't blacked out.) But I haven't heard the sound of any plane yet; nor have I heard anything drop, except shrapnel. . . . This morning there was already an air-raid warning, but it didn't matter, except that with the rigid rules here, you can't get out of doors, and all traffic in the street stops, and you are driven into a shelter. Lozovsky explained that the authorities didn't want more casualties than was strictly necessary; and, with all this shrapnel dropping, I suppose it is dangerous to walk about the streets in a raid, especially as tin hats for civilians hardly exist. But then, this morning, they weren't firing any guns; so where was the danger?

But tonight there was a real warning, and since then the oddest things have been happening. It was still quite light outside when the warning sounded. At first there was a flight of what sounded like a large formation of fighter planes; but soon afterwards the real fun started. Big booming bangs, and sharp light bangs, and the rat-tat-tat of a machine-gun, and then a loud *woo-oof* followed by a million dried peas being dropped on the floor; and when I looked out of the kitchen window, I saw a fantastic piece of fireworks—tracer bullets, and flares, and flaming onions, and all sorts of rockets, white and green and red; and the din was terrific; never saw anything like it in London. And searchlights, and more searchlights, all over the place; and Maurice said he could see a plane caught in the beams of the searchlight. I looked, but couldn't see anything. He said it was 9,000 feet up. How does he know? I am not convinced yet that it's a real raid. Perhaps they just want to show off their terrific barrage to the population; good for morale. . . .

Nonsense. It's a real raid right enough. There's the old familiar *woo-woo* of the German bombers—the old dentist's drill. And now, a long distance away, the old familiar swish of the incendiaries, one-two-three-four-five. They don't all come down at the very same moment. Will they use buckets of water, or will they use sand?

We've got fire-watchers on our roof; wonder what they'll do. Maurice and I asked the house committee if we couldn't take part in the fire-watching; but they immediately turned down the idea of any non-Soviet citizen being allowed to do any such responsible work. . . .

I've again looked out of the kitchen window. The Germans are dropping flares; not the decorative chandelier variety, but ordinary big vulgar sparks. Perhaps they are trying to locate the defences, the balloon barrage, and all that. But apart from that one packet of incendiaries, I haven't heard anything drop yet—nothing reminiscent of the rather sickening whine-crash, whine-crash, whine-crash, and then masonry falling, of the London blitz. . . . There's still nothing much to be heard, apart from the barrage, which comes on every few minutes (the amount of ammunition they are spending must be terrific), but now there's a glow in the sky; nothing much, though. They should have seen Fleet Street on May 10th! . . .

Somebody has just rung up to say they are dropping incendiaries in the centre of Moscow, round the Kremlin, and that old Dunlop at the Embassy has just put out two. . . . There's shrapnel clattering on the pavement outside.

So perhaps it's the beginning of the blitz, after all. But what a small beginning!

This ground-floor flat, with three solid floors above us, is pretty good. Even so, we ought to do something about these windows. It's more complicated than at home; for they've got double windows here, to keep the house warm in winter, and therefore a double quantity of glass; and I don't like glass in a blitz since Don Minifie, head of the London bureau of the *New York Herald Tribune*, got a piece of glass in his eye that night in the Strand. And the strips of paper Maurice stuck on when the war started are much too amateurish. . . .

Tuesday, *July* 22

Three times I nearly went to sleep, and each time there was another ear-splitting burst of gunfire and that kept me awake till after three o'clock. It was damned annoying; especially as I would *much* rather have slept through that hour between two and three when the dentist's drill of the Junkers got more and more insistent. However, I heard only one big H.E. coming down with the familiar London whine and crash. At three, during what must have been a longish interval, I got to sleep. The windows on both sides were a little disquieting, but I had put a lot of pillows between my head and the window, and that was better.

Bertha, the pathetic little maid, who has taken the place of Katya, said she had spent all night in the shelter. It was *"strashno,"* she said, *"otchen strashno"*—very terrifying. Katya left Moscow in a panic the other day; she left without saying good-bye, and didn't even collect her wages.

I have been feeling guilty about Bertha, though it has really nothing to do with me. But last Saturday she debated with some other woman whether she should go down to her Volga-German village near Stalingrad; and in the end she decided to stay. Maurice was very pleased. I felt tempted to tell her she'd be a fool not to leave Moscow if she had a chance; but it would have been "disloyal" to Maurice, and, from my own point of view, undesirable, since she had volunteered to launder my shirts for a small consideration. The regular laundries keep your stuff for a fortnight or more, and with my luggage as limited as it was, I brought only five shirts. And I grudge paying nearly two pounds for a new shirt. Not that any of this really occurred to me at the time—at least not as a problem.

10 p.m.

The second blitz is on. I am writing this in the shelter of the Narkomindel. What an infernal bore to have been driven down here at ten o'clock when the sirens went just at the end of Lozovsky's conference!

This morning, after breakfast, I walked along the boulevards and the Sretenka to the Nark. There were no signs of any devastation. The tram-cars in the Pokrovka were clattering along merrily. It was a sunny morning, and everybody looked quite cheerful—perhaps rather startled at the meagre results of the blitz. I wrote a piece saying it was what London would call a "medium blitz." Actually, it wasn't even that. However, the Moscow fireworks, whether wasteful or not, were much more impressive than the London barrage. In the Po-

krovka I heard a familiar sound: the clatter of broken glass
being shovelled from a lorry on to a not very impressive dump
of debris. . . . There was no sign of any damage near the
Kremlin, except a big bomb crater in the avenue north of it;
and already in the morning people were busy filling it up. By
two o'clock no trace of it was left. It just shows how easily
aerodromes can be mended.

I took the car along the Leningrad Chaussée, but didn't get
very far, for the road was blocked by the militia. They wouldn't
say what, if anything, had been bombed; but the Germans
must have tried for the airfield. . . .

Later, I went to see X. "Anglo-Russian relations couldn't
be better than they are already," he said, very cheerfully. He
assured me that, despite German claims, Smolensk had not
been taken. "Of course, I shan't prophesy," he said, "but the
situation has definitely been improving in the last few days."
He didn't think Leningrad in serious danger either; the Germans had been held up at Pskov, and the Finns hadn't made
much progress either on the Karelian Isthmus or round Lake
Ladoga (though today, for the first time, the Russian communiqué speaks of fighting "in the direction of Petrozav-
odsk.") It would be a nuisance if the Murmansk railway were
cut.

It appears that last night a lot of incendiaries dropped on
the Embassy—the General and the Admiral and some of the
others kept the fire under control for a long time, but in the
end they had to go and fetch the Russian fire brigade. When
the brigade arrived, the chief fireman said to the others: "Comrades, I rely on you to liquidate rapidly and energetically the
seat of the fire." This greatly tickled the fancy of the Embassy people. The damage done to the Embassy isn't serious;
none of the principal rooms has suffered.

I had lunch at the Metropole with Jordan and a bunch of others. The Latvian Legation (now housing the representatives of the Latvian S.S.R.) had, I learned, been completely wrecked, and some damage had also been done in the Arbat area. Later I heard that many Russians had been injured while putting out incendiary bombs; sometimes through inexperience but usually though sheer Russian foolhardiness. The young fellows would just pick up the bombs with their bare hands!

One of the people at the press conference this afternoon told me how he spent the night in the subway. He said it was comfortable, and in one section smoking was allowed, and there were lavatories with running water; women and children sat on the platform, while the rest of the public sat about in the tunnel, with the current cut off. Actually, the subway wasn't crowded last night. Either the blitz came as a surprise or people wanted to stay outside, as far as possible, to have a look at it.

On my way to the Nark I bought for two roubles the popular centenary edition of Lermontov's *Hero of Our Times*. It's been my favourite Russian book since I was ten. At two roubles they must print tens of thousands of copies to make it pay. It is well printed and quite decently bound; the illustrations are miserable, though. The popularity of the old nineteenth-century classics among the people of this country is truly remarkable.

And so here I am, in the Nark shelter. It is large and solid, well propped up, and a good long way underground. Just now I went and bought a bottle of lemonade from the canteen girls down in the next-door basement; they were very excited to hear I had been through the London blitz, and that it was I who had written that *Izvestia* article; and they wanted to know a lot more about London. It is curious how, in the last week or two, the Moscow people are becoming aware of all that the British people have done, and have gone through, in the last two years. Today I was reading the June number of the monthly magazine *Znamie*, and it was still talking about the "second imperialist war," and was deploring the fact that the French working class should have to go on suffering from the continuance of the war between Germany and England, and particularly from the British bombings of French ports.

The reason why I am down here tonight is that Lozovsky called a press conference at the unusual hour of nine p.m.; and this was to meet not, as usual, at the old Greek Legation place, but in his own office in the Narkomindel. It was a solemn occasion; for Lozovsky produced some first-hand documents seized by the Russians. They had been enclosed in envelopes sealed by the German General Staff, and were marked "secret." The documents proved conclusively that the German Army had already elaborately prepared the use of gas against Russian troops—and possibly civilians. Whether gas is actually going to be used is another matter; but it's just possible. It seems important that we should warn the Germans that gas will be used against German towns if they use gas in Russia. Everybody in Moscow has gas-masks; but the German documents show that the use of mustard-gas and other filth is also "under consideration." We would, of course, have sent off long stories about it tonight, but no sooner was the conference over than the warning sounded, and we were all chased down here. There was much gunfire, and some shrapnel was falling as we crossed the yard of the Nark.

This shelter is all right, as far as it goes; but it would be no fun to have to spend a whole night here. There are chairs here, and benches and other odd bits of furniture; but there is nowhere to stretch out. The place is pretty crowded; among those present are Palgunov, and the two censors, both of whom look overworked and are yawning all the time; and a couple of Japs, and Ilya Erenburg, who was specially asked to Lozovsky's conference, and the whole lot of us, of course—Philip Jordan, and Lovell, and the Americans. And Mrs. Bourke-White is running around with her camera, photographing this scene of misery and boredom. . . .

Pravda today tells a story from the front curiously reminiscent of the stories one used to hear in France about the frenzy of the Nazi shock troops. They go in for "psychological" effects, screaming like lunatics as they charge the Russians; and when they get into a village, they go all demented, killing cats, dogs, sheep, and anything that comes their way. And there is also the usual machine-gunning of villages, and of refugees; and hospital trains are often attacked by Nazi bombers. . . .

Regarding the actual situation at the front, I had a discussion with Philip today; he's been wondering whether the Russians may not, before long, get to a point where they will have to make the painful choice between losing Moscow and keeping their army in good fighting condition. . . . I think Moscow is too important to abandon, however strong the strategic considerations in favour of it may be; 1812 is all very well, but in 1812 Moscow was nothing but a big village, nor was it the Russian capital. I don't imagine the fall of Moscow would be necessarily fatal even now, but the shock to morale would be pretty terrible. This blitzing of Moscow is, I think, a healthy sign; the Germans would hardly bomb it if they thought they had a good chance of getting here soon. . . . Cripps is quite cheerful and confident. Generally speaking, the diplomats who like the Russians are also those who are most confident. It isn't a question of wishful thinking, but of faith and of a willingness to see the strong points of the Russians and of their régime.

I have been trying to sleep at the head of the stairs in the part of the shelter where it's dark, and where you can smoke. But the stone floor was damned uncomfortable, and people kept tumbling over my legs; so it was no good. In the dark I heard two voices talking in French (just now there was a big crash, which shook the building and made the electric lights twitch)—one was genuinely French, the other not. I heard them talking about Malraux. I recognized one of the speakers as Lucien, the other was Ilya Erenburg, Order of Lenin and all. A clever writer, but somewhat conceited. I foolishly remarked: "I think we met in Montparnasse some years ago," to which he replied, haughtily: "It's possible." However, we got on better after a while, when Jordan joined the party. Not that Jordan was any luckier than I with his first remark. "Erenburg . . . oh, yes, wasn't it you who wrote something called *Djulio Djurenito?* Read it years ago." "Yes," said Erenburg, "*Hulio Hurenito.* The Spanish 'j,' you know. . . ." Erenburg produced from his pocketbook the photographs of his three Scotch terriers—the only Scotch terriers in Moscow, he said; and he asked whether in London dogs were allowed into air-raid shelters. He was surprised to hear that they were not—at least not into public ones; for, said he, England was the paradise of dogs and smokers. In Russia neither dogs nor smokers got a fair deal; there were no smoking compartments in tram-cars, or on buses, or on the subway. . . .

J ULY 23

What a lousy night it was! The all-clear didn't sound till four o'clock, and we had to stay in the shelter till then; and then, of course, it was necessary to go upstairs to the Nark's press department to send a "flash" about the raid. . . . However, I left that to Lovell and went out to have a look at the streets instead. It was quite light at four. Blue sky, with rosy clouds; and the massive new Soviet buildings looked all spick

and span in the clear morning air, except the Nark itself with
the statue of Vorovsky in the yard. I don't know why he re-
minds me of the dishevelled old pianist, years and years ago
in Leningrad, who nearly broke the piano playing Chopin's
Scherzo in B flat. . . . There were people around, just out
of shelters, sightseeing. A fire was blazing somewhere off the
Sretenka, and somebody said a big bomb had dropped off the
Petrovka; that must have been the one that shook our shelter.
Somebody also said that a bomb had landed in the Red Square,
near the Lenin mausoleum. We went down the Kuznetsky
Mosst to the Central Telegraph office. Here some of the big
plate-glass windows were smashed, and fragments were hanging down from the strips of cloth. Otherwise no damage was
done to the building. . . . The girls behind the counters
looked quite unperturbed. . . . We didn't get home till seven
a.m. There was some broken glass on the way; and in the Red
Square there was only a small bomb-crater, half-way between
the Lenin mausoleum and St. Basil's, with no damage to
either.

In one or two places hoses were stretched across the street;
there were a few small fires still burning off the Ilyinka. It
seems that the Germans prefer using H.E.'s against Moscow,
the effect of incendiaries having, apparently, proved disappointing.

Bertha, the little maid, had been up all night, in the local
shelter. "*Strashno*," she again said, "*otchen strashno*." And
she asked how many more nights of this we were going to have.
"Oh," I said, "I don't know. Maybe a month or two." "And
in winter?" "In winter we'll be all right; it'll be much too cold
for the Germans to fly about."

JULY 26

Remarkably interesting article by General Krassilnikov on the new training of the Red Army, with numerous quo-

tations from the writings of Timoshenko. According to Krassilnikov, there is nothing more dangerous than to be conservative in one's military ideas; it is to this conservatism and easy-going optimism that he attributes the defeat of the French Army. The article must have been written just before the war, for he refers to it as the "second imperialist war," but adds that "our neighbours are all learning lessons from it," and "we also must keep our eyes wide open." "We must not be taken by surprise" is another theme running through the article; it rather suggests that at least certain people high up in the army were seriously expecting a surprise attack. Direct experience is absolutely essential to any army, he says, and he dwells at length on the enormous practical value to the Red Army of the Russo-Finnish war. He also summarizes Timoshenko's ideas on the necessary "realism" of manœuvres. While not going so far as to say that live shells are actually being used against troops in manœuvres, he says that bombing and shelling of the imaginary enemy targets is done with the real stuff, and that, during attacks in manœuvres, shells keep whizzing over the heads of the real troops, and bombs go on exploding very close by, so that the troops get the full sensation of real war. Timoshenko is quoted as saying that troops must be trained to suffer all the hardships of real war (short of actual death); they must do without food and without sleep, and must go on training in the severest frost. Troops must be made to march thirty miles or more a day, and to sleep in the open, even in winter. Timoshenko completely rejects the accepted old idea that five degrees Fahrenheit below zero automatically puts a stop to military operations.

Krassilnikov also gives the gist of the disciplinary statutes of the Red Army, as introduced in October last year. They are completely ruthless, and allow an officer to have any soldier guilty of gross indiscipline shot; an officer who, having been endowed with such powers, applies them inadequately, and fails to get his troops to carry out an order, is liable to be court-martialled for lack of firmness. No complaints can be made against excessive firmness on the part of an officer. And Krassilnikov says: "Present-day warfare requires such enormous moral tension that only the most firmly disciplined troops can face it and maintain their fighting power intact. That is why such drastic steps have had to be taken towards the final liquidation of the pseudo-democratic traditions in the army, traditions which only undermined discipline."

Since the war began, and since this article was written, the political commissars have, of course, had their powers restored; though not at the expense of the officers. Roughly speaking, the officer is, as before, responsible for the military operations; but the political commissar is the man who is in charge of the troops' morale, and, incidentally, also of the officers' morale. And in this most ghastly and murderous of all wars, the question of morale is of extreme importance; and it is important that at moments when retreating troops are on the verge of despair a political commissar should be there to pull them up, and explain to them why they've got to go on with it . . . and, when necessary, he's got to lead them over the top. I have been hearing of political commissars who have performed quite amazing feats of bravery in the most difficult conditions. By taking a personal interest in the soldiers' individual problems, the political commissar sometimes acts much in the same way as a regimental chaplain.

Perhaps a little discouraging is Krassilnikov's quotation from General Zhukov, the chief of the Russian General Staff: "Movement, continuous forward movement—that is the test of successful military preparation." The Russians haven't advanced so far; however, the Germans have got stuck at Smolensk. So it cuts both ways.

SUNDAY, *July* 27, 1.30 *a.m.*

I am writing this in the trench shelter under the tennis-court of the Stary Dom. Could anything be more dignified than being bumped off under an Embassy tennis-court? It looks like the first really big blitz over Moscow. Through the door of the shelter I have been watching the searchlights struggling with the clouds, and the bursts of gunfire, and, in the distance, the greenish haloes of exploding bombs. "Dot vos a bompf, and dot, and dot," I remembered, and I didn't think it funny. . . . A moment ago a packet of incendiaries landed somewhere fairly close. This is a nasty neighbourhood; I don't like to think of that big five-story house—just down Vorovsky Street—which they wrecked the other night, and hit the shelter and killed God knows how many people. The thought of those German carcasses I saw this morning gives me a slight consolation; only, how many more Russians—women and children and men—are killed each time these bastards come over? . . .

About those German carcasses. . . . The Nark people are getting much nicer to the press, and this morning we were taken on an excursion, to see two German planes which had been brought down yesterday. . . . We had to go in our own cars, though, which was a pity, for they are getting rather sticky about petrol—300 litres a month is all they will allow us—and today's trip must have used up a three or four days' supply. The party was conducted by a Red Army colonel, wearing a pince-nez and speaking with an aristocratic little burr. A very friendly person. The caravan consisted of some ten cars, including two Jap cars, one with a diplomatic number-plate.

We drove along the Leningrad Chaussée, which had been roped off by the police after the first raid. This gave one ideas of terrible damage, but actually nothing much was to be seen, and the aerodrome was, to all appearances, intact. We drove through Tushino. The Tushino Thief—wasn't that what the False Dmitri—not the first, but the second—used to be called? Here were *datchas*, with people sitting and walking about their gardens among the pine trees. We turned into another well-tarred main road and passed under a number of well-built concrete bridges, guarded by bayoneted soldiers. And then we drove into the countryside, with an occasional factory here and there, and a row of gabled *datchas* on the crest of a hill. Farther on we passed through various villages; the old log *izbas,* with chiselled window-frames, had, here and there, been replaced or supplemented by more modern and rational, if less picturesque, new Soviet houses. But even the *izbas* had paper strips on their windows. All place-names had been removed. There were many small rivers and ponds along the roadside, where naked little boys were bathing and waving at us as our caravan of cars passed. It was infernally hot, and there were five of us in the car: Misha, and Maurice, and Lucien, and Philip Jordan, and I. At length we drove into a fairly large town called Istra, with numerous golden domes glittering some distance away. Surrounding the church, which looked like the main building of a former monastery, were Kremlin-like walls with pointed turrets. It turned out to be the New Jerusalem, a famous old monastery which was being kept intact as a historical relic. The crosses on the domes had not been taken down. I remembered that Chekhov had often lived in this little town; he observed provincial life here, and the monastery must have provided him with the originals of many of his humorous priests and monks.

Along the road, lorries, camouflaged with foliage and crowded with smiling, fairly cheerful soldiers, were moving towards the front. There were also many soldiers in the main square of Istra. It was a rather nondescript town, with a fruit shop, where they also sold some tins; two or three lemonade carts, and an ice-cream stall, for which there were queues of soldiers and boys. We drove out of Istra along the same road. We passed through villages, where the hens were scuttling and the geese ambulating along the road, just as they must have done in the days of Gogol. And everywhere there was the same contrast between old and new. Striking was the enormous number of children, all healthy and cheerful-looking; the smaller ones waved as we drove past. Women were going about carrying large rye loaves, and cows sometimes got in our way and there were many goats and kids grazing by the roadside. The war seemed very far away. But then suddenly we turned off the main road on to a narrow country road—or rather path. *Proselochnaia doroga*—dear to the hearts of Nekrasov and Chekhov. Clouds of dust rose from the cars in front of ours. It was many inches deep. For a while we could hardly see where we were going; and the car bumped and jumped. . . . At last we stopped beside a large pond, and were then conducted up a slope into a small wood. "Heinkel 111," somebody said. The wreckage was scattered unimpressively over a wide area. A crater—at the foot of it were the tangled remains of an engine, and around the crater lay scattered pieces of metal—tubes and wires and what looked like the top of a camera. There was a sweet, sickly smell in the air—it wasn't the clover or the other flowers around. No, it came from the shapeless, longish mass off the side of the forest path—something black, with bluish-red flesh showing, and flies infesting it by the hundred. It was nauseating, and yet mildly fascinating. Yesterday morning he was still alive; like so many others, whose notes and records had been found, he may have spent the winter dropping incendiaries round St. Paul's, and H.E.'s in Bermondsey or Balham or Borough High Street; and now, but for this crash, he would, with the same cold-bloodedness and bloodiness, have gone on killing the little Russian boys cheerfully bathing in the ponds off the Moscow road. It was horrible; and yet I didn't object as much as I might have done. And the thought that it might have been a pleasant little fellow like young Wolfgang, whom I used to know in Berlin, didn't worry me—too bad for him.

We all stood round the crater, further up, and Mrs. Bourke-White insisted on taking innumerable photographs of us, as if *we* had brought down the plane. "*Tak karasho!*" she'd say in pure New York to some Russian whose position happened to take her fancy. "Don't move, just stay where you are!"

And an old peasant was turning over indifferently with a stick another blackened mass of putrefaction. *"Golova, znachit;* it's a head, I suppose. *Akh ty sterviatnik*—you carrion crow," he said grimly, but with just a touch of paternal reproach. Still, the man, dead or alive, was a *sterviatnik*; that was really all about it.

The colonel explained how it had all happened. Reconnaissance flight over the Moscow area; intercepted by fighter; brought down; crew of four. The villagers had taken away a lot of the stuff as souvenirs. . . . There was a village boy there; he described how he saw the plane spinning down, with smoke belching from its tail. "Ooh! he twisted and turned and then he came down with an *awful* bang."

We went back to the cars. There were heavy rainclouds in the sky; the village some distance away could be seen only faintly; it was raining there. Then the thunderstorm broke—torrents of water came down, battering the car. It was glorious.

Misha got philosophical. "Funny to think," he said, "that at six o'clock yesterday morning these chaps were still alive, and at nine o'clock dead." "It's funnier still," I said, with my tongue in my cheek, "that they were alive at five minutes to nine, and even at five seconds to nine." "Well, yes, I suppose so," Misha agreed, though he still seemed to think six o'clock more convincing. "You mean they were still at home in Germany at six o'clock," I said. "Yes, that's what I really meant," he said, gratefully.

The rain was magnificent; and when, after driving another twelve miles, we turned off the main road into a wood, the scent of trees and flowers was what I had expected from Russia. It was a beautiful thick wood of tall fir trees and younger birch trees; and in the glade the grass was high, and the raindrops glittered on it. And here, in this rural setting—it was so like my summer holidays in 1910 or '11—lay the helpless monster, the Junkers 88, its wings spread out, crocodile-coloured, and a swastika on its tail. Only, one of the wings was half shot off. No dead bodies around this time, thank God. But there was the same smell again; sweet, sickly. And pieces of cotton wool and lint were lying on the grass. The tops of the birch trees behind the Heinkel had been sliced off, untidily, over quite a distance. The radiator was choked with bits of wood and fir twigs. *O Tannenbaum, O Tannenbaum!* The tail was riddled with Russian bullets—good for the Russians! The giant carcass lay there, motionless, helpless, revolting, its inside revealing hundreds of wires and switches, and—like some diseased organ—large blue oxygen-containers. Efficient workmanship in every little detail, even in the serial numbers, and the tidy little metal plates, so-and-so Frankfurt A/M., so-and-so, A.G. Dessau, so-and-so Werke, A.G. Hamburg-Altona. The whole thing was almost intact. Only the mica bubble had been thrown aside, partly smashed; and one engine had been knocked out of place, and two of the seats had been flung out on the tall Russian grass. The two dead bodies had been found attached to these seats. They were young chaps. The other two were wounded. One was a colonel, badly wounded; the other less so. A Red soldier said: "They didn't say much, but the colonel kept asking for water. The other one wouldn't let him drink. We called out a doctor; he came and attended to them here. They're in the local hospital now. The colonel keeps on asking for the iron cross or something he lost in landing; couldn't we find it for him? Queer people." He was a good, simple-natured Russian. He spoke without malice. If only the Germans had the same sense of *decency*! The Russians don't fully realize yet what the Germans are.

We drove back, in a rather pensive mood. "Good story," said one of the Americans, "though not really a *news* story that proves anything." Apart from London and other bombings, it was perhaps my first taste of *real war*, and my first smell of it. How many people in England clearly visualize the meaning of "seven or eight or ten of our aircraft are missing"?

A little distance away from the Junkers 88 the air was full of the sweet smell of freshly mown clover.

We were, on our way back, taken to see a signalling station for aircraft detection. The Soviet colonel and lieutenants all seemed very efficient. There were little lamps on the wall, registering the location of planes, as detected by observation posts; phone lines to a central place in Moscow; an emergency radio station and an emergency power supply. It was all very impressive, though I don't understand much about these things. We drove on. In a wood I saw two girls peacefully reading: one was reading *Pravda*, the other a tattered old volume—Pushkin, perhaps, or Tolstoy. All the peacefulness of the scene contrasted so absurdly with these Heinkels. It reminded me of Winston's great speech of June 22nd—about the maidens who laugh and the children who play, and the simple joys of the Russian people, "despite Communism."

We didn't get back to Moscow until five p.m., all feeling very hungry. A crowd of us had a poor and expensive meal at the National; then we went to the Nark to write some "pieces"; and later I went for supper at Anna Mikhailovna's. Binkley also was there. Anna Mikhailovna is about fifty; she was probably very anti-Bolshie in the past, but, like a lot of people of her type, has become perfectly reconciled to the régime; she has a good translating and interpreting job, and even ventures to cultivate a number of friends in the foreign colony, with whom she likes to talk about "culture." She is violently anti-German, and thinks that a sacred mission has fallen upon England and on "our Soviet Union" to save civilization. What she regrets most of all, she says, is not to have had a chance since the Revolution to keep in closer touch with French literature. She once had a husband, and darkly hints that something terrible happened to him many years ago, but actually, I am told, he simply ran away from her. Once I said to her quite blatantly: "Tell me, would you like a change of régime

in Russia?" The good woman was horrified at my question.
"Good God, no. What other régime can there be, except a
German concentration camp? Our country has toiled for
twenty years, in appallingly difficult conditions, but now we
have achieved a standard of comfort and prosperity, and our
young people, who have never seen any other Russia, are
perfectly happy, and although we former bourgeois aren't as
well off as we were, the general level of education and culture
and economic well-being has improved so very much. . . ."
I really believe she means what she says, though she is inclined
to grumble about this and that; but that is a very common
failing in Russia, and not at all confined to the ex-bourgeois
class. However, that no more means disloyalty to the régime
than grumbling in England.

There was a well-laden tea-wagon of *zakuski* and drinks,
but, of course, she complained. "Terrible, the food conditions
in Moscow just now," she said. "A month ago you could get
thirty-six varieties of sausage at the Gastronom shops; now
there are only three kinds to be got." And the other night,
during an air-raid, she was chased into the underground, and
didn't like it. She had to *stand* in the tunnel for four hours;
and, in the end, she couldn't bear it any longer and sat down,
"in spite of everything"—meaning dirt and vermin—real
or imaginary. "This unhygienic sort of thing just won't do in
the long run," she said; "it'll kill off more people than any
bombs. Of course, it's the war; and don't think I am complaining; the Government is, of course, quite right to give ruthless
priority to troop trains; so it doesn't really matter about
the thirty-six kinds of sausages. . . . Do have a little more
caviar, won't you?" The flat was small—the upper floor of
a tiny old two-storey house off the Arbat—but well furnished,
with a lot of old-fashioned odds and ends, a Japanese screen,
and bound sets of Tolstoy and Maxim Gorki. There was a
ring at the door. "Oh, that must be Serezha," said Anna Mikhailovna, and ran out to meet him. In came a young lieutenant

with shaved head. "This is my nephew, Sergei Sergeievich"—
I forget what his full name was—"just home on leave."
"Gallant allies?" he said. "Well, well. . . ." He was very reserved, and didn't seem to think much of his "auntie." He
hardly said anything about the front, except that he had been
engaged in active fighting a week ago, and that casualties were
very heavy on both sides. There was something rather grim
about his face when he talked about the war; he gave one the
impression that, in his view, Russia was fighting with her back
to the wall, that she would do all that was humanly possible,
but that this war was a fearful calamity for the Russian
people, and that he was not expecting very much help from
what he called the "gallant allies." I asked about the civilian
population and the refugees. He made an evasive gesture.
"We are sending east as many as we can," he said, "but we
can't allow them to clutter up the roads; it's a ghastly problem; for by telling them to remain behind we know we may
be condemning them to a slow death. . . . However, it's a
sacrifice Stalin and the whole Russian people have agreed on
making. But it's tough on those who are left behind."

I asked if he thought the Germans would get to Moscow.
"No, you needn't worry about that," he said, with just a tiny
touch of sarcasm. There was a hard but tired look in his eyes.

I left about a quarter to twelve, but no sooner had I got
into the Arbat than the warning sounded. I had no car, so it
meant quickly choosing a shelter before the police drove me
into one. I wasn't in a copy-hunting mood, or I would have
gone into the Arbat subway. Instead, I decided to walk down
to the Stary Dom, in the Vorovskaya, only five minutes' quick
walking. Before I got half-way there, the guns were firing like
mad, and the sky was filled with the lights of exploding shells,
and tracer bullets, and all kinds of rockets—just as on the first
blitz night, and there was a droning of planes overhead, and
bits of shrapnel were falling. I felt fairly calm, and only

wished I had had my London tin hat. There was nowhere to sit in the crowded Stary Dom basement, so Maurice and Lucien (who had just arrived there from somewhere) and I went along to the tennis-court trench, which was quite empty.

And now the blitz seems to be dying down at last, after nearly two hours. Not that anything very big seems to have dropped anywhere round here, but there were plenty of planes about.

SUNDAY EVENING, *July* 27

Towards the end of the raid this morning Père Florent, of Leningrad, came over from the Stary Dom and joined us in the shelter, producing a bottle of excellent 1933 Pouilly. He is a tall, handsome man of about forty-five, with a large dome of a bald head. He had lived in Leningrad for a long time. He referred to it lovingly as *"ma ville, mon Leningrad."* He spoke good Russian, though with an accent. "What do you think will happen to Leningrad?" I asked. "No way of holding it. The Russians will destroy it before abandoning it." There had been some bombings of the outskirts of the town, he said, round the Obvodny Canal and the Narvskaya Zastava, round the Putilov Works; I knew it well, for when we went to the *datcha* by car we used to drive through it. I am told the shabby wooden houses have been largely replaced by fine blocks of workers' flats. Père Florent, who had declared his allegiance for Russia and for de Gaulle, is now living at the British Embassy, in a side building. . . .

The blitz had died down. Père Florent offered me a bed in the room next to his. I went there, tried to sleep, but the all-clear soon sounded. In the meantime, however, I had lost Maurice and Lucien, who had gone off by themselves, and I decided to walk. It was twenty to four. The streets were crowded with people coming out of their shelters, especially out of the Arbat subway. They talked quietly of their experiences. "Nothing much round here. All has been quiet in our street," a woman in the Vorovskaya remarked in a tone of relief. The Vorovskaya must be a little nervous about air-raids since that night when a five-storey building was smashed up and the shelter hit. The next day I saw women and children with bundles sitting on the pavement waiting to be taken away somewhere. . . . And that same day the maid said about some other place in the Arbat area: "And they sat there with their bundles and they cried, and cried, and cried."

It was a lovely clear lilac morning; there were balloons in the sky—rather more numerous than before. The Arbat was crowded. I walked down Comintern Street and Belinsky Street. No damage was to be seen anywhere. The Kremlin walls also seemed all right. I was hot with walking. When you've had no sleep you are apt to get hot much more readily. Blast that man in London who said I couldn't bring any more clothes; this tweed jacket is hopeless; I'll have to get something light to wear.

I went on to the Nark along the Kuznetsky Mosst, where in the last two or three days windows have been sandbagged and nearly all the shops boarded up. The street is more shabby and nondescript than ever to look at; it is hard to imagine that it was the centre of fashion in Moscow once—the Moscow Bond Street of last century.

The soldier outside the Nark now knows me, and I don't have to show my pass any more. . . . The agency men were all upstairs dashing off "flashes" about the raid. The communiqué said that "a small number of planes" broke through to Moscow, and that bombs were dropped only on the outskirts. It seems rather an understatement. From our shelter I could see many bomb flashes and count a good number of explosions. Four Hun planes were brought down, we later learned.

We didn't get home till six, in broad daylight.

MONDAY, *July* 28

The attitude of the Russian papers to England is improving. They publish glowing accounts of the devastation wrought by the R.A.F. in places like Cologne and Düsseldorf. Last night I heard Harry Hopkins's speech on the gigantic American support for Britain, and about the thousands of bombers which would destroy German industry no matter how far east it goes. He made no mention of Russia, though.

At the press conference today, where we were *filmed* for the Russian documentaries (millions of people read in the Russian press about these conferences, so they'll want to see what we foreign correspondents look like!), Lozovsky described the Russian front as "a gigantic continuous Verdun." The truth is that what is happening now at Smolensk and along the whole front is *the greatest event since the Battle of Britain.* It is beginning to look like Hitler's defeat No. 2, or perhaps No. 3, if we include the destruction by the navy of most of his capital ships.

What is it, I often wonder, that makes the Russians fight like this? They are defending *something*, their country, their régime, which, whatever one may say, are all part of the same thing. There is no longer a dividing line between "Soviet" and "Russia." Even the old people have accepted it, have become reconciled to it, especially since it has become a *national* régime. And though it is ruthless in some ways, even the most critically minded feel that, at least *potentially*, it is a good régime, with the Stalin Constitution as a basis for the future. The army's resistance is, of course, strengthened and supported by iron discipline. Timoshenko has the strongest views on that subject; but anyone who makes wisecracks—and I have heard some—to the effect that this war is "run by the G.P.U.," is just a fool. A thousand problems will, of course, arise when Russia ranks among the victors of Germany—as the chief victor, or as England's equal. Perhaps, almost certainly, some of our Tories are already getting cold feet at the prospect. They will not carry much weight, but our Labour Party will get alarmed at the idea of the Communists cashing in. Not that Harry Pollitt and Willy Gallacher, leaders of the British Communist Party, deserve the slightest credit for Russian resistance and an eventual Russian victory. They don't know much more about Stalin and the Russian people than I do about the Fiji Islands. Much depends on whether, after the war, the Comintern will be allowed to play any part in European affairs. It has seldom done Russia's national policy any good, and often a lot of harm, notably in Germany and France, and has played into the hands of Fascists and reactionaries. But the Comintern is one thing, and Sovietism another. The post-war competition (and the ultimate choice for Poles, Czechs, and even Germans) may be not between capitalism and Communism, but between two forms of democracy—capitalist democracy and Soviet democracy (with a progressive application of the Stalin Constitution). Here there is room for give-and-take, and for *rapprochement* between these ideologies. It is important to prevent a clash, and to prevent rivalries in Europe over the adherence of this or that country to one of the two ideologies. The social régimes of both England and Russia are going to evolve in the course of this war; they may become very similar in many respects, with Britain becoming more "socialist" (in the wide sense of the word) and Russia adopting more and more of those democratic liberties which her people would welcome and which they will expect from a full peace-time application of the Stalin Constitution. Perhaps the real difficulty will be America, which may, for a long time, still persist in being stubbornly capitalist.

What would be fatal to the future peace of Europe would be any sort of return by Russia to international Trotskyism, and any attempt to trotskyize Germany. It would be a boomerang. In a few years Germany would go Nazi again and start another war. But I think the Russians are becoming increasingly aware of the real nature of the German problem. Even with the Poles there shouldn't be much disagreement on that point.

The Russians are making a great deal of their air-raids on the Rumanian oilfields. Somebody even said that "there was nothing left of Ploesti but its name"; though a day later we learned that Ploesti—that is, "the name of Ploesti"—had again been bombed.

Actually, I am told by experts that apart from the destruction of the Czernowoda Bridge, which was a great Russian air feat, and has greatly been hampering Rumanian oil transport, the Russian bombings have knocked out only one or two oil refineries, but that this has left the refining capacity of Rumania almost unaffected, since the Rumanian refineries were not working at their full capacity at any time.

What I find disturbing is that when our people in Rumania were still in control of the oilfields, they should not have blown up the refineries the moment they saw that things were going hopelessly wrong, and that the British and Americans would be thrown out sooner or later. Just bad luck, or incompetence mixed with wishful thinking ("There'll be time yet"), or— long-term capitalist considerations? If it's that, then it's the biggest crime committed in this war by anyone on our side.

I went to see X. He was less overwhelmingly confident than last time. He said Smolensk was still in Russian hands—at least, so he had been told yesterday. What he said about the air-raids on Moscow was more or less common knowledge. The Germans had concentrated on engineering works and railways, though without much success; and they were also trying to terrorize the population to some extent. (Berlin radio last night painted gruesome pictures of panic in Moscow—"and that," it said, "is what Stalin has rushed the Russian people into!") Pskov is definitely in German hands, and in the Moscow sector the Germans claim to be near Vyazma, but the Russians deny it. It is not clear how far they've got into Estonia, and whether they are pushing on, *both* north and south of Lake Peipus. It is not easy to visualize this war. Apparently it's something like this: the tank thrusts are followed by mechanized units, then by infantry; at some point the Russians butt in, attempting to cut off the tanks; and then they counter-attack with their own tanks.

It looks as though, after failing in their frontal attack on Moscow, the Germans are now concentrating on Kiev. X thought the Russian equipment perfectly adequate; he wasn't quite sure about tanks, though. It was true, he said, that the Russian heavy tanks were first-rate, and that the Germans reluctantly recognized this; they had admitted that in a huge tank battle, in which fifty or sixty Russian heavy tanks were involved, only six were knocked out.

WEDNESDAY, *July* 30

I hear that Harry Hopkins is coming to Moscow. That's excellent. His speech over the London radio was given a lot of publicity in the Soviet press.

There was no blitz last night. But Monday's seems to have smashed up a lot of windows in various parts of Moscow; though nothing very serious. The Russians claim ten down.

Last night I went with Philip Jordan to the cocktail bar in Gorki Street—a sumptuous new place with nickel-tubed furniture and modern lighting, and crowded with Red Army officers. We drank vodka and had kilki (some kind of anchovy) sandwiches, and, perhaps in our honour—for they could hear us speak English—the band played *Tipperary*; a lot of the people cheered.

It's a nuisance: our petrol has run out, and there won't be any for the car until the 1st of the month. Maurice has tried to wangle an extra supply through the Embassy and the Nark, but it's no use. The food rationing is getting more difficult, too. We've been put on a special "foreigner's basis"—we are privileged to buy every week certain limited quantities of food at the Gastronom No. 1 shop; but the "limits" are quite generous; more so than for most Russians.

In the absence of a car, I decided to take a day off and to get away, for once, from the Nark, the Metropole, and all that. I took tram 24 at the Pokrovka; it was going to some place called the Baumanskaya Zastava, wherever that is—somewhere out east. The journey again showed what a strange mixture of different things Moscow is—a town in the making. First the tram went down Marx Street, which was nondescript, rather 1860; then it passed through a new quarter with huge and tidy-looking blocks of workmen's flats; after that came about a mile of nothing but wooden cottages, which looked like a seventeenth-century print of Moscow; the little houses might have been there since before 1812, for all one knew. Then, near the terminus, I got again into a large, brand-new district. On both sides of a wide avenue there were enormous nine- and ten-storey blocks of flats, with gardens and little fountains between them. Here also were workers' clubs and co-operative food shops, and a large cinema showing the *Chapaiev* film and news-reels; and a large shop crammed with books and pamphlets on *The Second Fatherland War* and on *The Role of Women in War-time*; and in the windows there were busts of Lenin and Stalin. There were many people in the avenue, particularly round the newspaper kiosk, where they were reading *Pravda*. They looked contented, or, rather, not discontented. A few windows, here and there, had been broken by bomb-blast, but there were few other signs of damage. Nor had there been any big fires anywhere.

I walked about this brand-new part of Moscow. These people have certainly built something; at a heavy price, perhaps at too heavy a price; but it is *there*.

I took a tram-car back into town—a different one, though. It went through another old part of Moscow, composed of nothing but wooden houses—a few of them were burned down, or rather half-burned out; the fire-watchers must have made desperate efforts to save what could still be saved. In England we should have let it go, I suppose. Opposite me in the tram sat a ginger-haired boy, a mass of freckles, and little red turned-up nose—a greasy cap and shapeless patched black trousers, and a belt with a school-buckle. I handed the conductress fifteen kopeks. She asked me where I wanted to get off; I hadn't the vaguest idea. Fortunately, somebody asked for the Kaluga Road, so after she'd grumbled: "Why don't you answer?" I said angrily: "I *told* you, the Kaluga Road." People in Moscow are very suspicious of anyone who doesn't know his way about. The tram went along a street called the Chaussée Entusiastov. They do give absurd names to streets. It was like the other day, on the trolley-bus, when they advised me to get off at the Bezbozhny Pereulok—the Godless Lane. . . . I hadn't the vaguest idea where the tram was going, until suddenly it crossed the river; far away west I saw the golden domes of the Kremlin. Eventually I got off at a railway station on the south side. It was called the Paveletzky Station and was painted pale-blue and white; its original name was the Saratov Station. Outside were crowds of people, apparently going off to the Volga. Here I got off and at last found my old friend, tram A, which took me back to the Pokrovka. On the Moscow Embankment a large bomb must have fallen—all the windows in a large seven-storey house were smashed—it was some kind of scientific institute—and there was some damage all around, but no houses had actually been flattened out. The bomb must have fallen in the street; and the crater must have been filled up. These wide Moscow streets are a great boon; nearly half the bombs must be wasted.

I notice that the new fire-fighting posters say *sand* must be used for incendiaries. That's what I call learning from experience!

At the same time, the fire-fighting here, for all its errors, is *better* because no shirking is allowed. Three fellows guilty of neglect, and so responsible for the destruction by fire of a large warehouse worth three million roubles, have been shot. I wonder what London would look like if, last September, a few City business-men had been shot for going off for the week-end with their office keys. . . .

Thursday, *July* 31

"The President asked me to come to Russia to see M. Stalin. I saw M. Stalin and M. Molotov this evening. I expect to see Stalin two or three times more before I leave. We discussed at some length the situation in relation to the war with Germany, and I told him, on behalf of the President, that our country considers Germany the enemy, and whoever fights Hitler anywhere is on the right side of our country. We particularly intend to help the Soviet Union with immediate supplies, and also in terms of the long-range aspect of this war, however long it may last. I expressed to Stalin the pleasure and admiration of the United States at the fight of the Russian soldiers. We discussed in detail supply and munitions problems. Obviously I can't discuss the details of the various items of munitions and raw materials involved. I am meeting various other Government officials later tonight, and am again seeing Stalin tomorrow afternoon.

"I shall go home as soon as my mission is complete. I cannot say if I'll go to England or direct to the United States. Stalin gave me several messages to the President—cordial thanks for offers of assistance. He was sure the American people and the President were not misplacing their confidence in the role to be played by the Soviet Union in the final downfall of Hitler. I spent two hours in the Kremlin.

"First, getting supplies here *immediately,* and secondly, on a long-term basis. These are the two distinct problems. I am confident there'll be no difficulty whatever, and no delay. Even if I hadn't gone to England I would have come here.

"I saw Ambassador Cripps tonight and had a long talk with him."

These notes were written at the U.S. Embassy, where we were summoned to meet Harry Hopkins. He spoke in a very soft voice, hardly audible from more than five feet. He seems a man with a very clear mind and is obviously conscious of the great importance of his mission. He stressed the word *immediately*. He looked very tired, though, which is not surprising, considering the kind of trip which brought him here! We sat in a circle round him, having whiskies-and-sodas, and Mrs. Bourke-White was, as usual, bothering us with her camera and flashlights.

As we were going out, I said to Hopkins: "May one assume you are working on the principle of 'first where it's most urgently needed'?" He said, "M-m-m-m——" which had an affirmative intonation but wasn't a straight "yes." Perhaps some of our people in London are objecting to British priority being in any way interfered with.

At eleven o'clock Lucien and I had, in the absence of a car, to walk home from the Nark. It was so dark that we had to hang on to each other's arms. Torches are, of course, completely prohibited. The black-out was absolute. We tripped and stumbled several times as we shuffled along the Ilyinka and the Maroseika. And we were perfectly sober. What Moscow's going to be like in winter I hate to think.

PART II

AUGUST

Friday, *August* 1

I haven't got that fearful foreboding I had on the 1st of June 1940 in Paris; even though the Huns aren't much farther from Moscow than they were from Paris then. Maurice and Lucien and I went to see the Père Florent last night. He had been for seven years in Leningrad, having settled there at the time of Laval's flirtation with the Soviets. During those years he had had a hard time and had seen a lot of life in the raw. He spoke of Leningrad in a manner that warmed my heart; but recently he left for Moscow. Before leaving he declared his loyalty to the Soviets and to General de Gaulle. Last night a telegram came for him to tell him he was to join the Free French forces in the Near East.

The *Père* is a reactionary at heart. He disapproves of Vichy, but he respects Pétain, and likes all the family-tradition business. When I went off the deep end about the French quislings, and said they had betrayed France's national tradition, he preferred to dwell on the wickedness of the Popular Front; he half-defended *Gringoire*, talked about the rotters who had invaded Paris, and winced whenever I said anything against the *Action Française;* he agreed that Bernanos had written a good book, but described the democratic Catholics of *Esprit* as a pack of frauds.

He is much better on Leningrad: there were 25,000 Catholics there with only two priests to look after them. Many of

110

them were Poles or of Polish descent; he used to christen 600 to 700 children a year. He talked about the fearful poverty he had seen, and mentioned a woman he knew who had ninety roubles a month to live on. He would let her do his washing so that, in coming to his house, she could eat something. "It is a city of scoffers," he said about Leningrad.

He seems to have met chiefly miserable people, and his ideas about Russia are therefore rather one-sided. It must be hard for him, of course, to get over the fact that even if this is *not necessarily an anti-religious régime, it is certainly an anti-clerical régime.* But victory over Hitler is now his chief consideration.

I found X looking worried, and he also seemed slightly irritated with Hopkins. "It's all very well talking about *immediacy*; but how does he know that anything can be delivered in time to affect *this* battle in any way? . . . Don't you realize the Germans are preparing a terrific drive in the south?" "It's a blessing, however," he added, "that there's Stalin at the head of things. He has a first-class grasp of military affairs; he is in close contact with the generals, has an alert mind, and an astounding mastery of *details* in every military problem. Everything depends on him. . . ."

The papers are making a big show of the agreement with Poland and of Harry Hopkins's visit. In all the papers there are pictures of Hopkins's arrival at the airport, with Lozovsky by his side.

I wrote a long piece about the Polish agreement, trying to show that it was perhaps an indication of Russia's post-war policy, attending to her own affairs as her first consideration. She has recognized the independence of Poland and Czechoslovakia; does that mean that she will let the Poles and Czechs build up their own countries, but take a paternal, Pan-Slav interest in their military security? The present boom in Pan-

Slavism in the Soviet press might be translated into both cultural and post-war reconstruction terms. Would not the Slavs —even the Poles—welcome Russian military protection against a new German aggression, since they were so badly let down when they relied for their security on the western Powers? But whatever may be the contradictions and the different snags in future Anglo-Russian relations, we've *got* to support Russia; we've got to do away with the suspicions and all that half-heartedness about the Russian allies that one finds even among some of the Britons here.

This evening I went to the popular cinema round the corner; it cost only two roubles. There were lots of soldiers in the audience. A somewhat dreary program. First there were some war news-reels—tanks, and marching soldiers, and firing guns. The people cheered loudly only once—when Stalin appeared on the screen. He must enjoy general popularity with the ordinary people here; for people don't cheer in the dark unless they really feel like it. The main film, called *The Boxers*, was amusing in spots. At first it showed a team of Soviet boxers training, and later the best among them are sent abroad for a great tournament in Paris. The director of the Salle Wagram, or whatever the place is called, is a villainous-looking Frenchman with a black moustache—how very like French Hollywood villains! "How do you speak Russian so well?" the Russian boxers ask. "Ah," says the Frenchman in comic Russian, "I went on a leetle journey to Russia. Sebastopol, 1919." . . . The Soviet boxer slaps him on the back. "Ha, ha! hardly a little journey that ended very well, was it?" The Frenchman supports with all his might Laus, the European champion; in the end, of course, Laus gets knocked out by the valiant Soviet boxer, amid cheers from the comic French audience. After their victory the Russian boxers are served supper in a luxurious hotel room, complete with brandy and wine bottles, and large bowls of fruit. One of the boxers gets up, opens a suitcase, and produces a little bottle of vodka, and they all stand up and drink to Russia. And at the same moment the girl friend rings up from Moscow to congratulate the hero, and to fix their wedding-day. For a second the Arc de Triomphe appears on the screen, and a mountain range, and then Berlin and Warsaw, all moving past in swift succession. The final shot is that of the Kremlin, and the boxers and all their friends join in a great song about being back in dear old Moscow again. All the sentiments and themes in this average "popular" film were very revealing.

The Kremlin is camouflaged with large splashes of black and yellow, and big canvases—with small houses and windows painted on them in what is said to be fireproof paint. At the Malyi Theatre they are using the old stage scenery of Ostrovsky's *Forest* for camouflage.

SATURDAY, *August* 2

There was no bombing worth mentioning, but we didn't get home till 3.30, with these infernal shelter rules. It was quiet and peaceful, and there was a glorious starry sky as we came out of the shelter. Got up late this morning. Coffee and bread and butter and cheese, and the last of Maurice's pot of marmalade. He says the price of food has gone up very considerably since the war started and that stuff is hard to get. However, I looked at the maid's regular ration cards for sugar, bread, meat, etc., and the rations seemed reasonable enough.

I spent the morning reading the Russian papers. Often one has to wade through columns of rhetoric or generalities for a few crumbs of fact or semi-fact. Important exceptions, though, are two papers which somehow seldom reach the ordinary civilian public—the army daily, the *Red Star*, and the navy daily, the *Red Fleet*. They are written mostly by service men, and are very instructive, especially if you know how to read between the lines. The thick military, naval, and air periodicals are also well worth reading.

We had chicken soup and frankfurter and mash for lunch, also raspberries. For years I had imagined—on the strength of childhood memories—that fruit in Russia had a much finer flavour than in any other country, that it was more "aromatic"; but I can't notice much difference, really. Maybe it's the fault of the régime!

Lozovsky gave a good snappy talk on the German promises and prophecies that haven't come true. At question time I must have made a bit of a nuisance of myself, for afterwards Lozovsky said: "*Gospodin* Werth, you always like to know everything, don't you?" "Of course," I said. "Oh, I sympathize, I sympathize," he said. "I was once a journalist myself." I asked (a) whether the release of Polish war prisoners had begun and if steps had been taken for forming a Polish Army in the U.S.S.R.; (b) whether, since the Soviet Government was willing to re-establish diplomatic relations with Belgium, Norway, etc., it would consider it desirable to have here a representative of General de Gaulle. He said that steps were being taken about the Poles, but a lot of practical problems still had to be settled; and he couldn't state how many Polish war prisoners there were, since these were to go into the new Polish Army; and that would give away vital secrets to the enemy. De Gaulle was not a government, and the matter would require closer consideration.

Very curious; I learn that every time there is a night raid on Moscow the Jap journalists go off to the country before dark. Inside knowledge?

TUESDAY, *August 5*

I spent Sunday in a different world. First, I went to see Ostrovsky's *Forest* in the Malyi Theatre. I hadn't seen it since Petrograd days. I am never quite clear about the different theatrical schools in Russia; but this one clearly isn't in the Moscow Art Theatre tradition. In this production of *The Forest* every one of the persons is a *character*; it's very much in the old Varlamov-Davydov traditions of the Alexandrinka of St. Petersburg. I liked the atmosphere of the Malyi. Here were, in front of me, two girls; both plain, but more natural, spontaneous, extravert than most of the people I had met here before. The plainer of the two, lanky, with big hands and a large grinning mouth, slightly monkey-like, bubbled with laughter and exuberance; she talked to her friend about the blitz, said she wouldn't leave Moscow, and chattered away so fast, and through so much giggling, that I missed part of the conversation. She also talked exuberantly about different plays. I wonder what her job is. The theatre was packed with soldiers. There was no feeling of dejection among them, but an air of complete self-confidence.

Before the curtain rose, Prozorovsky, the producer, came before it, and made a speech on the link between the army and theatre; he welcomed the army, "our great invincible Red Army, which is defending our great country and our beloved Moscow, where the remains of our great genius Lenin lie buried, and where that great man Stalin is conducting the destinies of this country." And he then announced, amid loud cheers, that Yablochkina was playing today. "Alexandra Alexandrovna has a weak heart and is in poor health. She has devoted sixty years of her life to the theatre; she worked here during the Civil War and during the later years of prosperity. We tried to persuade her to go to the country. But no; she said she was determined to stay on in Moscow, as long as the Government remained here. . . . Long live the Red Army, long live the Theatre, long live our invincible leader, Joseph Vissarionovich Stalin!"

Before the third act Prozorovsky again appeared before the curtain. "I made a mistake," he said; "we Bolsheviks always admit our mistakes. There was a phrase I used which may have given rise to some undesirable interpretations—it was when I said that Yablochkina had decided to stay on in Moscow as long as the Government remained here; what she said was that she wanted to be in Moscow because the Government *was* here." Some party person in the audience must have drawn his attention to the unfortunate slip.

How wonderful to see Ostrovsky's *Forest* again—after all these years! Generations of actors have cherished this role of Neschastlivtsev, the Shakespeare-spouting, ambulating tragedian of the fifties, with the soul of Don Quixote; and the part of Arkashka, his roguish Sancho-Panza-like fellow-comedian. The Soviet régime has made no difference; the actors make a wonderful show of the play, and the audiences are as delighted as ever they were; or perhaps more so, for the average age of the audiences is much younger, and they are fresher and more appreciative. While "walking from Kertch to Vologda," the tragedian meets Arkashka on his way, and he takes him along to see his—Neschastlivtsev's—aunt, an elderly, coarse-minded widow, who is being exploited by young Bulanov, her gigolo. The "forest" where the aunt lives is a forest of vulgarity, selfishness, and human injustice, against which the quixotic tragedian rebels, and which he denounces with Marlowesque rhetoric, in the play's great tragicomic finale.

What amazing actors they are, these "People's Artists of the U.S.S.R." and these "Artists of Merit of the R.S.F.S.R." —for it was practically an all-star cast. Even the smaller parts, like that of the old butler, and of the mischievous old Ulita, were played by first-class actors. The actor with the curious stage name of "Lenin" did not perhaps boom his Shakespeare-inspired oratory as loudly as he might; but in the scene with the unfortunate Astusha, robbed of her dowry, he was magnificent. Gurmyzhskaya, the selfish vulgar "auntie," was played with such vitality and psychological realism by nearly eighty-year-old Alexandra Yablochkina that I was continually reminded of some of the old émigré dames I used to meet in Paris! Throughout the play the blend of comedy and pathos was remarkably good, and how pleasant it was, during the intervals in the buffet, to talk to these soldiers, many of whom had come on leave from the front! They were not underrating the German war machine, but their calm self-confidence was impressive.

He's a great man, Ostrovsky. On Saturday I bought in the Kuznetsky Mosst a large one-volume edition of his principal plays, printed in 1935, which, the clerk said, was out-of-print, and a bargain at 9 roubles 50. It certainly was. One was never able to buy Ostrovsky before the Revolution, except in the expensive ten-volume edition. I also bought a new *Life of Gogol*, with a lot of recently discovered material, and also a book on Saltykov. But this, with its dreary, purely Marxist approach to the great satirist, I found disappointing.

The Poles have put their foot in it. No sooner had the Russians recognized the independence of Poland than Sikorski gave a broadcast in which he said that the Russians and the Germans had decided in 1939 to destroy Poland, just as they did in 1795. And then he added that Poland must have her 1939 frontiers back. This has greatly incensed the Russians, and, with a maximum of restraint, *Izvestia* today said that the general was all wrong. Russia, it says, had no desire to destroy Poland in 1939, but only to prevent the Germans from getting too near the vital centres of Russia—"It would have been much easier for the Germans if they had attacked on the first day, not Brest and Lwow, but Minsk and Kiev." Regarding Sikorski's assertion that no one would dare to challenge Poland's 1939 frontiers, *Izvestia* says: "Sorry, but frontiers are not immutable, and the British Government realizes this and hasn't guaranteed any eastern European frontiers. Mr. Eden said so the other day. But with goodwill on both sides, Russia and Poland will settle the question, as they have already settled so many other questions."

I am sure that on this question of frontiers the Poles mustn't be silly and should swallow their *panski honor*. It would be much more sensible if, instead of White Russia, they could get East Prussia and give the Germans the Corridor in return. Apply to both the great Hitler principle of transplanting populations. Why not? The Germans couldn't object; it's a great Hitler idea.

After the usual messing about with wires, etc., we at last managed at seven o'clock to get out of town to the Embassy *datcha*. As we drove along the outer circle of boulevards, something happened that shocked me out of all proportion to the seriousness of the event. I heard the sound of breaking glass, like a bottle being dropped on the pavement. It was some distance away, and I couldn't see the scene clearly. But I saw a pile of broken glass—and a little boy; he had fallen, holding the bottle with both hands. I saw he was crying, and he turned round and with a pathetic gesture of infinite helplessness he held out his two little hands to a man and a woman. Was he badly cut? Probably, though hardly anything fatal. But that child's simple gesture of holding out his two little cut hands—there was something deeply moving about it. I could not help thinking of that symbolic story Remizov wrote before the last war about the cat Murka who died from eating broken glass—Murka being the symbol of Russia; and, unreasonably perhaps, I inwardly protested against the idea that Russian lives, like Chinese lives, are less valuable than others. This little Russian child felt the pain as much as any other child when his hands were cut with a broken bottle. "The Russians love to travel." Sometimes I try to visualize the hundreds of thousands of Russian soldiers killed in the last month or so. Dead—as dead as that German carcass we saw that day. . . .

We drove on to the *datcha*. It was strange to be out in the Russian countryside. Actually, it was only an outer suburb;

but still—there were the pine trees, and the cones on the
ground, and the little garden round the *datcha* was filled with
the intoxicating evening scent of white tobacco flowers. It
recalled distant, very distant memories—but so distant that
they neither moved nor worried me much. We are living in
so harsh and stern a world—and so much has happened since
1939—that early memories don't much matter.

There were at the *datcha* a number of people from the
Embassy—mostly juniors, code clerks, etc.—some playing
tennis, others ping-pong. So I went for a stroll along the
unpaved country road. *Datchas* and more *datchas*; lads and
girls in bright summer clothes chatting in the streets; children
in the gardens of the *datchas*; women hanging out their washing on a line between two pine trees. Smell of pine trees and
flowers. Moscow seemed very far away. A boy of about ten,
with a fringe of fair hair and a sailor suit, was carrying a
kitten—Would I take it? he asked me. I said no. "Please take
it," he appealed; but I still said no; Moscow was no place for
kittens. I walked on to the pine forest. But there was a
bayoneted sentry there, and a lot of army lorries; so I turned
back. I lost my way in the tangle of streets with more or less
identical *datchas*; I asked for the *Angliskaya datcha*, and was
shown the way by a group of girls and lads, with a touch of
distrust, I think, for they continued to watch me for a while.
We had a cold supper with the chaps. Cold meat, salad, and
also a kind of mushroom soufflé made by the Volga-German
maid, and then ice and raspberries. And then we played a game
of bridge—there at the *datcha*. It brought back distant memories of the veranda with a view of the Gulf of Finland and
Kronstadt, and the same smell of flowers, and *tri piki, tri bez
kozyria* (three spades, three no trumps). . . . Never mind.

We drove along the dark, though moonlit, road to Moscow.
Misha was getting impatient and worried. As we were driving
into Moscow the *trevoga* sounded. Misha, more worried than
ever, raced down the dark streets, past sentries and police—

hoping to get home before being forced into a shelter. There was no gunfire, so nobody stopped us. We got home; the gun-fire started soon after. But it lasted only an hour or so; and, as distinct from the previous night, I didn't hear any bombs drop.

AUGUST 7

I wonder if Moscow is taking the blitz as well as London? People look grim; and there are mighty few bomb jokes. Perhaps the people here feel *individually* more helpless than they do in London. Ambulances are comparatively scarce, and perhaps too precious to risk in a big blitz, and they there-fore do not collect the wounded during a raid, but only after the all-clear has sounded. Until then, they have only the local first-aid to rely upon. And the fire-watching rules are very drastic, and a dangerous amount of sleep is lost; nor are most of the shelters adapted yet for sleeping. God knows what it will be like in winter. . . . In a Moscow tram-car the other morning I noticed a tired, drawn look on many faces. Nor is there proportionately the same elaborate organization as in England for looking after refugees and bombed-out people. The problem of evacuees and refugees is, of course, so much vaster here than the problem of evacuees in Britain.

I like Philip Jordan. I spent a good part of the day with him yesterday. He's a good fellow to have around here—fresh, open-minded, and *enfant terrible*; and although he knows no Russian, he has a quick grasp of essentials. And a pleasant malicious tongue. He has hired a car by the month—a dilapi-dated old 1932 Buick, painted blue and orange, and mostly paintless. It's driven by a Greek whom he pays, I think, 1,200 roubles a month. After the press conference, of which more later, we went to the Nark, to the Central Telegraph, and then to the cocktail bar in Gorki Street—the one where, the other day, they played *Tipperary* in our honour. Sitting on nickel-tubed stools, we drank red wine at the counter; the barmaid was meantime mixing fancy drinks for a couple of Red Army officers—a thing called Klaret Kobler, which is a mixture of various liqueurs, Russian Cointreau, Armenian brandy, and red wine. Then on to dinner at the Metropole, where we were joined by Monck and another of the Mission lads. Vodka and *pojarskie* "cutlets" and good strawberry ice. Amusing conversation, mostly non-political, with wisecracks, chiefly from Philip, about almost everybody. There was a gloomy chap sitting at a table very near ours; he seemed to be eating rather the way actors eat on the stage.

I got trapped by the air-raid warning and went to sleep in Jordan's room. I also had a warm bath, which I can no longer get at home, since they cut off the gas a week or two before the blitz started. Before going to sleep I put up a pyramid of chairs between the window and the couch, just in case. There was some stuff dropping.

It seems absurd not to be able to get to Leningrad. The Germans aren't anywhere near it yet, and trains are said to be running normally between Leningrad and Moscow. What an experience it would be for me to see Leningrad again! But it's considered a military zone, and for months now no foreigner, diplomatic or otherwise, has been allowed to go there. What harm could I possibly do? It would give them so little trouble and it would give me so much pleasure. . . . Jordan is also dying to get to Leningrad, though a feature-page article in the *News Chronicle* is his chief concern.

Jordan, who was in one of his *enfant terrible* moods this morning, said we must try shock tactics. So we went to see Palgunov and said we *must* go to Leningrad *tonight* or *tomorrow morning* at the latest. . . . When Palgunov heard this, he looked (as Jordan put it) as if he'd seen a ghost. He clearly thought it an impossible suggestion; said that everything was

normal in Leningrad, that there was, in fact, *no difference
between Leningrad and Moscow*, and he just couldn't understand what possible interest there might be in going there!
Unreasonable; and, to me, particularly disappointing.

I like these earnest, proletarian Komsomol girls. Five
women, who had won special distinctions for fire-fighting,
came to the press-conference place today. Two were typical
party girls—both very good-looking and in their Sunday best.
The others were an elderly woman; a young, fat, red-faced
matreshka in soldier's uniform; and, finally, Comrade Golu-
beva, who described herself as "a housewife." Each one had a
good plucky story to tell, and they also dwelt on the organization of the community for fire-fighting purposes and on such
problems as the emergency water supply, etc. They were also
unanimous in praising the pluck and the enthusiasm of the
young boys and girls in dealing with incendiaries. The pret-
tier of the Komsomol girls said: "We couldn't allow even a
little house to be destroyed by the Fascists; it also is part of
our Soviet wealth, and as our great leader, Comrade Stalin,
said . . ." The fat girl, on the other hand, was no orator, and
she said, stammering with nervousness and even redder than
usual: "Well, I just stood on the roof when the incendiaries
fell, but I stayed on even when a high explosive fell, only I lay
down flat and I was all right." She had clearly been very
scared, and she was proud of having stuck it out.

Comrade Pavlov, assistant head of fire-fighting of Moscow,
was also at the meeting. He talked about emergency water
supplies, and gave his arguments for using water against
incendiaries—"It can be done without negative results if one
tackles them at once," he said, "except for minor burns." He
explained that the stuff which exploded in contact with water
was in the *tail* of the incendiary; and if the bomb was put out
immediately after dropping, the difficulty didn't arise. (I

wonder.) All together, his way of talking suggested that we can learn from Moscow, not Moscow from London. Their system is, of course, to make every fire-fighter responsible for a certain section of the roof.

The fire-fighting girls dwelt on the voluntary nature of the whole organization, but, no doubt, as Jordan said in a piece he wrote today, "voluntary" doesn't mean the same here as in England. The fire-fighting squads are recruited by the house committees.

After the conference we moved into the elegant "Empire" drawing-room of the Greek Legation, where we talked to the girls. I told the pretty Komsomolka a lot about London—which on one night, I said, had had thirty thousand incendiaries—suggesting thereby that Moscow hadn't yet had any experience of a real fire blitz. She listened with very great interest, and admitted that, for her own part, she always advised her team to use sand rather than water. I asked her how the serious question of the loss of sleep was going to be tackled. "We don't all fire-watch every night," she said, "and anyone can stay up a couple of nights a week without hurting himself."

AUGUST 8, 1.45 *a.m.*

The all-clear has just sounded. There are no sirens here to make it known, but only those "local" radio sets, of which we haven't got one here. So I go by the voices on the stairs and the movement of cars in the street. There was a lot of gunfire, and I heard about half a dozen planes—at intervals—but I didn't hear a single bomb drop. I looked out of the window—a lot of tracer bullets, rockets, flares, and what not. I spent most of the evening in a heavy armchair, with its back turned to both the blacked-out windows. Maurice in the other chair was reading out some of the passages from *Mein Kampf* about Russia, which is always instructive. . . . "Fate has decreed that we, as a higher race . . ."

Lovell's German is excellent. Altogether, he is a most remarkable linguist. He even picked up Rumanian and Hungarian in a short time, can freely read the Russian papers after only five months here, and even talk the language in a small way. His political judgment is excellent; but that's rather a luxury for an agency man. His knowledge of the Balkans is so thorough that he sometimes almost looks like a Balkan politician himself. He was turned out of Rumania last year for saying that Carol was about to sell out to Hitler.

Later I read Ostrovsky's *Dowerless Girl*, of which I never tire. What a glorious Larissa Mrs. Patrick Campbell would have made, if anybody had had the sense to translate the play for her!

By the way, I've also been dipping at random into the ten-volume *Small Soviet Encyclopædia*, published in 1931. There's a later edition published in 1938, and the difference is said to be enormous. I haven't had a chance to have a good look at the latter, because the office here hasn't got it. But in the 1931 edition everything is still treated, as far as possible, from the standpoint of class war, and it is completely internationalist and almost Trotskyist in tone. The article on Moscow, for instance, is quite lamentable, and wouldn't have been published in this form under the present Stalin régime. It gives only half a column to Moscow's history, all the rest of the eight or nine columns being devoted to "the revolutionary movement in Moscow." Actually, this was never very important, and what there was of it was only a pale imitation of St. Petersburg, which always led the way. The height of absurdity is in the articles on art. Both Mussorgsky and Tchaikovsky are more or less dismissed as "representatives of the decadent gentry, reflecting in their music the defeatist moods of their social class"—or some such twaddle. I much prefer the present patriotic and even jingo treatment of any such national figures.

The other day I bought the first volume of the *History of the U.S.S.R.* It goes up to 1861, and is good straightforward nationalist history, with hard cracks at some tsars, but not at all of them. It is used as the history text-book in the upper classes of secondary schools and at universities. The second volume hasn't been published yet; it will be worth getting. I can see a definite national purpose in the current "interpretations" of 1917 and 1918. Trotsky's role is minimized by the Stalinites, but is not Stalin's role as the man who settled the vastly important nationalities problem in 1917 and 1918 totally ignored by the Trotskyites? And there's another point —though I forget whether the present official historians ever dwell on it: and that is that when Stalin arrived in Petrograd after the March Revolution *he wanted to go on with the war against Germany*, and only yielded on this point under strong pressure from Lenin. The university *History of the U.S.S.R.* pays lip-service to Marx by quoting him as an authority on totally uncontroversial matters: "As Marx says, the power and prestige of Kiev stood highest towards the middle of the eleventh century." (Or it may be the twelfth, I forget which.) And the authors sit severely on Pokrovsky, the historian-laureate of the internationalist days, for various alleged mis-statements—for instance, that the False Dmitri was, among other things, the leader of a peasant revolt in western Russia against Godunov and the Moscow boyars. The present historians treat him primarily as "a Polish interventionist." The *History*, by three or four professors, is a big volume of some six hundred pages, is well printed, includes a set of maps and costs only six roubles. That's good, subsidized education. By the way, the schools and the university were opened on September 1st for the year 1941–2. This year military training will take up a large part of the curricula of both; and with the partial evacuation of children from Moscow, and with so many young lads in the army, the attendance at both the university and the schools is much smaller than usual. But it's a cheering demonstration of optimism to have made all these educational arrangements in Moscow for a whole year ahead!

AUGUST 8 (*afternoon*)

There were a couple of fairly heavy raids on the industrial suburbs of Moscow the last few days, and today a number of us were taken round the famous Z.I.S.—the Stalin motor-works, in the south-east of Moscow. I went there in Philip's car. The idea was that we should deny the German story that the Z.I.S. had been destroyed by bombing. (The British technique in such cases is probably better: if, by any chance, the Germans really believe they *have* destroyed something, why deny it? It might only encourage them to come back.) The Z.I.S. is a huge plant, modelled on Ford's, and about twice as big as the Renault works in Paris. There were broken windows all over the place. We were first conducted into the office of the Big Boss, who turned out to be a typical party chap: fat, little Hitler moustache, and extremely tough-looking; over his shaved head he wore a cloth cap. There was an array of incendiaries on his desk. "Our workers are very brave," he said; "very, very brave; there hasn't been a single case of funking. None of our fire-watchers even runs downstairs, not even when the H.E.'s come down. There have been plenty of them, I can tell you, and the incendiaries come down just in showers!" He took us round the works. "This wooden hut," he said, "the only wooden building in the place, was hit the other night by twenty incendiaries, and every one of them was put out by our workers. . . . We've also had some incendiaries—great big brutes, a yard long—oil bombs is what they really are. Our men have learned how to tackle *all* such bombs and are getting used even to the H.E.'s. . . ." That was perhaps going a bit far; but still—. It didn't seem that many H.E.'s had actually fallen within the factory grounds, though there was some damage close by, and a lot of minor damage by blast. We didn't have a chance to see any of the fire-fighters. The Big Boss took us through four enormous workshops, each several acres large, which demonstrated the different phases in the mass production of cars and lorries. The most spectacular of the four were, of course, the first and the last. The first was a gigantic smithy, a hell of roaring furnaces, and crashing, thumping presses working on large lumps of red-hot iron and spitting showers of sparks and larger fragments of the glowing metal all over the place. Eight-hour day—a couple of hours in this inferno would do for me! The half-naked workers we saw in the red glow of the furnaces were like shadows; and they were too busy to take any notice of the crowd of visitors. It was much the same in the other workshops, where the larger parts were finished and the smaller parts made and assembled. Everybody looked busy and diligent, but completely noncommittal. All these men and women seemed to work with a great sureness of touch. Everywhere there were Stakhanovite tables of honour, and lists of voluntary "record" subscriptions to the war loan. Henry Shapiro, who has lived in Moscow for some years, later told me that in the past the appearance of any visitors in a Russian factory usually put a stop to the work for quite a time. The workers would crowd round the visitors and have long chats with them. The Stakhanovite piece-work system had changed all that. The attitude of the workers today did not, therefore, denote any unfriendliness on their part or any reluctance to talk to us. Especially in war-time—the Big Boss explained—the Stakhanovite principle was no longer a matter of individual achievement; the men and women were now working in Stakhanovite *teams*; I suppose that's only natural when hundreds of people work on the same assembling belt, for instance. The great assembling belt in the last of the workshops we visited was certainly impressive. Here the bodies were lowered down on to the chassis; then paint-sprays came into action, the glass windows were put in, the wheels and tires screwed on, and finally the tanks were filled, and off the army lorry drove into the great wicked world. Coming off the moving belt every ten or fifteen minutes, a brand-new lorry would drive out. Whether because there was rather a crowd of us, or (as I'd prefer to think) because the party included three Japs, or perhaps because he simply didn't care for foreign visitors, the Big Boss didn't really want to show or tell us very much. In reply to questions I asked, or Philip got me to ask, all we learned was that there were fifteen canteens and "hundreds of buffets" at the Z.I.S., and "a large number of first-aid posts," and that the works employed "tens of thousands of workers." We asked if the Z.I.S. also made tanks, but he ignored the question. The workers, he said, made anything from four hundred to two thousand or even three thousand roubles a month. I wish I could have gone into one of the canteens and talked to the chaps, but nothing like that was encouraged and, instead, the Big Boss had us put on a bus—manufactured right on the spot—and we were quickly taken round the Z.I.S. grounds, so that we could get an idea of its size. "The Z.I.S. people must certainly feel a great pride in this great big brute of a plant—built entirely since the Revolution," I said. "I agree," said Jordan; "not that I've ever really been much interested in ironmongery."

The Russians are, of course, right in "spectacularizing" industry. How many people in England, proud owners of a Baby Austin, have the vaguest idea—or even bother—how and by whom it is made?

"Wouldn't you like to live in that infernal smithy and feel the salt of the earth, Jordan?" "Now, none of your capitalist facetiousness here," said Philip.

We all wrote "pieces" about it. But who will write "pieces" about the vast, gigantic, horrible human struggle of Smolensk, and Belaya Tserkov, and Pskov? Only those who are there, and survive it. And not I, or Jordan, or Mr. Shapiro, or even

the war correspondents of *Pravda* and *Izvestia*. That's the
weak point of the journalism here.

SATURDAY, *August* 9

I wrote a long article for the *Sunday Times*, largely
a review of the week's meagre experiences; and, by way of introduction, a vaguely optimistic piece about Russian resistance, especially in the Smolensk and Kiev sectors.

Last night at the National Café I ran into that South
American, or Portuguese—I forget his name. I don't like the
look of him, though I am told that he's all right. He is supposed
to have a lot of contacts with "ordinary" Russians. He kept
telling me that morale in Moscow wasn't as good as it was a
fortnight ago; that the peasants had been saying that "Hitler
would die on August 5th and the war would be over on August
12th," and that they were disappointed it hadn't come off.
All together, he said, a lot of people in Russia were somehow
convinced that the war would be over before the winter; people
were very scared of bombs; and women were terrified of being
raped by the Germans; and if a girl said no nowadays, the lad
replied: "Saving up for the Germans, eh? . . ." I don't much
believe any of this. . . .

We went to Lozovsky's, of course. He talked about pessimistic German letters seized by the Russians, with confessions
of despair and lurid accounts of the bombings, "by the Tom-
mies," of western Germany; and he produced a few examples.
He concluded that civilian morale in Germany had been badly
shaken by the great uncertainties of the eastern front, and by
the tremendous German casualties.

At the Metropole, where I went to see Jordan, I tried to buy
a bottle of vodka, but in the end had to order it from the waiter
—half a litre, 22.50 roubles. Jordan has written an enthusias-

tic piece about the partisans, with some illustrations added from the Soviet press. Actually, partisans are quite important, but it's expecting too much from human nature if they're to carry on indefinitely. I wonder, though, if there's anything in the theory that they've got large munition dumps, which were prepared long ago. No doubt the Germans must be trying to mop them up; but does that mean that their presence is really holding up indefinitely the big offensive for which we are all waiting? There were partisans in Poland, too; but could the poor devils keep it up for more than a few months? Will the Russian partisans be able to last through the whole winter? . . . Wonderful as these fellows are (and to be a partisan requires more guts than *any* other job), perhaps too much military importance is attached to them. 1812, Denis Davydov; 1918–20, Chapaiev; we hear a lot about all that; but the conditions aren't the same.

No blitz tonight, despite a perfect moonlit night. Maybe they're scared of the night fighters, or are having a go at Kiev or Leningrad. Last night a lot of incendiaries were dropped on the Kremlin, but were all put out.

And all the time Russian soldiers are fighting and dying, not only for their own country, but for civilization, for Europe, for *us*. It makes me—unreasonably—angry to listen to the nondescript rubbish on the radio like tonight's "Iroquois, Oh, Iroquois," from a *Red Indian Suite* or something, or to think of one or two chaps in soft Fleet Street jobs who are still busy justifying their useless existence by hinting knowingly at the "coming invasion" and at the great work they are going to do then. As if there was going to be any newspaper work *then*!

Last night I headed my entry "September 7th" by mistake. Curious Freudian lapse—subconscious feeling that we'd be much more secure if it really were September 7th and not merely August 7th.

SUNDAY, *August* 10

I love Sunday in Moscow; it's so much brighter than any other day.

For hard-working Moscow there is not much chance for amusements and recreation on week-days other than in the evening, and the blitz, real or possible, has greatly restricted all entertainments after seven p.m. But on Sundays all Moscow's theatrical and musical life blossoms forth again. The list of Sunday entertainments, as announced by posters on the walls, is still most impressive. Today alone there were fourteen distinct theatrical shows; there was again the sumptuous production of Tchaikovsky's comic opera *Cherevichki* (for which, personally, I don't much care, at least from what I can remember of it), but it's a great favourite with the British visitors here, and each performance inevitably attracts several members of the Embassy and the Mission; another theatre was playing the old operetta *Les Cloches de Corneville*; at other theatres there were two or three Shakespeare plays on, and five other theatres had modern semi-propaganda plays, while the Children's Theatre (to which I must go some time) was showing a new patriotic play by the poet Svetlov, *Twenty Years After*; and there were several concerts, and a recital by the immensely popular Lubov Orlova, the Russian Gracie Fields, as Maurice described her the other day. I have only seen her on the screen; she's got vitality and personality and a good voice, but, on the whole, I like her about as much (or as little) as Gracie. But the most typical centre of the Sunday life of the Moscow populace is the Ermitage Garden, where thousands spend a good part of the day. It's the very Ermitage Garden where, in 1915, I saw them perform *A Life for the Tsar* on an open-air stage! Only now it's all freshly painted and well scrubbed and tidy, and there seem to be several more theatres and buffets in the place than there were then. Under the trees and between the well-kept flower-beds people sat in the sun, eating ice-cream, drinking beer, and hauling from the buffets cheese and ham and sausage sandwiches and sweets and chocolates, and plates of tomato and cucumber salad, and sugar buns. Incidentally, in the past week, after a temporary curtailment, supplies of such minor luxuries have reappeared in plenty, and even the subway stations have reopened their confectionery stalls.

The Ermitage Gardens looked their best this sunny afternoon, with the Soviet youths and girls in their summer clothes. Soldiers formed a large proportion of the public. The walls of the various buildings and pavilions were covered with gaily coloured, amusing posters. Some were practical pictorial posters concerning fire-fighting and blacking-out; others were satirical posters about Hitler and Mussolini. One showed Musso proclaiming to the Italian people: "I serve Italy well." On the second poster Mussolini, dressed up as a waiter, was shown serving Italy on a plate to his customer, Hitler. The entrance to the Garden was decorated with red banners and portraits of Stalin, Timoshenko, Budyenny, and other commanders, and the outstanding heroes of the war. A loudspeaker, transmitting some public meeting in Moscow, was just then blaring speeches in unfamiliar tongues by Czech and Polish representatives. The Pan-Slav drive is in full swing.

The Ermitage offers an embarrassment of riches in popular entertainment. People have the choice of four shows in four different buildings in the Garden: first, a Goldoni comedy played by well-known actors; secondly, the "Satirical Theatre"; thirdly, the operetta *Silva*, which has had one of Moscow's longest runs, followed later in the afternoon by a variety show at the same theatre; and lastly, in the half-open-air concert hall, the Symphony Orchestra of the Soviet Union.

It was too much for one day; but I started with the satirical show. It was simple but bright and amusing war propaganda. The audience was mostly soldiers. It started with a sketch of a stray Red Army soldier arriving in a Russian village and being received by a village girl. He asks: "Is the adjoining town called Holyhill?" "It used to be called that, but now it is Redhill," the girl replies. After several similar gaffes on his part, it occurs to the girl that the stranger is a parachutist, and after a lively struggle in which the girl incapacitates the parachutist by pushing a large jar over his head and knocking away his revolver with a broomstick, the villain is handed over to justice. The other sketch, called *Before and After*, showed an elderly couple sitting on a bench and complaining wearily of their old age and their innumerable ailments. The second tableau showed the same couple, after the outbreak of war, not only knitting for soldiers but also proclaiming their health and youthfulness, and finally going off to volunteer as fire-fighters. A girl then appeared on the stage and told the sad story of a little boy who was always crying because in the games played at school he was always given the part of Hitler. Later there was a sketch of two German generals drawing up a communiqué on the basis of "the other way round"; for example: "Two of our parachutists came down in a Russian village and captured all the peasants." One of the generals then said: "To cheer people up we had better add: 'We captured a hundred and twenty trucks of flour which have now been sent to Berlin.' " The other replied: "You're crazy! The whole of Germany will rush to Berlin."

I didn't have the feeling that any of these soldiers or these Moscow lads and girls were in the least nervous about the war, or that they regarded this as being perhaps Moscow's last really normal, almost peace-time Sunday.

From the satirical theatre I went on to the symphony concert. This also was typical of Soviet Russia. For here was a similar audience of soldiers, workmen, and the Soviet equivalent of A.T.S. girls. It was a perfectly civilized concert audience and was obviously enjoying what would be considered elsewhere an almost highbrow concert. Glinka's *Russlan and Ludmilla* overture, Rimsky-Korsakov's *Capriccio Espagnol* and *Coq d'Or*, and the Soviet composer Glière's *Solemn Overture*, with its numerous Oriental and folk themes. It was written to commemorate the twentieth anniversary of the Soviet Revolution. Glière was already fairly well known during the last war, and, like Glazunov, he stayed on. Rachmaninoff and Prokofiev emigrated, but Prokofiev returned some years later and was forgiven. He was quite right, of course. Rachmaninoff, without his native environment, ran almost dry; in the last twenty-five years he has written very little, and what he has written isn't first-rate. The U.S.S.R. Symphony Orchestra is composed of picked men with amazing clearness and lucidity of playing, and there were unforgettable solo passages, such as the clarinet in Tchaikovsky's *Swan Lake* overture.

The star turn was the eighteen-year-old infant prodigy Bussia Goldstein, the winner of many prizes in the international contests in Brussels and Warsaw not long before the war. On his lapel he was now wearing a high Soviet decoration. With technical perfection and restraint which was very like Heifetz's, he played Tchaikovsky's Violin Concerto.

I remember Zamoiski, the Polish sculptor, telling me about the amazing crop of infant prodigies—pianists and violinists —from the Soviet Union who turned up at that Warsaw contest. "Nearly all Jews," he added. They carried off nearly all the prizes; and I believe they did the same at Brussels. A pretty good recommendation for Russian musical culture and education!

But the concert was not altogether detached from the war. The second part started with an impressive and moving "declamation"—a sort of medley of war slogans alternating with famous patriotic passages from Pushkin, Lermontov, and more recent poets. It was recited by the famous actor Yakovlev, and visibly stirred the audience, who responded with bursts of applause. And later in this long musical program a famous contralto—I forget her name—sang folk songs and also a newly composed ballad, *The Partisan's Song*, with a perfect Russian folk-song texture. It was the song of a peasant who on returning home finds that his horse has been stolen by the Germans, his house set on fire, and his wife and children burned alive. At first he breaks down and weeps bitterly, but then the thirst for revenge prevails, and he joins a guerrilla band. This poignant song is one notable example in many showing how the present war has stirred the imagination of the Russian people and is acting as a powerful creative stimulant to artists. It is a most significant psychological phenomenon, and one which had no parallel in France. I believe that after several non-creative years Russia will produce, as a result of this war—if she isn't completely stunned by it—a rich crop of great music and great books—in the case of the latter, the censorship ought to loosen up, of course, when the time comes. I am told that in Leningrad, Shostakovich is already writing greater music than he has ever done before.

August 11

I persuaded Jordan to take the afternoon off, and we went in the car up to the Sparrow Hill in the south-west, on the other side of the river. We drove through the Zamoskvorechie and then along the magnificent wide new avenue north of the Park of Rest and Culture. Always the same contrast in Moscow: the impressive new blocks of the various scientific institutes off the avenue, and in the Zamoskvorechie the shabby, dilapidated old wooden and stucco houses, with the paint come off, and a derelict and rather indifferent-looking old church with "Kino" in large letters above the entrance. In one street a large number of houses had their roofs ripped off by blast, but there seemed to be little bomb damage otherwise.

We drove through the park, rising above the Moscow River,

to the top of the Sparrow Hill. There was a small church there, with an overgrown old churchyard round it. Most of the crosses were wooden, half-decayed, but at least one or two were fairly recent—1923 or 1924. This being a week-day, it was hard to find out whether or not the church was still used as a place of worship. Near by, with a terrace overlooking Moscow, was a small café, but it was closed.

The Sparrow Hill is famous for its panorama of Moscow. Napoleon looked at Moscow from here, and this favourite romantic spot is the scene of one of the acts in Andreyev's play about Moscow undergraduates. I often remember Andreyev; he is one of the few Russian writers who use Moscow, and not Petersburg, as their setting. But the panorama of Moscow that Napoleon saw, or even Andreyev's young people of 1910 or thereabout, was quite different from what it is now. Large concrete blocks and factory chimneys dominate the skyline of Moscow; and one can distinguish scarcely more than a dozen churches now, apart from the distant domes of the Kremlin. There were four hundred and fifty churches in Moscow before the Revolution, and their bells, if rung all at the same time, must have made a fantastic concert. No church bells are rung in Moscow now. The old *belokamennaya*—Whitestone Moscow—is gone for good. We wandered along the slopes of the Sparrow Hill, and left the car outside the little café. We noticed a girl in a red jumper watching us very suspiciously, and a few minutes later a militiaman came up to us and said that the parking of cars was strictly prohibited round here, and would we please drive away? The girl, perhaps hearing us talk a foreign language, had no doubt reported us to the militia.

Before going to the Ermitage last Sunday, I had gone in search of an open church. . . . I looked for one with a cross. At last I found one; it was a lovely little old church off the Upper Petrovka; but packing-cases were piled up under the porch—and the doors were locked. I must try again next Sunday.

I haven't seen the slightest trace of anti-religious propaganda here; and God is often mentioned in conversation. I don't think the Soviet régime will ever bother about anti-religious propaganda again; but it will remain anti-clerical. It is, of course, probably justified in regarding the clergy as an undesirable influence, and the obscurantist Orthodox Church as having done its best to prevent the spread of education. The existence of churches and priests will be permitted, but limited by the possibilities of having the priests trained and the churches financially maintained.

I saw a good selection of propaganda films yesterday. They were very ferocious; slapstick and Wild West—but ferocious for all that. There was more "snarling" at German prisoners. A group of Russian soldiers, eating sandwiches, are seen taking charge of a German airman. The hungry Hun looks enviously at their sandwiches. "No bread, no ham for you, my lad," one of them remarks, munching away.

It's a little different from the happy prisoners' camp, pictures of which are dropped over the German trenches, with the "safe conduct" attached.

But this is a totalitarian war, and whatever the Russians tell prospective German war prisoners, they certainly don't feel tender about them, which is scarcely surprising when one hears of the filthy way the Germans treat *their* Russian prisoners.

The dastardly German soldiers and officers in the films on German atrocities in Yugoslavia and Poland—yes, Poland!— all make good hate propaganda. I like the monster who snatches a mouthful of milk from a sick Polish child and pours it into his coffee!

Lozovsky today handed out some tortured corpse photographs; they are too sickening to be good propaganda, I think. What was much better was the letter he produced from a bitch of a *Hausfrau* called Lotte. It was written in tidy Gothic script to her *"lieber guter Gottfried"*: "Couldn't you pinch me a fur coat from some filthy Jew? These swine can afford to lose one. There must still be things to be got in Russia. . . . It would be a little compensation for the bad times through which we are passing. Would you also try to get me a pair of snowboots, size 39, so that at the end of a winter day my feet aren't cold in bed, and you don't call them *Eisknödel*." [1]

Lozovsky laid down something of a principle for settling the German "problem": "we should start by shooting the S.S. and other Gestapo chaps—that is, some 300,000; they are Hitler's immediate fellow criminals. . . ."

But what about Lotte?

Philip Jordan (looking at the plan of Moscow in his 1914 *Baedeker*): "There wasn't a Sverdlov Square before the Revolution, was there?" Very angry at my laughing: "Stop giggling. Of course I know it wasn't *called* that."

FRIDAY, *August* 15

The "August crisis" which we had expected has come. The Huns are sweeping across the Ukraine, right towards Dniepropetrovsk, Kherson, Krivoi Rog and Kremenchug. Last night's communiqué admits the loss of Kirovograd (ex-Elizavetgrad) and Pervomaisk (whatever it was called before). It all looks nasty on the map. The Germans have advanced very rapidly. Is this the big crisis, or will the situation stabilize itself again after five or six days, as Lovell expects?—that is, once the German drive has exhausted itself

[1] Ice dumplings.

and the communications have got too long? One or two things I don't like—for instance, the arrival of Hitler at the front. The Germans always time these arrivals of his for the eve of some great "final" success. Or is it this time merely intended to prop up German morale, which, at least until a few days ago, was beginning to sag?

The Germans claim the capture of Krivoi Rog—with "61 per cent of Russia's entire iron-ore production." They claim the encirclement of Odessa and Nikolaev; they have certainly cut off the former by rail, and probably the latter, too. The claim about Krivoi Rog is probably still untrue. I am not sure whether the Russian retreat is planned so as to avoid a pitched battle on the unfavourable terrain of the western Ukraine; where, by the way, in the absence of woods, there aren't many opportunities for partisan activity. Can the Russians establish a line, roughly running from Kremenchug to Kherson, so as to save the vastly important industrial area inside the Dnieper bend? The Germans aren't claiming anything much in the way of prisoners, so it can't be a Russian rout, a *débandade*. At least, I hope not.

Russian morale is being put under a severe strain. People in Moscow were rather shocked and depressed at the news of the fall of Smolensk. Minsk—well, that to them was a frontier town; but Smolensk is rather too near home. Some of the simpler people are rather shocked that any territory should be lost at all; they had been told for years about the invincibility of the Red Army. The German radio today quoted the report by a "Danish journalist"—one of those "moving" accounts of how a church in Smolensk was opened after twenty-five years; and an old priest—who had been a stonemason in the interval —was fished out from somewhere, and he conducted the service in his tattered old robes, and all the people wept and wept and wept. (No doubt with joy at seeing the Nazis.)

There have been no air-raids over Moscow these last two

nights, though they were clear and starry. Bad sign? Don't the Germans bomb towns continually only when they think they have no chance of getting them?—Moscow until three days ago, and London?

On Wednesday I went with Jordan and Sulzberger to one of the hospitals. The pince-nez colonel, who had already taken us to see the two German planes which were brought down, turned up at the Nark again. He strikes me as a decent and sensible fellow, and he talked to me like an ordinary human being, very reasonably, and without propaganda effects. He said the Germans hadn't caused any military damage of any importance in Moscow; but he said: "It's tough on the people. . . . Shelters—the subway shelter is very unhygienic. People need sleep if they are to carry on; it's going to be a great problem this winter. . . ." He also said that most of the doctors had gone to the front: in Moscow he knew some famous specialists who had to be on duty for twenty-four hours on end; operating, operating, operating; then twenty-four hours off.

How grim war can be! It wasn't one of the biggest Moscow hospitals, but a school building transformed into a hospital, from which, soon after their operation, the wounded are moved farther inland. Moscow is not considered a healthy spot for the wounded, and it is mostly severe cases requiring specialized handling that are brought here. It was a cheering thought, though, that even this improvised hospital should be able to give such excellent care to the wounded. The place specialized in some of the saddest cases of all—face, jaw, and eye injuries. It was clean. The children's bright watercolours were still on the walls. The medical staff appeared to be most efficient, and as he took us through the sterilizing, X-ray, washing, operating, and dressing rooms (here the dressing of wounds was in full progress), the chief surgeon talked about the modern methods they were using. He dwelt particularly on the direct application of vitamins to wounds, and also on plastic surgery, which is one of the most important branches of this hospital. There was certainly a great need for this. I saw men whose mouths were nothing but a large gaping hole, others whose noses had been blown off and who had a dressing over the flat space. But the chief surgeon explained how, with the use of the bones and tissues of corpses, disfigurements could be eliminated. Apparently it is no longer necessary to graft a piece of the patient's own flesh.

Most of the patients were too ill to speak, but I was able to talk to a stocky young man of twenty-seven. His jaw was swollen and his speech thick, but he volunteered to tell his grim story. I write it down just as he told it. . . . He had been in the Red Army for a year, and came from Konotop in the Ukraine. Before joining the Red Army he had been working as a carpenter. "Well," said he, "I may as well tell you the whole story from the start. Our platoon received the order to occupy the village of Demidovka, near Smolensk. As we moved along a country road we met two women. They said: 'We've just come from there. The Germans have just occupied it. They are having their lunch now.' Our commander decided to attack. We crept carefully forward along the edge of a wood, established firing positions, and after opening fire proceeded to attack. It was the afternoon of July 16th. We broke into the village, turned out the Germans, and killed several. They left dozens of cars and motor-cycles behind them. Having thrown out the Germans, we proceeded to build entrenchments round the village.

"But our commander decided that we ought to occupy a further stretch along the Smolensk road. It was getting dark when we set out. Most of our men had stayed behind in the village, and only a small party moved on. We crawled along the edge of the forest and reached a field, when suddenly we were attacked by heavy gun and mortar fire. I was wounded by a splinter which went through my thigh. The commander ordered me to return to the village, but I was in charge of a machine-gun and wanted first to find someone who would replace me. I somehow lost my party, and my mind wasn't very clear. Our men must have gone away after searching for me in vain.

"So I remained lying half-conscious in the wood. Suddenly I felt a hard kick that made me look up. I saw an officer and two soldiers. The officer, in broken Russian, ordered me to get up. I was too weak to do it. So the two soldiers raised me to my feet. The officer then asked questions about the Russian troops. I didn't answer. He got more and more irritable, finally became furious, and, judging from his tone, swore foully in his own language. He then struck me in the face and knocked me down. With his rifle he then fired at me at point-blank range. The first bullet ricocheted from my tin hat and merely stunned me, but the second went through my temple and face, coming out through my lower jaw, smashing my teeth and my tongue. The Germans thought I was dead, and went away. Strangely enough, I didn't lose consciousness, though I was losing a terrible amount of blood. When I fully realized what had happened, my moral depression was acute. I lay in the grass waiting. It was now dawn. I heard a German motor-cyclist driving along the road. The grass was not high, so I decided not to try to dress my wounds, as the Germans might notice me. I began to have hallucinations—I imagined my own comrades were there, and I couldn't understand why they weren't dressing my wounds. Then in a moment of greater lucidity I realized that it was still light, and I waited for night-fall. When it came, I crawled in the direction where I thought I had seen a river. I was very thirsty. I didn't find the river, but, still crawling, I got to a village, where I asked the peasants where the Russian troops were. They said they didn't know, and that the Germans were all over the place, but they advised me to spend the night in a barn. I did so, and through sheer weakness and loss of blood I managed to sleep. In the morning I heard Russian speech and saw our men. They took me to a first-aid post, and then to a hospital train."

I am at the Embassy *datcha*, sitting in a thicket in the wood, under a pine tree. I've just left the Embassy chaps to their local gossip. Grass and purple flowers around me, and heaps of pine needles. I've walked through the garden, smelling the tobacco flowers—with a faint nostalgia for twenty-five years ago. . . . What's the good? . . .

After supper we spent the evening playing bridge. A lot of the fellows here held various diplomatic and consular jobs in Hungary and the Balkans, and haven't much to do here. They amuse themselves however they can. Then I went to bed in one of the *datcha's* spare bedrooms and had to undress in the dark in the absence of black-out curtains. I was wakened about three by gunfire—it was still dark. I looked out of the open window at the pale purple twilight and the motionless pine trees—and I breathed the fresh night air, with its scents of pines and tobacco flowers. And quite near, there were guns, going hard.

SATURDAY, *August* 16

The German drive in the south doesn't look too healthy, and the Soviet communiqués are very secretive. There's a big battle going on at several points, but especially in the south. In the north they are trying to cut the Moscow-Leningrad line, pushing east of Staraya Russa. At Smolensk they have stopped for the present. According to *Red Star* they *bury* their tanks and use them as pill-boxes—that's the latest form of "digging in." That article also contained an implicit confirmation that Stalin's son has been taken prisoner, while in charge of a battery that had run out of munitions. . . .

After a lot of routine work, including a "flash" about the

Cripps-Steinhardt meeting with Stalin and the Roosevelt-Churchill message they handed him, I went and had a caviar "lunch" in Jordan's room at the Metropole. Foster and Monck were also there. I was very late, and gulped down the caviar and white wine and then we walked up Gorki Street to the Moscow Art Theatre.

Anna Karenina. I had always been a bit prejudiced against it (perhaps because I had read it *after War and Peace*). The only characters that really interested me were Steva Oblonsky and Karenin himself. In this dramatized version of *Anna Karenina,* Steva is only a subsidiary character; the whole thing is rather reduced to a triangle play, and the best thing of all in it is the husband. Khmelev is a remarkable actor, perhaps almost *too* consistently perfect; he must have practised for weeks *every* word and *every* gesture. According to the little booklet they sell at the theatre, Khmelev spent months studying Tolstoy's numerous notes on the appearance, clothes, character, historic and social background, etc., of the great bureaucrat that Anna's husband is. The chief actors get together and discuss all these points. The Moscow Art Theatre very carefully studies not only the externals but also the man's psychology, all his inner reflexes. The crowd scenes, on the revolving stage—the tea party, the grandstand at the races, the theatre with outlawed Anna in one of the boxes—were superb; the best thing perhaps was the grandstand, where one really got excited about the race one didn't see; the crowd was, however, treated rather more satirically by the M.A.T. than by Tolstoy, and the writer of the booklet dwelt on the degeneracy of the society Tolstoy had described, with Lenin's authority in support of all this. Anna, however, did the regular characteristically Slavic sob-stuff in a very, very human way; it was just female suffering all through the play; and not a moment of cheerfulness. Rather a bore, Anna, really, and Elanskaya, though a great actress, was rather old for the part; and Vronsky, the lover, was very commonplace. The great masterpiece was Khmelev's Karenin, really a superb performance, and psychologically, amazingly subtle. But Anna provided the sob-stuff; and she was deeply moving—especially in the scene where she pays her clandestine visit to her child. The theatre was sobbing; I looked back—two young girls behind me were weeping buckets, really *enjoying themselves*. How much sentimental *tendresse*, natural human emotion, there is in these ordinary Soviet girls; their souls haven't been toughened by the hard fire of Stalinist propaganda; they haven't been made impervious to ordinary human emotion, far from it. . . . The old butler and Annushka, the nurse, who took Anna along to see the child despite their master's orders, seemed the most decent people of the lot. These "common people" alone responded naturally and humanly to Anna's troubles. . . .

Amazing was the finale. When the curtain dropped, after Anna had been duly run over by the railway train—a bit Grand Guignol that!—hundreds of young girls swarmed to the front of the stalls, shouting frantically for Anna. How much youthful spontaneity, what a fund of generous instincts there is among these young people of Russia!

I went back to the Metropole and read out to Jordan in English the three columns about Smolensk from the *Red Star* for his "feature" article. Then I walked to the Nark, and thence home along the Sretenka, and the Chisty Prud Boulevard. Near the pond I saw an old beggar with a white beard and a fine wrinkled old face, like an ikon. "*Na propitanie*" (for some food), he said gently, holding out his cap. I gave him one or two of those dirty paper roubles. "*Kormiletz*," he said, genuinely moved; "*Gospod' tebya ne ostavit*" (God will not desert you). His whole appearance and his vocabulary were almost seventeenth-century! Touching. I must try to see him again and talk to him. As usual, overwhelming thanks from beggars make me feel very self-conscious and quite dumb.

People were sitting on benches round the Chisty Prud. In the sunset the place looked singularly lovely, though all the buildings around it, with the exception of one or two old stucco Empire houses, are extraordinarily nondescript. I love the week-ends in Moscow; it's the only time I get away from the artificial foreign-journalist existence. . . .

Symonds and Croad, the Home Office experts, have gone back to London. Symonds seemed a little disappointed; the Russians have not adopted his stirrup-pump, apparently owing to a shortage in certain metals. Actually, the Russians think they know quite enough about A.R.P. themselves. As one of them told me the other day: "We've got a lot to learn from your navy, and quite a lot from your air force, but not much from your A.R.P. people, and nothing at all from your army. We could teach *them*."

I like Lieutenant-Commander P., who came to lunch today. He's shy and boyish, not very talkative, but intelligent. Only after a while you discover he's been in the *Nelson* and has done a lot of convoying work, and knows all about how the *Bismarck* was sunk. "It must be pretty good," I said, "to belong to the Royal Navy, to feel you are—how shall I put it?—one of the great powers of good in this world. Aren't you *told* you are that, just as the Red Army is told it is?" "No; we aren't told it. It's just as well we aren't, but," he laughed, "at heart we know it. We just do our job; that's all. . . ." He admitted, however, that the men in the merchant fleet weren't getting nearly enough credit for their work. "However," he said resignedly, "it was just the same in the last war." P. himself hadn't yet seen the Russian Navy; but he thought the naval men he had met were pretty good, and those members of the Mission who had gone to see the navy at Sebastopol thought highly of the ships and very highly of the officers and men.

MONDAY, *August* 18

The news from the front is bad. The German drive in the south is very serious, and also fairly serious in the north. On Saturday night the communiqué admitted the loss of Nikolaev and of Staraya Russa.

Yesterday, Sunday, was an altogether delightful day, apart from the usual routine, which I disposed of in the forenoon. From the Nark I went to the Metropole to have lunch with Foster. Another caviar lunch; very tasty, though not very nourishing. On the way there I met the Moats with a man called Steele, who has just arrived in Moscow from the *Chicago Daily News*. I naturally fired fond inquiries at him about Richard and Edgar Mowrer. Steele had come from Shanghai *via* Alma-Ata. "Must be a job getting to Alma-Ata," I said. "Oh, that's nothing. Got there by direct plane—right across China. The real job is to get here from Alma-Ata. They've stopped the plane service, and the train took about a fortnight." I decided not to go on the press trip to the A.A. batteries and to go to *Eugene Onegin* instead.

Outside the theatre—it was the "annex" in Pushkin Street of the State Opera, which is under summer repair—there was a seething mass of young people who accosted every new arrival with the words: "You haven't got a ticket to spare?" These are the musical enthusiasts who had the misfortune to find that all the seats were sold out and were hoping against hope for a last-minute "return." It's the same at nearly every show in Moscow, but especially at the Opera and at the Moscow Art Theatre. It so happened that Foster had an extra ticket, and he gave it to somebody, but I didn't see to whom. I thought it was the wrong thing to do; for no self-respecting Soviet citizen would accept a ticket for nothing, least of all from an obvious foreigner. I was interested to see who our lucky neighbour would be.

I was all sentimentally keyed up for the sweet sad melody of the opening bars of the *Onegin* overture; but instead there was a blare of brass, and the curtain went up on a patriotic chorus of women dressed up in sarafans, and bearded warriors in glittering *vityaz* helmets and mailed armour, and resting with both hands on enormous swords. The chief *vityaz* stood in the centre and boomed away in a *basso profundo*. It was the patriotic prologue to Glinka's *A Life for the Tsar*, now called *Ivan Susanin*, after the main character. However, once that was over, I was able to settle down to *Onegin*. The singers were all admirable—dreamy, romantic Tanya bred on Richardson and the *Nouvelle Héloïse*, and her playful sister Olga, and "Byronic" baritone Onegin, and young poet Lensky, "with exalted speech and black curls falling down to his shoulders."

Poor Lensky disappears after the third act, in which he is killed in a duel by Onegin; but until then he certainly gets a run for his money—or rather the young girls in the audience do. Kozlovsky, the sweet tenor, is the idol of the youth of Moscow, or rather one of the two idols, the other being the tenor Lemeshev; and Moscow is really divided into two camps, the Kozlovsky fans and the Lemeshev fans. There is a parallel feud among the ballet-goers, between the worshippers of Ulanova and those of Lepeshinskaya, the two rival *prima ballerinas*. Only in a country where the theatre is really part of life, and not just one of the frills of life, can people feel so strongly about such matters.

Onegin: it was all very lovely. The scenery and the costumes were all very "period," very 1820, and the country-house ball in the third act was treated with the appropriate Pushkin irony. As it was to us, before the Revolution, *Onegin* is still part of the young Russian's emotional equipment, almost a teacher of human conduct and a guide to emotional reactions. I think it quite possible, judging from the frantic enthusiasm shown by the young women in the audience, that flappers' love letters, more or less modelled on Tatiana's, are still to be found in the Soviet Union today. Crude eroticism, which was fashionable in Russia for a few years in the '20's (wasn't it the same in England, for that matter, just about that time?), has undoubtedly, in recent years, given way to a much more emotional form of sex-relationship. One or two Englishmen who have lived here for some years have told me that Russian women were "very troublesome" and "got attached to you."

But to return to the *Onegin* show: Tchaikovsky's music to *Onegin* corresponds perfectly with the gently ironical lyricism of Pushkin's poem, just as the more dramatic and sombre tones of his music in the *Queen of Spades* express the spirit of Pushkin's weird St. Petersburg story. Perhaps I knew the score of *Onegin* a little too well. Even so, I found the letter scene musically very thrilling. The bass aria by Tatiana's old general of a husband—who is the librettist's invention and the only real departure from the Pushkin text—I found as commonplace and detestable as ever; but the final Onegin-Tatiana duet was superb. Its orchestral accompaniment is one of Tchaikovsky's great moments.

The stranger to whom Foster had given the ticket turned out to be a lanky, rather stupid-looking lad of twenty-five or so, in an embroidered shirt. There were many members of the British Mission in the audience. "What kind of uniforms are those?" he asked me. I said they were British. "Very pretty uniforms," he said. He said he was a house-painter, and was working on the present repairs at the Bolshoi Theatre. After the first act he suddenly asked me what was "going to happen now" and what this play was all about. "Why, have you never seen *Onegin*?" I asked. "No, I haven't." "But, surely, you've read Pushkin's *Onegin*?" "No," he said, apologetically, "it wasn't among our books at school—*ne prokhodili*." This was a blow: a Russian who had never read *Onegin* was like an Englishman who had never read *Hamlet*. It was certainly unusual; but, after all, I said to myself, this fellow was at school ten or twelve years ago; the Soviets were just then building

up thousands of schools out of very little; all the teachers were
overworked and some were incompetent or had no experience.
Before the Revolution this fellow would perhaps never have
learned to read at all, and he would certainly not be sitting
through an opera today.

When, later, I told a few Russians about this "phenomenon"
who had never read *Onegin*, they could hardly believe it. "He
must have been a mental defective," they said. Well, perhaps
he was. In fact, he rather looked it. (But when one comes to
think of it, how much literary education, compared with this
fellow—who was an *exception* in Russia, or at least in Moscow
—does there come out of our elementary schools in England?)

At the theatre I was perhaps a little irritated by the Mission
lads going into raptures over the "wonderful show." What
did *they* know about Pushkin, *Onegin*, and Tchaikovsky for
that matter? What did the lovely verbal felicity of those
Pushkin lines mean to them? In the intermission after the first
act G. said he was enchanted with Lensky's aria "*V vashem
domie.*" I said it was the sugary variety of Tchaikovsky, want-
ing to explain further that the Lensky role had been treated
by Pushkin with deliberate irony; but I didn't get beyond
the word "sugary" when he already began to protest. "Oh,
one always says that about Tchaikovsky," he said disapprov-
ingly.

The finale here was just the same as at *Anna Karenina*—the
young people simply went frantic over the tenor, Kozlovsky.
Then they crowded outside the stage door. It so happened that
the Mission cars were there too, and some of our Mission
people thought the crowd had assembled for their benefit.
What they had come for was another glimpse of the adored
tenor. It's true that they also gazed into the Mission cars with
some interest. But an old woman with a wart on her nose
commented: "Allies, aren't they? What an ill-bred crowd
we've got here, don't you think? Instead of cheering, or pre-
senting flowers, they just *stare* at the cars!"

In the evening, I had supper at the Moskva restaurant with Monck, Foster, Philip Jordan, and Sulzberger. Very pleasant. Good *selianka* (sturgeon soup), *pojarskie* cutlets, etc. There were several Soviet generals at the neighbouring tables; this hotel, the biggest one built since the Revolution, is architecturally much more agreeable than the other hotels, nor has it their Intourist atmosphere. (Not that I mind the Metropole atmosphere as much as I did at first; in fact, I am quite pally now with the dark lady behind the Metropole counter who treated me with such suspicion the day I arrived in Moscow.) Most of the Moskva customers are Red Army officers. We naturally talked about the war; also about France. Foster, who is an oil expert, thought all the German conquests would be of no avail, as they would run out of oil in a very short time. They've got to get to Baku, and get it intact, or croak. That's cheering enough. It's a long way to Baku.

Tuesday, *August* 19

Vera Maximovna, the woman with whom I sometimes chat on the stairs, seemed very upset by the news this morning; she thought the Russians, who had gone through the last war and the Civil War, and years of famine, couldn't stand this war for very long. "You see," she said, "Russians are people who like to eat and enjoy themselves. They can't stand as much as the British." That point of view was quite new to me, though I could see her point. I assured her that the British also liked to enjoy themselves and that, if anything, they could not put up with food shortage nearly as well as the Russians could. "Yes, you are probably right," she agreed, "and I suppose if things start going really badly our people will pull themselves together. . . . Only the food situation isn't too good, and the famine of the Civil War years is a very frightening memory. You can't judge from Moscow; people who've had their people evacuated to the provinces get very discontented letters. Surely that doesn't happen to people in London whose children have been evacuated to other parts of the country?"

I said there was one thing that would cause defeatism in England, and that was a desperate food shortage. So the Government was doing everything to keep enough food in the country; it might be of the wrong kind—too much bread and not enough meat and fats and vitamins—but still nobody went hungry. "Unfortunately," the woman said, "there's no such guarantee here."

I don't think it's elderly women who are going to decide how long Russia can or cannot stand the war. But the hardships it is bringing to civilians are certainly pretty serious. Vera Maximovna thought the loss of Leningrad would be a terrible blow. "And *such* a beautiful city. Not as *uyutny* (cosy) as Moscow, but so much more beautiful. There's nothing much to see in Moscow, is there, except the Kremlin?" she said; "but then, the Kremlin is *so* Asiatic!"

The Germans are certainly closing in on Leningrad from three or four directions. Will Leningrad repeat the miracle of 1919? Yudenich and Hitler are not quite the same, I fear. Still, we'll see. . . . And down at the Dnieper bend?

I am getting to like Misha more and more, though sometimes he talks a little like Smerdiakov, the lackey in *The Brothers Karamazov*. But his hankering after European "culture" is typical, even though his own particular idea of "culture" may be a trifle limited. "London must be wonderful," he said. "Luxurious, aren't they, all those bars and restaurants? People enjoying themselves till six or seven every morning?" I described to him the London pubs; just as ordinary as any *piteinye* here. And I gave him a lecture on closing-hours. "You don't say so!" said Misha; "but there must surely be *other* kinds of drinking places? It must be a great life—people enjoying themselves all night long!" "After all, Misha," I said, "you must remember there's been a war on in England for two years, and also there are lots of very respectable and married and hard-working people." "But," said Misha, "they can't *all* be married and respectable?" "Well, of course, they aren't *all* that, but still—" I then told him about Paris and the Paris cafés. "That must be lovely, very beautiful," said Misha. "But tell me this," he continued, "what about the girls in England? Very beautifully dressed, aren't they, in evening dresses? And are they—accessible?" I couldn't help laughing. "About the same as here. There are the accessible ones, and the less accessible ones. But with your gifts, Misha, you'd probably be all right wherever you were."

He read out with relish an article by Lavrenev describing Hitler as a murderer, sadist, and degenerate. "He must be a perfect ape, that Hitler," Misha laughed; and he looked more than ever like an ape himself. . . . He can't take his eyes off my wrist-watch. "Real gold, is it? Very expensive, I suppose." In his covetous, greedy little monkey eyes the blessed wrist-watch has become like a symbol of Western glamour.

I saw Y. this morning. "In the Ukraine the Russians are sure to blow up everything; they're made that way. The Dnieper Dam—yes, of course they'll blow it up." "Do you think they might try a counter-offensive at Smolensk?" "Oh, Lord, they'll be damn lucky if they manage to hang on till winter. . . ."

I went to a second-hand bookshop in the Petrovka, but failed to get the *Kniga Otrazheniy*, Inokenti Annensky's book of literary essays, which I've tried to get for years, or his poems. Pity. The woman, rather *ancien régime*, was sympathetic and wanted to be helpful. She got rather impatient with a young man who complained of her stuff being "old and rusty"; another young man came in, asking in vain for Essenin's poetry;

and a girl—whom the woman addressed first as *baryshnia* (miss) and then as *grazhdanka* (citizen), wanted a second-hand school-book on physics.

I went on to Jordan's, and then to the Caucasian restaurant, where I was "throwing a party" for Jordan, Lovell, Foster, and Monck, of the Mission, and Jeffries. Jeffries, a British official, thought it was a great problem whether Budyenny could get his troops across the Dnieper, and he thought the outlook in the south pretty nasty. He also said he was no longer so sure that we'd stay on in Moscow. Otherwise he was very amusing, while I told a number of so-called "Armenian" stories, and items from the Russian "alphabet"—smutty schoolboy humour, all of it much appreciated by Jeffries. Incidentally, the funny stories I've heard from people since I got to Moscow have long whiskers; I heard nearly all of them twenty-five years ago.

Listened to the eleven o'clock (that is London nine o'clock) news. They spouted at me at great length on Leningrad, etc. I suppose one has to be thankful for small mercies; half a dozen sentences heard by fifteen or twenty million people must be a justification of sorts for one's existence.

AUGUST 20

I don't know how it happened, but nobody could be bothered going on that trip to the kolkhoz, except me and three Japs. With us came Palgunov and Kozhemiakov, and I went in their car, as Lovell was needing ours in town. The place is some twenty miles out of Moscow, near Mytystchi. It's a big kolkhoz, and one which, I suppose, they like to show to strangers, though from the look of many other collective farms we passed it can't be altogether exceptional; and they tell me there are many more like it in the Moscow area.

Here there were acres and acres of tomatoes, and more acres

and acres of cabbages, cauliflowers, and cucumbers. Till 1931 they used to grow rye here, and the village was small and poor. Now it is one of the best market-gardening kolkhozes in the Moscow region. Beyond the hundreds of vegetable-growing acres were farm buildings and pastures with cows and huge pedigree pigs in whose company Lord Baldwin himself would, I am sure, be proud to be photographed. Through the pastures meanders the River Kliazma; and nude kolkhoz children were bathing there.

There are four hundred homesteads in the kolkhoz now and some four hundred active collective farmers, the others being children and old people; and there are also the young people who still go to school and others who attend the university in Moscow or the famous Timiriazev Academy of Agriculture. Many graduates of this school have in recent years returned to their own kolkhoz, bringing with them their knowledge of the latest agricultural methods. Highly scientific and elaborate methods are applied to the hot-beds, fertilizers, manuring, watering, anti-frost protection, etc. . . . But I needn't go into that. The principle is "no matter what the weather"; and the results may be judged by the acres of tomatoes with thick clusters of fruit, many of the tomatoes weighing nearly two pounds.

We walked through the grounds on this hot summer day with the podgy, bespectacled kolkhoz chairman, Comrade Rusin, the moving spirit of the whole place. Later he took us to his cottage for "tea." In reality, it was an enormous rustic meal, everything excepting the tea itself, the vodka, and the salt herring being the product of the kolkhoz.

Before that we had talked to some women who were attending to the cows. All their husbands were at the front. They mentioned it in a matter-of-fact way, with almost deliberate casualness, but there was anxiety in their eyes.

Among the people at Rusin's tea-table was an impressive figure, the secretary of the *Raikom*, the regional committee of

the Communist Party, a tall, gay, extraordinarily handsome
fellow, a native of this village. He wore a high Soviet decoration.

"What is that for?" I asked. "Tomato-growing?"

"No, more important than that," he laughed.

"The war, then?"

"No, more important still—or at least as important—mu-
nition-making."

As the meal progressed he grew more talkative. Pointing
across the veranda at the chairman's pretty garden, with the
phlox beds and the acres of potatoes and cabbages beyond, he
said: "Prosperity! Look at the prosperity of this place. Damn
the Germans! But for this war we'd be living in a world of
ever-increasing plenty for everyone." He talked about the
numerous men who had left the kolkhoz for the army, about
the German advance, etc. "You had a tough time in London,
hadn't you? Yes, but now the whole weight of the monstrous
German machine is turned against us. It won't be easy to stop,
but," he added angrily, "we shan't give up even if we've got
to retreat to the Urals. But, no, we shan't need to do that.
And I am damned if they get anywhere near our Moscow. I
know Moscow hasn't had any very severe bombings yet, but
our morale is good; I know that from my own big armaments
works—and we're prepared to make every sacrifice. And
Leningrad—oh, I know the proletariat of Leningrad—that
city won't fall. The Germans will break their necks there, lose
half their troops." And suddenly changing the subject: "But
tell me, your Churchill is perfectly reliable, isn't he?" I replied
that he was a great man and perfectly reliable—"as reliable
as Stalin." "Well then, he couldn't be better than he is," said
the comrade, reassured.

There was more talk of how Nazi Germany would be repaid
tenfold for all she had done to other people. The secretary of
the *Raikom* also remarked that it was a pity the Paris prole-

tariat had not been given the opportunity by its treacherous government to defend Paris, "with its great revolutionary tradition"; while a young kolkhoz woman, looking a little concerned, kept repeating that England ought to strike harder, much harder, at Germany to draw off some troops from Russia. And she asked: "Why can't America do more, since she also is committed to victory?"

Altogether it was a most interesting meal, and it had its comic side. Everybody was very cheerful. The woman expert kept questioning the Japs on how tomatoes were grown in Japan, and of course they hadn't the vaguest idea and merely giggled. The kolkhoz chairman, Comrade Rusin, in pouring out more drinks for them, kept mispronouncing the Japs' names, calling Mr. Kuga "Tuga," which means "tight" in Russian. And the secretary of the *Raikom*, who got a bit uproarious towards the end, said to me: "Let's go and hang these Japs. They're probably just a lot of Nazi spies." I said I quite approved, but suggested it might create a diplomatic incident. Addressing the Japs, he nevertheless said: "Now, frankly, do you Japs really disapprove of the German attack on Russia?" And the Japs hissed and giggled. One of them, meantime, had actually got rather tight, and when, after the meal, we were taken to see the prize bull on the dairy farm, Kozhemiakov took him under one arm and I took him under the other, and so we walked across the field. We all admired the bull, and our Jap, looking at the animal's powerful equipment, exclaimed in pidgin Russian: "What a beautiful cow, and what a lot of milk you must get from her!"

Later we were taken to the kolkhoz office, with its elaborate graphs of working hours and output, and its Stakhanovite tables of honour; and then to the school library and the infirmary. We then walked back to our cars on the main road. The air was filled with the smell of hay. It was a lovely summer evening. A crowd of children returning from their bathe were waving coloured towels. It was hard to imagine that not so many miles away other prosperous farms, the fruit of years of skill and labour, were being shelled, bombed, and annihilated by the Germans.

I drove back with Kozhemiakov. He is a particularly good fellow. How deceptive appearances sometimes are in this country! I scarcely thought this good-looking youth human at first. He struck me as a particularly "tough baby." Perhaps he is; but he's human for all that. He is intelligent, speaks good English, and has been out in the Far East. He is, I imagine, a fairly good specimen of the Stalinite Government official, very conscientious and hard-working. He is well-read and probably not of strictly proletarian origin. In any other country one would take this tidy, good-mannered youth for a "white-haired boy."

As we drove back to Moscow he talked about the interesting time he had been having during his long vacations before the war. "One can enjoy oneself in Moscow," he said. "I usually used to spend the first fortnight of my vacation having a really good time in Moscow—theatres and concerts and parties; and then I'd go down to the Caucasus to 'recuperate.' Lovely sanatoria at Sotchi, for instance, and glorious bathing in the warm water of the Black Sea. I'd take down the wife and the kid; it used to be great fun." We talked the rest of the time about the Caucasus, and romantic Kislovodsk, and we quoted Lermontov at each other. Young Russians today feel just as romantic about Kislovodsk and the Caucasus generally as I used to. In addition, they attach special importance to it as the homeland of Stalin. However, they never fail to stress the great development under the Soviet régime of cities like Tiflis and Erivan. Erivan used to be just a romantic spot; now it's the capital of Armenia, with huge steel and concrete buildings and wide avenues.

THURSDAY, *August* 21

      Voroshilov's appeal to the people of Leningrad reveals the gravity of the situation there. "The enemy is at our gates," it says. "Stand up like one man; train to use rifles, machine-guns, hand-grenades. This is the cradle of the Revolution; the factories we have built, the beautiful buildings and gardens we have made, shall not fall into the hands of the Fascists." Why this over-emphasis of the revolutionary greatness of Leningrad? Why nothing about its greatness as a city, as a centre which for two hundred years radiated civilization, and which never did "lie at the proud foot of a conqueror"? . . . The only never-conquered European capital —except London. Does this propaganda mean that Voroshilov is relying more on the highly "conscientious" Leningrad working class than on the population in general? Why nothing about the Fatherland War, or—about the Bronze Horseman? But perhaps I'm not objective enough where Leningrad is concerned. . . .

The grim memory of the famine of 1919 must be terrifying to many Leningraders. Can the Moscow railways and the Vologda railway be kept intact? That is the great problem. As for industry, there was a decree published at the time of the Finnish war instructing every factory to keep in reserve a year's supply of raw materials. I wonder if this has been strictly applied?

Today I told Jordan what I thought of the Voroshilov appeal—namely, that it was rather one-sided, and did not constitute a sufficiently *general* appeal. All the Leningraders I have seen have a deep sentimental love of their city, and they very largely think of it in terms of literary associations. "Oh, come on," said Jordan, "you don't die for Anne Hathaway's cottage." "A very pretty Jordanism, I admit," I said, "but you are missing the point, if only because you have never read *The Bronze Horseman.* What you call Anne Hathaway's cot-

tage, which, in Leningrad terms, means the whole of Leningrad, represents something profoundly vital to the Russian
people." Jordan was very pleased with "Jordanism." He
works infernally hard; it is, of course, much more encouraging to work for a paper than for an agency; apart from the
Sunday Times, I can see no trace of any of my work here in
the English newspaper cuttings the Embassy have been getting. . . .

Monck asked me to go with him to Scribe's *Verre d'eau* at
the Malyi Theatre. I advised him against it. It turned out to
be even worse than I expected (I had expected a funny,
slightly smutty French vaudeville). Instead, an imbecile *kup-
chikha*-like Queen Anne, and a miserable leading juvenile, and
an equally miserable ingénue, all of them used to doing Ostrovsky parts. And the villainess was the Duchess of Marlborough.
Nobody in the audience seemed to realize the family connec-
tion with Winston, but everybody seemed about as bored as I
was. These youthful Russian audiences adore the theatre, but,
by heaven, they are not uncritical. I heartily cursed Monck for
having dragged me there, when he could have gone and seen
Onegin instead.

Magidoff of the *Exchange Telegraph* was very pessimistic
in the morning; he said the B.B.C.—or some military expert
on it—was talking about the "tragedy of Russia moving to its
climax." Monck said it wasn't half as bad. The Germans had
claimed only 60,000 prisoners in the Ukraine, and it seemed
that Budyenny had got most of his troops across the Dnieper.
The bridgeheads, which, the Germans say, the Russians are
still holding, "though they are being mopped up," suggest
that the main Russian forces are getting across the Dnieper
all right. The loss of the industries on the right bank—including the iron ore, seven or eight huge engineering plants,
and the principal aluminium plant in Russia—is very serious,
though.

Lozovsky today said: "Heaven protect us from our sympathetic pessimist friends," meaning, no doubt, the B.B.C. He wasn't as exuberant as usual, though; he admitted the strength of the German Army, and declared that the Soviets were *Realpolitiker*—witness Voroshilov's appeal. . . . He said that some of the bloodiest, fiercest fighting was now in progress around Odessa, where the Rumanians were losing many tens of thousands of men.

AUGUST 23

There was a hullaballoo last night. We were having dinner at the Metropole, when a phone call came from somebody at the Nark, saying that the Japanese Ambassador had just seen Molotov. I went down to the Nark. The Jap who had distinguished himself at the kolkhoz the other day by mistaking a bull for a cow, now looked like the centre of the universe. Standing between the map of the United States and Lenin's portrait, he was handing out "inside dope" about the alleged demands the Japs had just made on the Russians. Very confidentially—but to everybody. The Japs, he suggested, had asked that the Russian Far Eastern Army be demobilized, "as a token of goodwill," and that no American shipments be made via Vladivostok. "Failing which—?" I said; at which the little scoundrel hissed and giggled. I don't think there is much in this story; the Japs are simply trying on a little war of nerves, with our expert on cattle trying to get the American journalists all worked up. . . . The Russian censors wouldn't pass any of the "conjectures," and merely passed the bare statement that Molotov had received the Jap Ambassador.

It was a bore getting here through the dark, at the risk of being run over by a blacked-out tram-car, and all for nothing. And then, to add to my troubles, the night communiqué arrived and announced the loss of Novgorod.

At one a.m. I went to the Metropole and slept on Jordan's sofa. The trouble is that our car broke down three days ago, and it's about as hard to get a car quickly mended in Moscow as it is to get a pair of shoes resoled. Bertha, our maid, said it would cost eighty or one hundred roubles from a *chastnik* (a private artisan) ; anybody else would keep it too long. . . .

It's difficult to get other odds and ends; for instance, note-paper. Five thousand Woolworth stores in the Soviet Union would, I think, greatly add to the people's happiness.

MONDAY, *August* 25

Ochnaya stavka—"The Confrontation"—is a good thriller of a play. I saw it last night at Tairov's Kamernyi Theatre. The scenery was in the real Tairov tradition: simple, suggestive, and slightly cubist. A German plot, a murder, the theft of secret blueprints from an arms factory; the discovery of a clue by a comic Jewish tailor who, in the process, makes a little speech about the improved status of the Jews under Soviet rule; the gradual tracking down of the German villain, and then the impressive propagandist finale, in which the German spy is confronted, one by one, with all the characters of the play. In the end the German breaks down and bursts into imprecations against "this cursed country. . . . I can't do anything . . . *they are all united* . . . they have all shown me up."

I hear important steps are being taken to develop the port facilities of Archangel, and that several of the British are go-ing there to organize all sorts of things. . . . A big convoy is expected in shortly. Incidentally, I hear Vernon Bartlett, of the London *News Chronicle*, is on his way here. He is to act as liaison officer to the M. of I. and also as correspondent of the B.B.C.

Good news about the Anglo-Russian invasion of Iran. It would be amusing to see some of the Blimps from the Near

East meeting the *tovarichi*. . . . Perhaps they won't get on too badly. Anyway, this invasion of Iran is very cheering. (The Russians say that in their case it is merely an application of Article 6 of the 1921 Treaty—directed at the time against England. Their present technique is much the same as that of our entry into Iraq.) The Russians are delighted to see Britain taking a big initiative for the second time. Syria was the first.

The Germans have taken Novgorod, and claim Dniepropetrovsk, and also Luga on the way to Leningrad. The resistance in the Leningrad sector is very strong, it seems; and the Germans are paying a heavy price for every inch of useless ground. I wonder if the Germans are pushing across the difficult terrain between Novgorod and Leningrad and avoiding the Moscow-Leningrad railway, lest the Russians bring up a lot of troops from Moscow and strike at their rear? But on the map the Luga and Novgorod pincers look disquieting.

The small space given in the Soviet press to Churchill's speech today suggests that the Russians are not too pleased with England. They must be annoyed by the delay of the Economic Conference, and by Beaverbrook's statement in America some days ago suggesting that he did not wish to be rushed. A certain amount of stuff has been reaching Russia from England, including some planes (some of which are since said to have bombed Berlin), but it doesn't amount to very much so far. In the literature dropped by the Russians over the German lines there is hardly any reference to the British allies. The only leaflet relating to Britain is the text of the Atlantic Charter, which the Russians have O.K.'d.

Large-scale economic aid to Russia is, apparently, being planned for the spring, but nothing wonderful for the immediate future. No wonder the Russians aren't over-enthusiastic about Churchill at the moment. . . . They also cut out from their press reports all he said about Japan.

The German radio is reported to have said that the Germans have lost one-third as many men as the Russians, and they put the Russian casualties at five millions. If the report is true, this is a tremendous admission, and greatly exceeds all the official German casualty figures I've seen so far. The Russians admit 750,000 casualties. The terrible thing, of course, is that the Germans have trapped so many of the Russian wounded; and they are certainly not going to treat them properly. Obviously, with the Russians retreating, they are likely to lose more of their wounded to the Germans than vice versa.

Today, by the way, Krantz, an American reporter, was screaming his head off because the Nark had handed out the note to Iran in Russian only. I said: "Now, look here, this is a country of 180 millions, and it's no use treating it as a nigger republic. The least qualification they can expect from a journalist coming here is that he has at least a smattering of the language." . . . A bit low, I admit.

I saw *Volga-Volga* at the local cinema tonight. There were lots of young people screaming with laughter. How the Russians like to laugh, and how little chance they get! Actually it's not a very funny film, but it's jolly. Good slapstick, slightly surrealist, especially when old Byvaly is chased all over the place by ballets and dance bands, and singers and drummers come popping out of doors and windows. And the little boy conducting the band is superb. I don't much like Orlova; but it's all very good fresh fun, with a nice touch of craziness; it would be extraordinarily good Russian propaganda if it could be sent to England.

On Saturday I saw the general; he had just come back from his first visit—his long-awaited visit—to the front, and is very pleased. He was well impressed by everything. He was taken for a day or two to the Smolensk sector, where he watched a local Russian offensive.

He received us in his office at the Embassy. The flags on the big map showed bulges into the Dnieper bend and towards Leningrad. Not pretty, but perhaps not so very alarming after all. Unfortunate about Dniepropetrovsk, though—if the German claim is true. If only the Germans could be held up before winter! And then, oh boy, won't it be lovely in Berlin with three hundred planes overhead every night . . . if we do it. . . .

Yesterday I went and had tea at the Red Square café with "the Moats," who is the correspondent of *Collier's Weekly* here. It's the most pleasant place in Moscow. It is quite plebeian, and the tea costs thirty-five kopeks—the cheapest "meal" I've ever bought anyone, especially in Moscow. I also bought some sweets—very expensive—in the shop attached to the café. Alice-Leone Moats (I don't know why they call her "the Moats," or "*la* Moats"), who likes to snoop around Persian and Turkish diplomats, said the Persian Ambassador had been dragged out of bed by Molotov at 3.30 a.m. The Ambassador had advised Teheran not to offer the Russians any resistance. Last week, apparently, he was still claiming that the British and Russian stories about the Germans in Persia were "greatly exaggerated."

The latest news-reel shows more arrivals by air of Polish, Czech, and Yugoslav diplomats. The Polish general was wearing one of those rather absurd square caps. The Soviet audience didn't react in any particular way. But they recognized "Creeps," as they call him, with visible approval.

WEDNESDAY, *August* 27

Pity it's fine: it means that General Mud has gone out of action for the present. However, in four days' time it'll

be September, and it mayn't get so funny for the Germans.
. . . The Russians have not yet admitted the loss of Dniepropetrovsk. The advance into Persia is rapid, no doubt with
motorized troops. *Pravda* published a somewhat "Marxist"
documentary article on Iran, in which it described it as a
feudal country, and said that the feudal lords are charging
the peasants exorbitant rents, and that the Germans had tried
to prevent all industrial development and wanted to use it as
an agricultural and raw-material "colonial appendix" to their
Lebensraum. The Russians are very tactful about the British,
but isn't that roughly the policy some of our boys have been
pursuing in Persia for years? Never mind, the "two great
democracies" are now co-operating in Persia, and whatever
they may do to the Persians, it won't be anything so bad as
what the Germans would do. . . .

The report in one of the Soviet papers about the entry of
Russian troops into Iran was pretty funny—especially the bit
in which an old Persian comes up to the Russian commander
and welcomes him "in the name of Article 6 of the Treaty of
1921"!

Moscow is taking an increasing interest in England and in
the R.A.F. There is a new poster showing an R.A.F. man and
a Soviet airman shaking hands over Berlin; English gram-
mars are sold on the bookstalls, an exhibition of English books
"from Chaucer to Shaw" has been opened in the West European Library; a new news-reel about British A.A. defences
is showing in the cinemas, the Moscow Art Theatre is playing
The School for Scandal, and good prices are offered for
English books by the second-hand bookshops.

Pleasant little episode in the tram-car in the Ilyinka today.
A little soldier, who was quite tipsy, was soliloquizing while
looking out of the tram-car window—much to everybody's
delight. He said he'd come from the front for just two days

and was going back tomorrow. "*Matushka Moskva!*" (little Mother Moscow!) he exclaimed. "You're just as you always were; one has to be gas-bags like our Russians to say that the German bombs had knocked you flat. There it is, the Ilyinka— just the same as ever!" "And now," he added, "I am going to a *vecherinka* (a party) with my friends, and tomorrow I'll go and catch the train at eight o'clock—mustn't miss it, mustn't miss it!"

In a second-hand shop in the Kuznetsky Mosst I picked up a charming first edition (1863) of Polonsky's *Kuznetchik Muzykant* (*The Musical Grasshopper*), with pictures, in the original gold-embossed cloth binding, in very good condition, for five roubles. In it is the *Madman* poem old P. N. loved to recite. Poor old boy. . . . It's hard to imagine he may still be alive. God knows, Paris seems so infinitely far away.

I also bought a Soviet book of *Kamchatka Tales* by one Melnikov. It's curious how for many years now the Arctic has been a constant source of literary inspiration to Russian writers—as if they had only just discovered the vast expanses of their country. A chap came up to the counter and asked if they had any Dostoevsky. Only second-hand, the assistant said. Apparently the reading of Dostoevsky is not greatly encouraged.

There's a good article in the *Literaturnaya Gazeta* by Kornei Chukovsky, the famous critic, who, years ago, introduced Kipling, H. G. Wells, and Oscar Wilde to Russia. He is an old Leningrader, and speaks lovingly of his town. "Every street in it," he says, "is a quotation." He recalls Pushkin, Belinsky, Nekrasov, Blok, etc., and says that St. Petersburg was a source of inspiration to nearly all the great Russian writers—and an everlasting source of Russia's *generous* ideas; "*essentially an anti-Fascist city.*"

Magidoff, who takes a civilized interest in Russian books, lent me the other day Chukovsky's very amusing book on "child speech"; also Pasternak's *Poems,* which, with their far-fetched imagery, I still find hard to follow. T. S. Eliot is lucid in comparison, and Edith Sitwell simplicity itself.

At the Metropole the other day I met Captain Billotte, a son of the general who was killed in a car smash at the time of Dunkirk. He had recently escaped from Germany and had some remarkable stories to tell of how he had made good use of German stupidity. He had travelled across half Germany, and every time he and his two pals were at a railway station they made a point of sitting next to the Gestapo chap who was looking for them. He is now going to join de Gaulle. . . . Like all other escaped war prisoners, he cannot speak too highly of the Poles, and of the risks they took to help them. He's a French officer of the very best type—full of guts and personality.

The number of casualties resulting from the twenty-four raids on Moscow in the last month has just been published: about 750 dead and 2,000 seriously wounded. Very few of the raids were heavy—I don't think there were ever more than fifteen or twenty planes actually over Moscow—the casualty figures are, therefore, fairly high. It's probably largely due to the very thorough fire-watching.

I've just been hearing on the radio some trade-union boss saying that there may well be an invasion of England in the next few weeks. He even said he was sure of it. Germany, he said, would abandon the eastern front for a time to a slender defence force. I doubt it; but it seems that this kind of propaganda is deemed necessary, (a) to counteract any public demand for an invasion of France, and (b) to discourage that complacency which is getting hold of many people in England. The very "hits" the B.B.C. keeps on repeating interminably are significant—for instance, that altogether idiotic appeal to a chicken "to lay an egg for my tea." Its success may be due to the egg shortage, but perhaps also to a growing lack of seriousness.

AUGUST 29

Y. had some "bad news" for me, as he called it. Somebody told him that morale was getting very poor, that people had their tails between their legs, that there was discontent with the Government, and much disappointment because the Germans had managed to invade Russian territory *at all*. And then, he said, somebody had come from Dniepropetrovsk, and had seen many Russian soldiers there *bare footed*. That *is* bad, if it's true.

I mentioned this last point when I saw Z. this evening. "Oh, that, at any rate, is all right," he said. "Three million pairs of army boots have just arrived. Think of it—48,000 tons of boots!" "British or American?" "All British," he said. There was something thrilling about it. England, bombed, bombed, bombed—and producing three million pairs of boots for Russia!

I gathered from Z. that the entry into Iran had not been properly thought out in advance, and that, unless we were careful, there might be some misunderstandings between us and the Russians. When I asked him what he thought of the outlook in general, he said: "The big, the enormous problem now is going to be the problem of British and American supplies. It's absolutely vital . . ." and he added that he was more confident about British than about American determination to help the Russians. "Are the Russians to get the stuff under the Lease-Lend Act?" I asked. "Oh, God only knows," he said, rather peevishly.

It rained cats and dogs all yesterday. In the morning I looked out of the window—the roof of the old stucco house across the lane was all glossy with rain, and the women were toddling along to market under their umbrellas, jumping over the puddles. A cheerless sight; but cheerful when one thinks of the infernal mud in the Ukraine and the swamps round Leningrad. The Germans may get stuck in the mud for weeks.

I had a job getting to Lozovsky's in the afternoon. The car was still out of order, so I waited under torrents of rain for the "A" tram at the Pokrovka. At last the tram appeared in the distance and a swarm of citizens came from under a gateway and there was an infernal scramble. However, they all took it fairly cheerfully, and only an old woman resented the pedantic remarks of a citizen who said we must get out from the front platform; for the tram was packed like nothing on earth. ("Compared with Moscow trams, a tin of sardines is just a vacuum," Jordan said the other day.) We got off from the back platform, the pedantic citizen still laying down the law. "You try yourself," the old woman said, and others joined in till he shut up.

It poured like the devil all the way down the Mestchanskaya. I was half an hour late for Lozovsky. It didn't matter very much; he had been talking about the Italian seizure of Dalmatia, "while the Germans weren't looking." It was only from his casual answers to casual questions that we learned that the Dnieper Dam had been blown up. It must hurt a good Five-Year-Plan enthusiast, and perhaps every Russian, more than the destruction of St. Paul's would hurt James Bone [London editor of the *Manchester Guardian*]. Although the whole foreign press naturally cabled the news, the Russian papers this morning made no mention of it.

At night Lovell's two pals from Teheran dropped in. They had had a long, tedious railway journey, and no chance of reading from nightfall till dawn. Somewhere near Orel, while standing at a station, with a large ammunition train alongside, they were attacked by a German plane flying very high;

but it dropped its bombs five miles up the line. They waited for five hours before the line was repaired. . . .

SATURDAY, *August* 30

This rainy weather is very welcome from the military point of view, but it's a nuisance not to be able to get one's shoes soled when these shoes are letting in water; and the house is getting all damp and cold. I have been using the quilt from Lovell's bedroom; until then I couldn't sleep for cold. How this house is going to be heated will be a problem.

Lovell laughed at Reuter's new brain-wave—a wire came from them suggesting I go to Leningrad, which, in their opinion, "would make a first-class story." As if I didn't know it.

There's a cigarette shortage in Moscow. Misha said he'd gone all over the place trying to buy some. Nothing doing. I gave him a few of mine—grudgingly. The cigarette shortage would be the worst thing of all, and we've got to draw on the surplus stock of cigarettes and whisky which the American Embassy are selling off to their friends. For some reason they have bigger stocks than they need. Maurice also has a few good bottles which he picked up from the various legations when they were turned out of Moscow, shortly before the war.

Misha was telling me that the huge Moskva Hotel had been built on the site of the Okhotny Ryad market, and the equally huge Sovnarkom Building on the site of a church, blown up in 1924 or so. Both places used to swarm with vociferous tradeswomen selling cucumbers and salt fish, and what not. The Trubnaya Square, now quite uninteresting, used to be the dog, cat, and bird market. Moscow has gained in efficiency, but has lost in picturesqueness.

Long letter from M. Sad to hear that the Wren Cloisters and Pump Court and other parts of the Temple burned out by the blitz are being pulled down, and that I shall never even see their ruins again.

I spent the evening indoors re-reading Alexis Tolstoy's *Peter the Great* and listening to the B.B.C. One has to live in Moscow to regard the wireless as a blessing. I never felt much need for it before. I wrote an article for the *Moscow News*— the English weekly, which has now started coming out three times a week. Jordan and Ralph Ingersoll, editor of a New York paper, have also written pieces. My article was called "Looking Back"; it was a description of the Battle of Britain, of the London blitz, of the Battle of the Atlantic, and led up to the *third* great German set-back, the Battle of Smolensk. But it's useful to remind the Russians we've been at it for two years. What is so cheering is that they welcome articles of this kind.

PART III

SEPTEMBER

TUESDAY, *September* 2

On Sunday I went to see *Onegin* again—irresistible this atavistic desire to hear Tchaikovsky!—and took Jordan with me. It was as lovely as last time—the sighs and the heart-beating in the orchestra and a less decorative (too fat) but better Tatiana, with a good voice, good acting, and a beautiful diction for all those lovely Pushkin lines. What verbal felicity Pushkin had! The young women in the audience were as rapturous as ever about Lensky, though Lemeshev in the part wasn't, in my opinion, as good as the Kozlovsky I saw last time. We left after the duel scene; Jordan admitted he knew nothing about music, but thought it "a very pleasant noise." . . . Later I wrote a longish article suggesting that since the Germans had failed to (1) capture Moscow, and (2) smash the Red Army, they were now trying the next-best thing —to reduce Russia's war potential as much as possible. They had succeeded in this to some extent. I estimated the reduction —very modestly—at twenty-five per cent, taking account of the agricultural losses in the Ukraine, particularly the sugar-beet areas round Vinnitza, the industrial area west of the Dnieper, and the effect in the Donbass of the loss of the Krivoi Rog iron ore. Also, on the strength of an official Soviet publication, I enumerated the main industries on the west bank, notably the big aluminium plant, and, quoting the same source, I said that Leningrad represented (including shipbuilding)

173

seventeen per cent of the total industrial output of the Soviet Union. I also dwelt on the high quality of Leningrad labour, a quality achieved by the generations-long industrial tradition of St. Petersburg. If the Germans get to Bryansk, with its 100,000 workers, it'll be a serious matter, even if the Russians manage to evacuate in time most of the plant and the workers to the Urals. It'll take time to get it started again.

Somebody told me that winter clothes would be scarce this year, and since I am probably going to be here a good part of the winter, I decided to go on a shopping expedition, taking Misha with me as my guide. Shops in Moscow are very unattractive-looking just now, for all the windows are either sandbagged or boarded up with rough planks. The job was done with astonishing speed in the two or three days following the first air-raid on Moscow in July. The Mostorg, near the Bolshoi Theatre, and the big shops in Gorki Street, and all the shops in the Stoleshnikov Lane, the Petrovka, and the Kuznetsky Mosst are all boarded up in this way, and it is sometimes a job to find the shop you are looking for. We went first to the Stoleshnikov Lane; Misha said it had the best shop for winter clothes. The Stoleshnikov Lane has many "commission shops," where people sell their valuables when hard up, and a shop of *Russkie Samotsvety*—various objects made of semi-precious Ural stones, such as amethysts, topazes, etc.; and boot and shoe shops—where, I discovered, a very ordinary pair of shoes which would cost about 25*s*. 0*d*. in London, costs about £5; [1] and several second-hand clothes shops, as well as one of the principal shops for winter clothes and fur coats. We went into this one. The attendant said that their stocks were very low just now, but that they might get a consignment of reindeer coats from Archangel in a week or two; he was rather indefinite about it, and I thought I had better see what they

---

[1] At the present time the pound may be considered as approximately equal to four dollars; hence a shilling as equal to about twenty cents.

had. The few reindeer coats they still had—pretty light-brown fur with a soft silky texture—unfortunately didn't fit me; and I was left with the choice between some long, second-hand padded cloth coats with fur collars, at about £30, and a fairly short jacket (a *polushubok*) made of some kind of white fur, with a rather doubtful astrakhan collar. I tried it on; it looked rather like Father Christmas, but it fitted. What kind of fur was this, I asked. "Dog," the assistant said, "Siberian dog." Siberian or not, it smelt like any other dog. He assured me it was "the warmest fur in existence," and said it was a bargain at 337 roubles—which worked out at about £7. So I bought the dog coat. I then went into another department of the same shop and chose an astrakhan hat—of much better quality than the collar of my coat. There were plenty of them and I got one for about £3 10*s*. Now for galoshes. We could get none in any of the shops in the Stoleshnikov Lane, and went to the Mostorg department store. It may have been all right before the war; but just now a Moscow department store compares very unfavourably with any similar establishment in Oxford Street. Parts of the shop looked rather like a jumble sale. The toy department was very measly. Most of the "domestic ornaments"—inkstands, paperweights, and the like—were outrageous-looking objects; there were queues in the department dealing in stockings and women's underwear; and there seemed to be a shortage in all these things. The men's shirts were of fairly good quality, but expensive—an ordinary shirt costing about 100 roubles (i.e., £2, even at my semi-preferential rate of exchange); an ordinary suit cost about £20; and the quality and patterns of the ties were of the Woolworth standard with Bond Street prices. Misha assured me that three months ago there was much more to be got at the Mostorg, and prices were more reasonable. I suppose that's true; but I still think that a few thousand Woolworth stores in Russia would make life much simpler for the housewife and the ordinary citizen. Concentrating on heavy industry, they hadn't much time for the rest. We couldn't get any galoshes; but I was offered a pair of enormous *valenki*, felt boots, going right above your knees. They were good-quality felt, but cost about £6. "What do you say, Misha?" He laughed. "With your dog coat and *valenki*," he said, "everybody will think you've come straight from a kolkhoz." So I decided against the *valenki*. On our way out, we passed through the perfumery department; there was still plenty of soap there, and bottles of scent and eau-de-Cologne, all made by "T.G."—whatever that means.

I have also noticed that chemists' shops are fairly well stocked. Natalia Petrovna, Lovell's secretary, the other day bought a large and efficient-looking first-aid box for 20 roubles.

Storm in the journalistic tea-cup. Ralph Ingersoll has been here a fortnight or more, and he is determined to see Stalin. He has been pestering the life out of the American Embassy, bothering Ambassador Steinhardt, spending a fortune on urgent cables to Sumner Welles, and Oumansky, and, for all one knows, to Roosevelt himself. The line he takes is that, since he specially travelled nearly round the world to see Stalin and to get an interview from him for his New York paper (*PM*, I believe, is its name), it would be *very wrong* of Stalin not to see him. None of us has been received by Stalin, and there is no reason at all why Ingersoll should be. He suspects the British press of having expressed this view to all kinds of people; and, in short, of trying to sabotage his trip. To millions of Russians this war is a matter of life and death; but to Mr. Ingersoll it's an opportunity for a scoop; and people don't like this attitude. Ingersoll is particularly furious with Jordan, whose wise-crack must have been repeated to him. "Ingersoll didn't take Moscow, and knows it," Philip said, parodying Ingersoll's melodramatic article about the London blitz last September, which he called "Hitler took London and didn't know it."

Anna Mikhailovna asked me and Binkley to spend the evening at her *datcha*. It turned out to be a little bungalow in a pine wood, with a lot of other *datchas* all round. I can't be much bothered with Anna Mikhailovna; but I liked the old maid, Astiusha. She was very *ancien régime*, and kept on invoking God in her conversation—*akh gospodi*, and *gospod' s'vami*; and there was a nondescript young female at the party whom Astiusha persisted in addressing as *baryshnia* (miss). "Why don't you call her *grazhdanka* (citizen)?" I said jokingly. "Never again," said Astiusha. "Some time ago Anna Mikhailovna had a friend here, and I called her *grazhdanka*, and she said: 'Excuse me, but I am not a *grazhdanka*, I am a *baronessa*.' " She was a dear old thing, but she must have seen better times and seemed slightly embittered about the present wicked world. We sat under a wooden "umbrella" and had supper—tomato salad and *borsch* and veal chops and watermelon and a variety of drinks. It was a glorious warm moonlit summer night—though it was already the 1st of September—and the air was filled with the strong, intoxicating scent of the tobacco flowers, and the crickets were chirping their dry, yet sweet crackle. A bright full moon was shining through the pine trees—how still and lovely the Russian countryside was—even with the mosquitoes! Yet I felt restless, at the thought of the war, at the thought of all the uncertainty on this 1st of September; I wished the rain would pour down in torrents; every moonlight night, every sunny dry day, was so much gain for the Germans. I gathered from the conversation that there were still a lot of *staroregimny* people (Tsarists) about in the Arbat area. They had all adapted themselves to the new régime, more or less, though they still kept sighing for the "good old times." Thousands had wangled permits for Tashkent. As for Moscow, Anna Milkhailovna said, oh, she *hoped* the Germans wouldn't get there, but she wouldn't express an opinion. "And do you know," she said, "there is a Jewish division which has won a great victory and has captured three large towns—

Sverdlovsk, Omsk, and Tomsk." It was a favourite Moscow joke, she said, and it was quite true that most of the important Jews had beat it to Siberia.

Curious talk, the next morning, just as we were going back to Moscow, with two old muzhiks, who were janitors, or something, attached to the *datchas*. One of them reflected on the wickedness of "that wicked man" Hitler: "Just think," he said, "of all the millions of people he has killed and ruined. How, I ask you, can God allow such a man to go on living? Think of all the suffering he has brought on the whole world." He had three sons, he said, and two of them were in the army, and now he was living with the third one, who was half-witted. "But I devote my whole life to him now; and if they are going to call him up, I'll just go and join up, too, although I am past sixty. It's terrible," he went on, "what these Germans are doing to our people; but we'll beat them all right in the end. Our Red Army pushed them back from Moscow last month—now, didn't they? I was in the last war; our soldiers were good soldiers, but they weren't so certain then what they were fighting for; but now they know." He was sure the war would be over in November. The other muzhik, who was wearing a cloth cap, and had a broom in his hand, said the war would probably last a little longer—till January. "Last time, Grisha, you said it would end in August; I told you it would last longer, and you see I was right. And so now you say it'll end in November. I tell you, it'll go on till January." I didn't like to disillusion them, but suggested that it might last rather longer even than January.

We drove back to Moscow, passing through villages with quaint little wooden houses, built God knows when, and a village church which was in a good state of repair and was obviously being used as a place of worship. There were many army lorries on the road, and the soldiers looked very cheerful; and the horses drawing the numerous army carts were well looked after.

Got my shoes back from the mender's at last. The new soles and heels look fine, but cost 70 roubles, nearly 30*s*.

SEPTEMBER 5

Ingersoll has seen Stalin after all. He pulled so many wires in Washington, and made such a nuisance of himself to everybody, with his pestering and arguing, that Stalin was finally persuaded to see him for a few minutes. Ralph was warned, however, that no interview would be given him for publication. We all had a good laugh; and I am told he has left Moscow full of praise of the Russians, but very angry with the British. Before leaving, he wrote a slightly patronizing piece about the Russian people for *Moscow News*. What does he know?

Called at the Yugoslav Legation. I like Gavrilovich, the Minister. He has a sad but very intelligent face; he seems to feel the tragedy of his country very deeply. He produced a German paper, with a full page of violent denunciations of himself, under the huge headline: "Gavrilovich." He was treated as a "Bolshevik" and his wife, according to this German paper, had a Jewish aunt, which, of course, explained everything. I also like young Miletich and that enormous jovial mountain of a Bogich, the two counsellors. We talked about the present "Pan-Slav" propaganda drive in Russia. I think the Yugoslavs are willing to see Russian influence after the war strengthened in the Balkans; and, in the military sense, they would certainly welcome it. There still remains the moot question of the post-war policy of the Comintern (if any); but, as somebody remarked, bourgeois democracy, Sovietism, and capitalism are all relative terms, and the Balkan countries, full of admiration for the Soviet Union, might well produce a tolerable blend of all kinds of things which would in no way alienate their national independence. I don't think the

Serbs—and all the people here are Serbs—think very highly of either the Croats or the Slovenes.

Vernon Bartlett has arrived after a three weeks' sea voyage. The new arrivals also include Mrs. Haldane and Topolski, the Polish artist. Interesting talk with Vernon about public opinion in England, the effect of Churchill's speech in which he spoke of "our Russian allies," the B.B.C.'s decision not to play the *Internationale,* and the curious reasons behind it, the "cashing-in" by the Communists, and the Government's decision not to raise the ban on the *Daily Worker.*

It seems that the German attack on Russia has greatly delayed America's entry into the war. German propaganda in the States is exploiting as hard as it can the "godlessness" of the Russian Government; and it seems to be carrying some weight.

Damn funny about Citrine going all pro-Soviet.

MONDAY, *September* 8

I've just come back from the Caucasian restaurant, where I had dinner with Jordan and Topolski. Topolski is planning to go down to the Polish camps on the Volga. The Poles have had a tough time since 1939, when thousands of them were deported to Siberia and Central Asia; but as Germany is—even to *these* Poles—*the* enemy, they are now only too keen to fight on the Russian side, if they can get the equipment. Probably some of it will have to come from England, as the Russians haven't quite enough for their own troops. How much finer the attitude of the Poles is than that of the Finns! Because the Finns had a grievance against Russia they joined up with Hitler. There, perhaps, is the real difference between a civilized people and an uncivilized one. Clean lavatories— such as they have in Finland—are not necessarily a criterion of civilization, and of high spiritual values.

Philip has bought himself a good radio set, and we've just been listening to the English news. Very good, that story about the "anniversary" raid on Berlin—the anniversary of the first big London blitz. And it was great fun to hear the German wireless squealing, with great moral indignation, about British inhumanity, and the bombed-out women and children of Berlin crowding into rest-centres set up in school buildings. I seem to remember a few last year—especially that one off the Old Kent Road.

Strange to think of this time last year—that Saturday evening when, after leaving the *Sunday Times*, I took a bus down to the East End to look at the fires. There were panicky crowds in Commercial Road East waiting for buses to get out of town; the docks were blazing; then I walked along to London Bridge and looked at the burning docks—there were three or four gigantic fires, and on the other side of the bridge there was a red sunset. And then, through the darkening streets near the Monument (all those houses were then still intact), I walked back, feeling rather nervous. They were dark and enormous, those big blocks of offices, standing out against the red sky, with a sunset at one end of the street and the glow of fires at the other. . . . And then the sirens sounded and the massacre in the East End began.

The Moscow ballet season opened yesterday at the annex of the Bolshoi Theatre. The place was packed, and there were the usual crowds of unluckies outside the theatre hoping for a stray ticket. The Embassy, and the Military Mission, including all the juniors, and the American Embassy, and the various legations (which, with the return to Moscow of the now Allies, have greatly swelled the ranks of the diplomatic corps) all turned up in force, doing a good couple of hundred Russians out of their ballet seats. Lots of uniforms throughout the theatre; it made this opening of the ballet season look a very brilliant affair. The stage of the annex is, of course, rather inadequate for the ballet, but it couldn't be helped, as the Bolshoi is still under repair.

I am not greatly interested in the ballet, least of all in this kind of ballet. After an hour or so I get bored—except for the music. Not that the *Swan Lake* music is uniformly good; it contains a lot of rather trashy Tchaikovsky—especially all that Hungarian and Spanish stuff in the third act—but it's got lovely stretches of five or ten minutes. The *corps de ballet* did good, if not exceptionally good, team work; the hero, Prince Charming, or whatever his name is, did his stuff very well, though he looked fatuously pansy with his powdered face and pink tights, but Lepeshinskaya, the *prima ballerina*, was charming, and the clown had great rhythmic vitality. The scenery was conventional, and so, of course, were the "dying swan" costumes, and the colour schemes of costumes and scenery in the acts other than the Swan Lake itself were a trifle incoherent. However, it was pleasant enough, though Act III I found almost unbearably dull. Perhaps I was in the wrong mood. Later, there was a party in the Moats's suite at the National. With its dozens of champagne bottles and its enormous buffet it must have cost the woman a fortune. Everybody and everybody's brother was there, and she even managed to get some Russians to come—a young ballet dancer, and a Leningrad film producer and his wife. The little ballet dancer was charming, and spoke fairly good French, and some of our sex-starved colleagues stood round her with their tongues hanging out, until she said she had been married for only a month. But the person I was really interested in was Comrade Miliutin and his little dark wife. They had both just come from Leningrad, where he is one of the leading lights of the Leningrad film studios. He said he was going back to Leningrad at the end of the month, and said he "simply loathed" Moscow. "It's colourless," he said, "it's nondescript. It will probably be magnificent in a few years (or it would be, but for this war); but just now it's neither one thing nor the other. We Leningraders used to like Moscow for its quiet idyllic provincial calm—it was such an *uyutny* place; but now it's got none of its old cosiness, and little of its colour left. But Leningrad is quite another matter. Yes, Leningrad is still what it was; if you went there now you wouldn't find it any different from what you knew it before the Revolution. I know our Leningrad people well," he went on, "I know the spirit of the Leningrad working class, I know they will fight to the last man. But what gives me nightmares is the thought that these German swine may bomb Leningrad, destroy one of the most beautiful things of human civilization. You who saw so much destruction in London, and who also know Leningrad, must know how I feel." I said I did. The little brunette joined in the conversation. "So you lived in Leningrad before the Revolution," she said. "Petrograd," she corrected herself, "or rather Petersburg," she added. "You know a lot of us still call it that." "By the way," she said, "what school did you go to?" I said it was the Reformatskoie. "Good heavens, that's where I went," she said. "And do you know that old Arthur Alexandrovich Brock is still alive?" "Is he really?" I said. "Now that *is* extraordinary. You know, about five years after I left Russia, I had a letter from him, quite out of the blue. He told me that he was very happy to be in Russia, and to be teaching—not bourgeois schoolboys, but workers." He was running some kind of evening lectures.

I never felt sentimental about the Reformatskoie, where, I always thought, I had wasted a lot of my time; but I had admired Arthur Alexandrovich Brock very much. He was the headmaster of my school, one of the three "German" schools in St. Petersburg. The two others were the Petrischule and the Annenschule; and all three (which were attached to the three Protestant churches) had been, for many years, an important source of supply to the bureaucracy, the bar, and the liberal professions. Arthur Alexandrovich, the headmaster, was a real scholar and humanist. Of German culture he thought in terms of Winckelmann, Goethe, and Hölderlin. Despite his German origin, he was a true Russian patriot, and one of his sons was killed in 1914, serving in the Russian Army. The teaching was done partly in Russian and partly in German, and the Reformatskoie was the most "modern" and the most Left-wing of the three. Brock was a good liberal. It was said to produce good, civilized Europeans. What it did teach its boys well— later it also had a girls' school attached—was modern languages, particularly French and German. When the war started in 1914, the teaching in German was abolished, and the wretched German-Baltic teachers—and about fifty per cent of them were that—were made to give their lessons in broken Russian, which amused most of us enormously, and completely undermined the teachers' authority. About half the boys were Russians, and half Baltic Germans. All my friends —not that I made any lasting friendships there; few people do at school—were Russians, with only one exception. But this exception I often remembered in later years. My best friend was Sasha M. His father was a colonel and they lived in an old-fashioned house in the Millionnaya. Sasha looked like a Jap; he was small and lively, and he had a yellow skin. At twelve he wrote very good comic verses, and in the summer we were often together, riding cross-country, or wandering about the woods at Oranienbaum. I could never understand why Sasha looked like a Jap, or, for that matter, why his mother did; for she was a very snobbish woman, and loved talking of her ancestors. Sasha spoke good English and a very affected French. The English was one of the bonds between us; none of the others in our form could speak it, and we were very proud of being exceptions. The only German schoolmate with whom I had a lot to do was called Robert Germann. His father was the chief surgeon of the eye hospital. They hailed from Riga. He was a good chap, Robert, but he had always very poor marks, and he had a disgusting habit of biting his nails and the flesh round them. For all his good looks, there was something mentally defective about him. At heart, he knew that Sasha and I were mentally more alert than he, and I think he respected and admired us for that reason, and always wanted to learn from us, often repeating as his own remarks we had made. But in one respect he felt very superior to us, and that was that he was a real, hundred-per-cent German. He despised the Russians, ridiculed the English, and said the French were completely degenerate. One day I found him standing in front of a mirror. He was passing his chewed fingers through the large lock of fair hair falling over his forehead. "It's a great thing to have fair hair," he said. "Why?" I asked. "Well, you see, it's a question of race; the German race; Nordics, you know, superior to all other races." He was unable to develop his theory; he had, apparently, just picked it up from some relation of his; but he felt very pleased about it, all the same. I pointed out that there were many fair-haired Russians, and some dark Germans; this rather puzzled him, but he said something more about "the Nordic race." And when, much later, during the Great War, we went in a tram-car, crowded with Russian soldiers, he used to say in French (for he liked to show off his French): *"Les animaux"* ("The beasts"). . . . . And, throughout the war, he frequently referred with admiration to General von Falkenhayn and to General Ludendorff. Sasha and I treated him rather as an amiable crank and didn't take much notice of his nonsense. One was tolerant in those days. But in later years I often remembered Robert Germann. About ten years ago I heard from him. He was in South Africa. He had had a thin time since he left Russia, but he still believed that Germany would reassert herself. He sent me a snapshot of himself, looking like the lord of creation, as he stood there, between two wretched black men, with a cigarette hanging from a corner of his mouth. I am convinced that, if he hasn't been locked up, he must be up to some mischief in South Africa. Perhaps I should be grateful to him; he gave me an insight into Nazism long before any-body had heard about it.

I told much of this to Miliutin and his wife. (I had got them into a corner and we talked for a good long hour.) "Yes," she said, "what an odd assortment of people the Reformatskoie produced! Do you know, for instance, that Alfred Rosenberg, the Nazi 'philosopher,' received his education at the Reformatskoie?" "Good God, so he did." I had vague recollections of him. He was a few years ahead of me. "And Major Pole-zhaiev—did you know him?—who was killed at Smolensk only a few weeks ago. And Ilyish, who is the leader of the orchestra of the Leningrad State Opera. And you, coming back to Russia as a British correspondent, after twenty-four years' absence, and coming back not, as one might expect, full of White Russian ideas, but as a supporter of the Soviet Union. For you are a supporter of the Soviet Union, aren't you?" "Of course," I laughed. "Do you imagine they would have let me in if I wasn't?"

Petersburg, Petrograd, Leningrad; it was all mixed up in my mind. I could not help it. I asked Miliutin and his wife a hundred questions about the town, about the Summer Garden, with its marble Greek goddesses with their chipped noses, about the Nevsky Prospect and dozens of other streets and places. Miliutin was an old Leningrader, and loved the city. He was a typical Russian intellectual; and spoke the good old Leningrad Russian, without that Moscow singsong intonation. The man was so friendly that I ventured to touch on one or two sore subjects.

"You've made mistakes," I said, "but, in spite of it, you have built up something which is magnificent. Soviet Russia is a great country. You've achieved that. I've been away for twenty-four years. And I know in my bones that this is still Russia, but in many ways a better Russia—though in some respects a Russia that is less good. I'll talk to you quite frankly. I think

if you had a satirist of genius like Saltykov, you wouldn't, like
the Tsarist régime, allow him to write all sorts of scurrilous
things about you. You'd simply lock him up in a concentration camp or shoot him." "Yes, probably we should," said
Miliutin. "But you've got to remember that, for the present,
we can't afford the luxury of such freedom. In time all that
will change; but not now; there are too many things to build
up, too many things to do; anything that undermines the collective effort, the collective enthusiasm, is bad. But remember," he continued, "we've got the Stalin Constitution, out of
which a democratic Soviet Russia is going to evolve. It answers
the aspirations of our people. Its application would be in full
swing by now but for the present war, and the menace of war
that has hung over this country for years. And when I say
democratic Soviet Russia, I mean democratic *Soviet* Russia,
not a strict imitation of your parliamentary bourgeois democracy." "What is going to be the position of the party?"
"Well, the Communist Party is that *apparatus* of national
policy which will bring into full existence that Socialist Democracy, that Soviet Democracy—that is, democracy without private capitalism—which is Stalin's aim. There is no
dividing line any more between the party and the nation; the
two are becoming more and more parts of the same thing. And
in this war you have seen how our people—who are easy-going
in many ways—have had their discipline and morale constantly kept up to scratch by the party."

"Yes, I entirely agree. But the Comintern?" "Well," said
Miliutin, a little evasively, "we don't really see much of the
Comintern these days, do we? And have you seen the last issue
of the Comintern monthly?" I said I had, and that I couldn't
help chuckling at the glowing tributes it was paying to the
British people and to the British Government. "So you see,"
Miliutin laughed, "there isn't much to worry about." "Well,"
I said, "not at the moment. But you will admit that the British
Communist Party pursued a pretty absurd and anti-national

policy before June 22nd." And I quoted a few examples. "I dare say," said Miliutin. "But, frankly, I don't think anybody in this country is in the least interested in what the British Communist Party is doing. We never even hear about it these days."

"Do you mean to say you don't care whether the ban is lifted from the *Daily Worker* or not?"

"What's that?"

"You know, the Communist Party paper."

"Oh, I don't know about that. But I don't think anybody worries. No, the way I look at it is that the world is going to change a lot in the course of this war; that we are going to become increasingly democratic—though there will inevitably be a few years' reconstruction, after all the damage the Germans have caused; and that you, too, will develop a new kind of democracy, which may be quite a big departure from the present capitalist democracy. But I don't think the Communist Party or the Comintern need worry you. The Comintern may be of considerable use in the occupied countries still —for instance, in France—but England needn't worry. Our people are not interested in the world revolution in the old sense of the word; you know the famous old story—for it is fully ten years old, or more—about the young man who boasted of having got a job for his whole life. His job was to climb to the top of the Kremlin every morning and see if the world revolution had started." I said I had heard the story ages ago, and ventured just one more question. "When the new Stalin democracy comes fully into being, will the G.P.U. be abolished?" "G.P.U.," said Miliutin, "there's no such thing any more. There's the N.K.V.D." "Well, isn't it the same thing?" "No. It's all quite different since the liquidation of the Yezhov crew. But anyway, the police, the secret police, has been absolutely essential. Do you imagine that if the Trotskyists hadn't been liquidated we shouldn't have a Fifth Column in this country now? I don't know if you know much about the

Spanish war—we film people took a passionate interest in it—
but remember that the worst sabotage and the worst defeatist
propaganda in Republican Spain was done by the Trotskyists
—they called themselves the P.O.U.M." "Yes," I said, "I remember very well. We even had a pro-P.O.U.M. M.P., an
I.L.P. fellow called McGovern, whom I met in Barcelona, and
who furiously denounced to me what he called 'the Stalinist
G.P.U.,' who, he said, were committing all kinds of atrocities
against the P.O.U.M. people."

Miliutin looked at his watch and said he had to go. I said
good-bye to him and his little wife and we agreed to meet
again. "If you really go back to Leningrad at the end of the
month," I said hopefully, "couldn't it be arranged that I go
too?" "Well, perhaps," he said; "we'll have a talk about it."

I liked the man very much; and thought his ideas were not
only sound, but that he had summed up very nicely a great
number of points and tendencies I had observed elsewhere in
Moscow. The Moats's party was a distinct success, from my
point of view.

SEPTEMBER 9

X was more pessimistic than I had ever seen him before. He suggested that Leningrad was in a desperate plight.
The Germans are boasting that they will get Leningrad in a
fortnight. I don't believe it; though, if it is true that the Germans have got Schlüsselburg—which the Russians deny—
they may easily paralyse Leningrad's principal electric supply, which comes from the Volkhov hydro-electric plant, and
also cut off the city's normal water supply, which, apparently,
comes from the upper reaches of the Neva. It would also mean
that they were in control of the Leningrad-Vologda railway.
All together, X said, the situation was "definitely serious," and
the problem of maintaining the cadres of the Red Army was
becoming an increasingly serious one. Equally serious was the

question of supplies; to a large extent already the Russians
would have to depend on British and American supplies; and
these would not be easy to get to Russia . . . even with the
best will in the world.

Moreover, he said, the Germans had succeeded in establish-
ing two "as yet unimportant" bridgeheads on the left bank of
the Dnieper; they had failed in this for a long time; the Russians had bombed their pontoon bridges to blazes; but in the
last day or two the Germans had rushed up a lot of fighter
planes, and these had shot down the Russian bombers, or
driven them away. The Germans were trying for Kharkov
and Rostov.

The Russians no longer seem to believe very much in "good
Germans." About ten days ago a decree was published—
though not in the daily press—ordering the deportation to
Siberia and to Central Asia of the entire German population
of the German Volga Republic. Six hundred thousand people
are affected. The Russians are not taking any chances with
any Germans, especially with Germans living round Saratov,
on the main river and railway route connecting the southern
front with the Urals. Probably quite correctly, the Russians
claim that there have been several attempts at railway sabotage in the Volga Republic, and that every precaution must
be taken against such Fifth Column activities. I imagine the
deportation of the Volga Germans is going to be a pretty
brutal affair, rather like the deportation of the Poles in 1939,
and of the *kulaks* before that; but this deportation is, surely,
less a departure from the principle of "equality of nationalities
and races" than a realistic approach to the problem of a German minority—a problem the essence of which was demonstrated only too clearly in the Sudetenland and elsewhere. No
doubt, it's going to be hard on a lot of innocent people, but
still——. Some of the British residents here sometimes talk about
the Volga Germans as being "the most civilized people on the

Volga." What does it mean? It means they have cleaner villages, and better sanitation. And, because of that, they have always looked down on the Russians, have consistently refused to marry Russians ever since they got here in the reign of Catherine, and have disdained the Russian language. They continue to talk their absurd German, and to feel civilized Europeans. I dare say some of them are quite harmless, such as our little maid, Bertha, pathetic little creature who must be so undersized as a result of going through the Volga famine as a child. Perhaps she will be exempted from deportation because her father fought on the side of the Reds in the Civil War. But it doesn't follow that all the Volga-German domestic servants who are employed by so many foreigners in Moscow are altogether harmless. Maurice told me about one of his predecessors here who had a Volga-German maid. One day he sacked her. Half an hour later, "quite accidentally," he was rung up by somebody he knew at the German Embassy and was asked whether he knew of a job for a particularly good Volga-German servant. The German Embassy hadn't quite as easy a time in Russia as elsewhere organizing the German minority, but there had unquestionably been contacts between it and the Volga Germans. And old Katya, Maurice's first maid, who fled in a panic in July, was pretty suspect to me, anyway.

Jordan has made a big story of what he called "the greatest forced migration in history"; and the *News Chronicle* has naturally splashed it all over the place. Very unwise, I think. It'll only encourage the anti-Reds and also our more tender-hearted Liberals to talk about Soviet brutality.

Actually, I am told that each household has been allowed to take two tons of belongings with it.

SEPTEMBER 10

Two warnings last night (I didn't hear the second one), and a certain amount of stuff was dropped in the industrial suburbs. Fairly serious damage in one place.

The war situation is serious both in the south and the Leningrad area, but, partly to make up for it, the Russians are making a big display in the press of their offensive on the Smolensk front, where, after four weeks' intense fighting, they claim to have recaptured a large slice of territory and the small town of Yelnya. They say that in the course of this counter-offensive they demolished eight German divisions. It's the first fairly important counter-offensive, perhaps the first piece of country *recaptured* from Hitler.

I spent the forenoon at one of the Russian artillery schools in the Krasnaya Presnya district of Moscow, where we were taken by our friend the pince-nez colonel. They looked such fine earnest fellows, all these young cadets with their closely cropped heads, as they attended their ballistics and higher math classes, and answered questions, and worked out angles and distances in front of a miniature battlefield inside a large glass case, with a voice behind the case registering "in," "out," or "hit." Many of these cadets were clearly of proletarian origin; it didn't look, judging from the keenness with which they were working out difficult problems, that an intellectual pedigree was of any importance. We went through the clean, but very Spartan-looking dormitories, with small iron bedsteads and thin mattresses; we looked at the menu in the refectory; the menu for the four daily meals looked very adequate, and it also showed the number of calories contained in the dishes: a daily average of 3,538 calories for cadets, and of 3,200 for soldiers. This does not include the bread, which is unrestricted. Impressive display of red and black charts and posters and pictures on the history of the Russian Army, and maps of important battles like Izmail, Borodino, Perekop, etc., in the library. This also had its Lenin corner. The corridors of the school were decorated with pictures of famous Russian artillery experts of the past—in Tsarist uniforms. There were also numerous pictures of Stalin and Timoshenko.

As we were about to leave, the school band played *God Save the King*, and, for the benefit of the Americans, *The Star-Spangled Banner*, as well as the *Internationale*, and, as an encore, a Tchaikovsky waltz. These Russian lads playing *God Save the King*—weren't they, in a sense, England's soldiers? And America's soldiers, for that matter?

To put an end to opposition and passive resistance in the occupied areas of Russia, the Germans are, I am told, resorting to the queerest tricks. They circulate fake editions of *Pravda*, with completely defeatist articles; they also tell the people to keep the portraits of certain Soviet leaders, who have set up a pro-German government in Moscow, but to destroy others, notably Stalin's; they also undertake to deliver letters and parcels to Kiev, Moscow, and Leningrad, which, the people are asked to believe, are already under German occupation.

SUNDAY, *September* 15

Great big luncheon given by Lozovsky to the foreign press at the Moskva Restaurant, in a big dining-room with murals of the Caucasus and the Crimea. Bottles all down the table, and horses made of butter. I sat at the top table between Palgunov and the general manager of Tass. Both overdid their vodka-pouring—especially into my glass—to such an extent that when, towards the end, I stood up to propose a toast, I said all the wrong things—or rather, I said the right things in the wrong way. After making the usual remarks about the solidarity of the three great anti-Hitler powers, I added that the Soviet Union was fighting heroically and was suffering fearful casualties, that Britain, which had already been at war for two years, was doing great work, especially at sea and in the air, and that while Mr. Roosevelt was a very great man, our American friends should put more backbone into their share of the work. Tanks for Russia, I said, were much more important, from America's own point of view, than the continued manufacture of joy-ride automobiles. It was all wrong. The Moats was very annoyed, and so was Mr. Sulzberger, and the Russians looked—or tried to look—rather pained; and Hatanaka, the Jap, hissed and giggled and said he had found my remark about joy-ride automobiles "most embarrassing." Of all the Americans Cassidy alone, I think, took it in just the right spirit; perhaps because he's lived in Moscow long enough not to attach too much importance to speeches made at Russian vodka banquets.

Lucien and I managed to find the right tram in which to get home; only we were rather absentminded, and forgot to pay our ten-kopek fares; but just as we were getting off, an inspector came up to us and asked us to produce our tickets. I said we hadn't any; whereupon he said I'd have to pay a fine of three roubles. These I meekly surrendered. Lucien meantime was trying to lose himself in the crowd on the pavement, but the inspector sighted him, and I paid up another three roubles for Lucien. I got two green receipts. "Imbecile!" said Lucien, when I joined him, "don't you know the customs of the country? You should have made yourself scarce."

Very nasty outlook round Kiev.

I've just seen a circular signed by a German general deploring the unduly indiscriminate shooting of civilians in captured Russian towns and villages. "Even Communists should be shot only with your officer's approval." He emphasizes the necessity for Germany to keep Russian agriculture going as much as possible, and says the German soldiers should try to sound friendly to the Russian peasants, and to refrain from looting in villages and on collective farms. The Russian peasants are not being taken in by any German smiles, and the German plans for starting a quisling movement in the Ukraine have proved a complete flop. I've noticed, however, one reference in *Pravda* to "kulaks and Petlurovites," [1] whom they are using as their agents. But they can't be numerous.

The Russian papers are full of rape stories, while the *Krokodil*—which is quite amusing at times—embroiders on the theme of Nordic stud farms which the Germans, it is said, are planning to set up so as to keep up the birth-rate in war-time. Good comic poem about dreamy sentimental Gretchen looking at the moon and thinking of her fiancé, and suddenly receiving a summons to present herself at the stud farm at six p.m. the next day.

Hundreds, or even thousands, of Latvian partisans are said to be still active in Latvia. With their own local Fascists to help the Germans, their job must be even more desperately difficult than that of the Russian guerrillas. Several trains are said to have been wrecked in Latvia.

[1] Followers of Petlura, the Ukrainian "separatist" who, in 1918, secretly co-operated with the Germans in the Ukraine. His bands were famous for their Jewish massacres. Petlura was assassinated by a Jew in Paris in 1928.

PART IV

Men and Women At the Front

SEPTEMBER 16 *to* 25

At last, at last, at last. . . . .Palgunov called a "confidential" press conference a week ago last Sunday. Only eight or nine people were invited. "Tomorrow," he said, "you will go to the front. Now, you must take with you plenty of warm clothes, and high waterproof boots, and galoshes, if possible, and an absolute minimum of luggage. The cars you are going to travel in are very small; you can't go about our country roads in luxurious Z.I.S.'s, you know. But remember the warm clothes; tomorrow night you will sleep at a hotel in comparative comfort; but after that you may have to spend some nights in the cars. . . . And you will start out from here at 7.45 in the morning. Very punctually—7.45. And don't talk about it till then; we just can't take everybody who happens to have a press card."

I went down to the Mostorg—the big department store in the Petrovka (didn't it once belong to two Scotsmen called Muir and Merrilees?)—to try to buy a pair of galoshes. "Sorry, only ladies' galoshes." I tried another shop in Gorki Street. "Sorry. Only children's galoshes." Couldn't be helped; I decided to take just an extra pair of shoes. Also my dog-coat, just in case. It would do well as a sleeping-bag. And the

196

old blitz tin hat—not that there was likely to be any need for it. But it's the only military object we wretched civilians possess. Only I wasn't going to be bothered with the gas-mask.

7.30 was, of course, much too early to disturb Misha; he doesn't like starting his day till 11. So, with dog-coat over my arm, tin hat, and a typewriter case in lieu of a suitcase, I took the tram-car to the Sretenka and walked from there to the Nark. It was a cold grey morning, with a nip of autumn in the air. Outside the Nark stood four or five little four-seaters, like Baby Austins, one of them painted khaki, and all Russian-made. It is remarkable how the Russians have built up a pretty substantial motor industry in the last ten years, almost literally out of nothing. The thousands of lorries one sees are particularly impressive.

By about 7.55 everybody was there. Bearded old Cholerton, and Jordan in his old war correspondent's uniform, and Vernon Bartlett, and Wally Caroll, star United Press reporter, looking the good, tidy boy that he always looks, and Charlotte Haldane, with beret over one ear, and little Cassidy, and Sulzberger, all dressed up for winter sports, and Steele of the *Chicago Daily News*, and the Caldwell-Bourke-White *ménage*, cameras and all. And then there were the Russians, the *sympathique* pince-nez colonel—Baltin is his name, I later learned —and a tall, dark, handsome political commissar, aged only about thirty, but with the high rank of brigade commissar, which is apparently the equivalent of Lieutenant-general. He looked rather stern and grim, like a revolutionary hero of Erenburg's early novels. And also Anurov, the censor.

We drove out of Moscow on to the Mozhaisk highroad. It was to be expected. The papers had been full of the Russian counter-offensive south-east of Smolensk; fighting had gone on for a month. The Russians had driven the Germans some ten or fifteen miles back along a front of sixty miles or more and had smashed up eight German divisions. Many villages, and at least one fairly important town, Yelnya, had been retaken. "Yelnya—is that where we are going?" I asked the driver. "Yes," he said, "but not right away; and I think we are spending the first night at Vyazma." Vyazma; I knew it from childhood days as a place where they made gingerbread, with the white crust of sugar on top—*Vyazemskie pryaniki.* . . . They used to sell it at the *Verba*—the famous Palm Sunday fair, the joy of all schoolchildren. . . . But in July, Vyazma had been in the news. The Germans had claimed to have reached Vyazma. At least they suggested that one of their armoured units had got there, or very near it. That was during the week when people in Moscow were beginning to feel a bit uncomfortable, though the Russians never said anything about Vyazma. We drove along the Mozhaisk highroad at full speed; a wonderful road, wide, and as smooth as a billiard-table. I could write notes in the car without my pencil jerking once. It occurred to me that this road would really be *too* good, if ever the Germans got near Vyazma again. . . . The weather was clearing up. There were large white cumuli in the sky, and bright streaks of blue. And on both sides of the road was the large expanse of the Russian countryside, usually with a wood some miles away, or ahead of us. Nearer to Moscow we had passed a number of *datcha* places, and then several villages. But this was not a rich or densely populated part of the country; sometimes one drove for several miles without seeing much human life except a few dark grey huts, with thatched roofs, some distance off the road. Or else we'd drive through a forest—and there was one, not very far from Moscow, which must have stretched over ten or fifteen miles; quite good as a natural obstacle, I should think.

There was, however, a good deal of traffic on the road. Army lorries were travelling in large numbers in both directions; and then a lot of peasant carts, driven by bearded muzhiks, and with the old-fashioned wooden *duga* over the horse's neck.

They were going towards Moscow, laden with vegetables. Now and then we would pass a tank going towards the front, or a couple of tractors going towards Moscow. Were these being evacuated from the "scorched-earth" regions?

Our chauffeur was a young army driver, with fine features, perfect white teeth, and a stubbly chin—which reminded me of poor old Oleander, the army driver who took me and Richard Mowrer from Barcelona to Madrid in the winter of '37, and told me all about his family he had left in Seville. Oleander—that's what Richard used to call him, I never knew why—also seldom shaved. I wondered what had happened to him. . . . After all, Andrei Pavlovich was carrying on the same show. . . . Andrei Pavlovich, though looking so young, turned out to be thirty-five. Since the beginning of the war, since the 22nd of June, he had driven army cars; and "had seen things," as he put it. But he had had ten years' experience as a driver, and spoke with knowledge and enthusiasm about cars and all the different gadgets. Something the Soviets had taught the Russian people—a love of mechanics, and of machinery. . . . Poor Oleander was a dreadful driver, and a wretched amateur in comparison. Spain—Russia. There was a big difference. Andrei Pavlovich talked volubly about his wife and his two little boys he had sent to the country—to a kolkhoz near Ryazan—at the beginning of the war. You have to get a Russian to talk about children, and he will never stop. There is nothing I don't know about Vanya, aged eight, and Petya—"He's quite a little one, *sovsem malenki*"—aged three and a half. And the "*sovsem malenki*" was said with infinite tenderness. How these people must loathe Hitler! . . .

Andrei Pavlovich had just been in Leningrad. "What a beauty of a town!" he said. "Do you know it?" I said I had known it many years ago. "What a glorious, majestic sight that river is! I left Leningrad just a week ago; life was going on perfectly normally, just as in Moscow." "Were there no bombings?” “One or two little raids, but nothing much.” And he talked about the Summer Garden, and I asked if the trees planted in the early years of the Revolution in the large, useless parade ground of the Marsovo Pole were quite big now. He talked about the shops in the Nevsky Prospect and of the nice big cinemas. . . . “No, they will never give up Leningrad,” he said with conviction. “*Otstoyat!*”

We passed a number of large army haycarts driven by Mongol soldiers. “Who are they?” I asked Andrei Pavlovich. “*Asiaty, Mongoly,*” said he. “The Germans imagine they’re fighting only the Russians; but they’ve got nearly the whole of Asia against them, too. Very good chaps, these Asiatics, very loyal, and marvellous fighters. I saw them in the Smolensk battle last month.” He hadn’t done any actual fighting himself, but had travelled along some “pretty tricky roads” driving “commanders” about under shellfire. In Russian the word “officer” has been abolished, and the word for an officer, irrespective of rank, is “commander”—*comandir*.

The road was following the Moscow River, some five miles south of it. The town of Mozhaisk was somewhere off the main road, and we did not see it. The country round Mozhaisk was open, but hilly in spots. We saw on the crest of a hill a village church, and some houses around it; and Andrei Pavlovich said it was Borodino. I don’t know if it actually was, but the church was overlooking a large plain, which might well have been the scene of the famous battle. Then we passed through another wood. Two peasant women, with coloured scarves round their heads, were sitting on the roadside, sorting mushrooms and putting them into an enormous basket. Many crows were flying over the road, and above the fields clouds of starlings were performing their amazing exercises before departing for the winter. . . .

After six hours’ almost continuous driving we got to Vyazma. After the first sixty miles the road was no longer so good, and speed was reduced.

Vyazma looked almost normal, except for the large number of soldiers about, and a few broken windows here and there. Why bomb it? It seemed such a harmless little town, with a few Government buildings in the central square, and a couple of derelict churches, and a statue of Lenin, and the rest of the town a mass of quiet little provincial streets, with wooden houses and little gardens in front of them, and rows of rough wooden fences. And in the gardens grew large sunflowers and dahlias; and old women, with scarves round their heads, chatted in front of the garden gates. The place cannot have changed much since the days of Gogol. Our caravan of five cars attracted some attention, but not much, as we stopped at the "hotel." This was very Gogol-like, too, except that it was now some kind of army or governmental guest-house, and was run by a youngish man in a *french*—that semi-civilian, semi-military tunic which Stalin himself wears—and by a staff of young women. But the rooms were much in the Gogol tradition, except that there were no bugs. The furniture was primitive, and the mirrors played strange pranks with even the best of faces, and as you looked down the dark corridor you could well imagine the immortal Pavel Ivanovich Chichikov emerging from one of the rooms, stroking his chin, or hear the Gamblers having a quarrel next door. . . . The sanitation was a little on the primitive side, too, and you washed under a tap at the end of the passage.

We had a quick meal downstairs, where some more army officers joined us; to the Anglo-American party, except Chol and myself, it was heavy going, since none of our hosts knew any language other than Russian. I had by now learned to distinguish between ranks, and between the different kinds of pips (the ones rectangular, the others diamond-shaped) as worn by officers and political commissars, and that also was a great help. Next to me sat a young captain, with closely cropped hair, who had been stationed at Vyazma for some weeks. He declared that the Germans had never got anywhere near Vyazma; but that the place had been bombed a number of times. However, they had usually aimed at the railway station, but had missed it every time; he thought the marksmanship of the German airmen very poor. There had been no raids on Vyazma for nearly a month now. . . . Altogether, he said, at this part of the front at any rate, the Russians had marked air superiority over the Germans, and the roads were no longer infested by enemy planes trying to bomb and machine-gun troops and cars. But it used to be an infernal nuisance at the beginning of the war; only it wasn't as dangerous as a lot of people imagined. He had been machine-gunned on the roads nine or ten times, and had never got as much as a scratch. "But you must have seen some others killed?" "Yes," he said, "but astonishingly few, considering the persistence with which they attacked roads." He admitted, however, that it was a very unpleasant sensation. I told him various machine-gunning stories I had heard when I was in Spain. "Pity about Spain," he said. "In the Red Army we were intensely interested in the Spanish War. One of my comrades went out there as an instructor. Pity the British Government let us down so badly." "Yes," I said, "and the French. . . ." "Ah well," he said, "what could one expect from a country like France? Rotten to the core. So many Fifth Column people, one sometimes wonders where the other four columns were!" I tried to assure him that there had been columns other than the Fifth Column in France. . . .

I went out for a stroll through the Vyazma streets. Opposite our "hotel" in front of a wooden cottage a small crowd had gathered, obviously speculating about our five cars and the party they had brought. I particularly remember a youth, and two old women, and an elderly man. They were all interested to hear that the visitors were British and American, and asked me no end of questions about England. The elderly man—a carpenter by trade—said he had fought in the last war, and the English were already allies then, and "against two such great powers as England and our Soviet Russia" the Germans hadn't a chance. They had tried to get to Vyazma, but they wouldn't try again. It had all been very quiet for nearly a month now. "Three weeks tomorrow," one of the old women said. The youth, fifteen, and a trifle pimply, belonged very much to the new generation. He said pedantically: "There's no Fifth Column in the Soviet Union. The Fifth Column has been the downfall of all the countries the Germans have attacked so far. Now, it's just as well we and the British marched into Iran; for if we hadn't, the Iranian Fifth Column would have sold the country to the German Fascists." "You are very well versed in present-day politics," I said. "Where do you pick it all up?" "Ah," said an elderly matron, who turned out to be the boy's mother, "he has been taught all this at school." "And we also have discussions at our club," said the boy proudly. The other old woman, yellow and haggard, and with a black knitted shawl round her head, was in a weepy mood. "Oh, this war, this war, these cursed Germans; I could scratch every German's eyes out." And she began to weep. "Three hundred people killed in the last raid on Vyazma. Oh God, oh God. . . . *Gospodi, Gospodi.* . . ." "Oh, stop it," said the matron. "And where is your God, anyway?" "God is up there," said the weepy old thing, "and He is looking down on us." "Up there is a long way away," the boy said, and laughed. "And besides," he added, "it isn't true there were three hundred people killed at Vyazma. There were fifty-two, all buried in the common grave. Everybody knows there were fifty-two." "No, there were three hundred," said the weepy old thing. "Three hundred. If only God would help us against these brutes! . . ." Again the boy laughed, and assured her it would be all right, because the Red Army would take better care of her than any God ever would.

That evening some of us were driven to an aerodrome some miles out of Vyazma. On our way there, we had a look at the important railway station which the Germans had tried to bomb so often, but which was functioning normally, despite some minor damage. But in the fields, near the station, there were numerous bomb craters; and the bombs had penetrated deep into the soft clay soil. We drove bumpily along muddy country roads, and through enormous puddles. It was getting dark when we reached our destination. There was a purple sunset in the west—Smolensk way—and the sky was a strange pattern of purple and green. We walked across a stretch of marshy ground, alongside a pond, and passed two miserable-looking huts, both blacked out. It was growing cold and a thin mist lay over the fields. In the distance the peasants' watchdogs were barking. The air was filled with the scent of wet earth. At last we reached the aerodrome. From a distance we could see the shapes of several fighters; then, suddenly, we heard the drone of engines, and, despite the growing darkness, a Russian fighter swooped down and landed gracefully on the airfield. A crowd of airmen on the ground ran up to the new arrival. Soon we joined the crowd. So here were the "Stalin Hawks," the *Stalinskie Sokoly*. How often had I seen them on the screen! What good, fine, strong, and yet human faces they all had! We were presented to a colonel, in a smart pale-blue and gold-braided cap, and to some of the others. The newly landed plane was a fighter, but had been adapted to dropping bombs, and to doing other, more original, stunts. The young pilot, who had by this time got out of the plane, was busily examining one of the wooden wings which had been pierced through the middle by an anti-aircraft shell. He had dropped bombs on a German aerodrome near Smolensk, and there had been some heavy anti-aircraft fire. He had set fire to a hangar, and seemed very pleased with his raid. He was about twenty, but had done a good deal of flying. "How many Germans have you brought down?" one of our party foolishly asked. The boy looked embarrassed. "I haven't brought down any," he said. I asked how much flying a day he did. "From here to the German lines—oh, five, six, seven raids a day; only takes about an hour or so, there and back." He said it perfectly simply; with nothing to suggest that he was actually risking his life "five or six or seven" times a day. We asked if he was badly shaken by the shell that hit his wing. "It was a bit unpleasant for a moment," he said, "but I saw at once that it was all right." It was strange to be here, among these young fellows, these *Stalinskie Sokoly*, of whom one had heard so much in Moscow, but never seen in their real surroundings. "So you often bomb Smolensk?" somebody said. "No, we never bomb Smolensk at all," a short, stocky little fellow replied. "We bomb airfields near Smolensk; but Smolensk is Russian, and we shall want it back ourselves." There was a young, fair-haired airman, with a boyish face, whom I asked how he liked this dangerous life. "I love it," he said with conviction. "It may be dangerous, but every moment of it is exciting. It's the best life there is. It's worth it." They all wanted to hear about the British Air Force, and we told them that a wing of the R.A.F. had landed in northern Russia. The news was received sceptically. Then an argumentative young fellow butted in. He thought the British weren't really doing enough. "What's a wing, anyway?" he asked; "thirty, forty planes?" I said I was sure there would be more coming. We talked about this and that; and then the argumentative fellow said: "Now, tell me this—why is it that, since our alliance is so essential, you wouldn't make an alliance with us *before the Germans invaded Poland?*" "Why didn't *you* make an alliance with *us*?" I replied. "Oh, that's quite simple," he said. "Your people didn't want it." I referred to the Anglo-French Military Mission which had been sent to Russia in August 1939, but I failed to convince him. "Eyewash—they didn't mean business." For a moment I seemed to see Bonnet's froggy eyes looking out of the marsh; the light was very odd, and one could, of course, imagine things. . . . "No," I said, "*really*, why didn't you have an alliance with us?" "Oh, let's drop it," he said; and we both laughed.

The pince-nez colonel asked if we could be shown one of the latest inventions which the Russian Air Force has been using with remarkable success. One of our air experts in Moscow had actually told me that it was, in his opinion, the most successful of all the inventions this war had produced so far. It was actually a kind of shell which the Russian airmen were successfully using for attacking not only enemy aircraft, but also tanks, and the mechanism of the whole thing was remarkably ingenious. The "tank-buster's" aim was, of course, much more accurate than that of a bomb. But I cannot go into details. . . .

We said good-bye to the *Stalinskie Sokoly*, and assured them that Britain and America were doing, and would do, their utmost and their damnedest. . . . How many of these fine fellows will live till after the war to tell the whole tale? It had got quite dark; it was damp and very cold; in the west there was one faint streak of light on the distant horizon. There was a dog still barking on a distant farm. The two hovels near the place where we had left the cars looked dark and uninhabited. We drove back to Vyazma in silence, except for occasional curses at the bumps on the road, and clinging hard to the side-straps.

At the Gogol-like hotel at Vyazma that night we received a visit at supper from General Sokolovsky, Marshal Timoshenko's Chief of Staff. It, obviously, was a great honour the Russian High Command were doing the foreign press. The general was no propagandist; though his appearance alone was excellent propaganda. He was young, barely forty, remarkably handsome, and had a charming smile and manner, which might partly be attributed to his Polish origin. And long, delicate hands, like a woman's. Such was the appearance of the Chief of Staff in the one army in the world which, since the beginning of the war, had not only stopped, but driven back, the Germans, and had recaptured territory from them. . . .

He spoke in a quiet, even voice, describing what the Russian Army had done on the central sector. Several German armies had been smashed up in the last month; in the first few days of September alone they had suffered 20,000 casualties; 1,950 German planes had been shot down in this sector over a number of weeks. "The German *Blitzkrieg*," he said, "has become a *Blitzkrieg* for the destruction of German men and equipment." The process of "grinding down" the German war machine was in full swing. . . . The Russians were now twenty miles from Smolensk; and among the reasons why the Germans had to give up their attempt to advance on Moscow was that their rear was unsafe, with the hostility of the population and the activities of the partisans, who were constantly interfering with the lines of supply. Off the main German lines of communications, convoys of foodstuffs were being continually seized by partisans. To check the Russian counter-offensive on this front the Germans had to rush up reinforcements from the Bryansk, and possibly from the Leningrad sectors. All along the front the Germans were digging in; and there was no doubt that Russian artillery was greatly superior to that of the Germans, and that it was mainly responsible for the casualties inflicted on the enemy. German gunnery, on the other hand, was very diffuse and inaccurate.

The general then talked of the prospects of the coming winter. "All our troops," he said, "have their *polushubki*, and other adequate clothes, and they can stand even 50 degrees of frost; the German will not stand up to it. There is a historical example of this—I don't mean 1812, but a much more recent one. In 1919 the Japanese tried to occupy parts of Siberia, but they had to clear out, because they couldn't stand the winter. And our winter here is not so much milder than the Siberian winter; we get anything up to 30 degrees below zero Fahrenheit. . . ."

I asked Sokolovsky whether the Russian Army was short of any war material. He replied that "he couldn't say, at the moment, that it was"; that the number of planes in this sector had doubled in a month; and that there was no immediate shortage of anything, with the possible exception of tanks. "But," he added, "the more stuff you can send, the sooner will victory come."

As an afterthought, General Sokolovsky said that he was competent to speak only of the central front; and he could not speak with first-hand knowledge of Budyenny's armies in the south, or of Voroshilov's in the north, but what information he had suggested that these two had the situation well in hand. I asked whether, in view of what he said, a new German offensive on the central front was now out of the question. "No, of course not," he replied. "They may always try a last desperate gamble; or even a few 'last desperate' gambles. But I don't think," he added firmly, "that they will ever get to Moscow. . . ." And he added an interesting reflection—which, unfortunately, may apply to the Germans elsewhere. In this sector, he said, the Russians had superiority in artillery, planes, and even tanks; and although they were advancing, their casualties were only half those of the German casualties. So it did not follow that an advancing army necessarily suffered heavier casualties than a retreating army. . . .

There was a bang. . . . "These impetuous Slavs; why have they got to knock on the door like this?" He looked at his luminous watch. "It's late, anyway; we told them to call us at 7, and it's 7.30 now." Vernon Bartlett was indignant. Whizz, crash. It was much louder this time. "Hell, it's a bloody air-raid," one of us at last said. We were on the top floor of the little Gogol hotel. There were three of us in the room—Bartlett, Jordan, and I. "Hadn't we better get under the beds," said Vernon. It was pitch-black in the room and the floor was damp and cold. "Oh, hell, where are my socks?" I said. "We'd better keep away from the window," said Jordan. It was a narrow room, and the window at one end was as black as the door at the other. "Where *is* the bloody window? I want my socks." Whizz, bang; that one was a beauty; it landed just outside; the window went to pieces with a clatter of broken glass. "That's better." I, at last, knew where the window was and was able to find my socks. "You all right, Philip?" He was still in bed, near the window, with the blanket over his nose. "Yes, all right, thanks; the glass just missed me." Vernon was sitting on his bed, in his pyjamas, and with a tin hat on his head. "Very unpleasant," I said. "Yes, very," said Vernon. "And quite outside the Nark's program of our trip," said Philip. . . . It seemed to be over; the Russian fighters must have chased them away. It was just a smash-and-grab raid. Outside the window there was nothing but a cloud of brick dust. Through it I could see only the faint outline of a tree.

One feels elated after getting safely through a bombing; and we were all very cheerful and talkative round the tap at the end of the passage, and round the breakfast table downstairs. . . . A bomb had hit a house some thirty yards away; several people had been killed. Mrs. Haldane had dashed along to look at the dead bodies, and Mrs. Bourke-White had gone to photograph them. . . . They arrived back late for breakfast; two young girls had been killed by the blast just outside the house, and an old woman, and there was an old man who was wounded, and whom they saw being taken away on a stretcher. And the mother of the two girls sobbed over their bodies, and there was a crowd of people round the house, and many of them were weeping. . . .

We drove out of Vyazma in a rather more subdued mood. When we got to the main square, another air-raid warning sounded—actually, there hadn't been one in the morning—but this time there was no raid. However, our colonel insisted that we get out of the cars, and we were ushered into a well-propped-up air-raid shelter, a sort of tunnel, with benches, inside a small hill, with a church on top. The people in the shelter did not look particularly excited; we learned from them that about a dozen bombs had been dropped in various parts of Vyazma, and somebody said that thirty people had been killed—though, clearly, it was only a piece of hearsay. . . . Our political commissar said that there was a great deal of air activity about today.

For three hours we drove along the Vyazma-Smolensk road. It was mostly open country, with only a few woods here and there. In a wood, a little outside Vyazma, we stopped to camouflage our cars with branches. Already at Vyazma the colonel had ordered the drivers to keep a distance of two or three hundred yards between the cars; but, in practice, it somehow never worked. Just as we were helping the drivers to cut some branches and to cover the cars, we heard the faint droning of a plane, and two explosions followed, and two pillars of earth and fragments of wood went up in the air a short distance off the road. Very high up, scarcely visible, a German bomber was flying west. It then disappeared behind a cloud. The sky was overcast except for numerous blue holes; the worst possible day for surprise attacks—that is, the worst from our point of view. However, nothing more happened that day. Many miles west of Vyazma we crossed a modest little river, which turned out to be the Dnieper; and then we drove through a wide wooden gate, decorated with red flags, with portraits of Stalin and Timoshenko, and inscriptions telling Red soldiers that they must "do their duty to the last"; "Victory will be ours," and "The Fascist Reptile Must be Crushed." It was strange to enter the front zone through an arch as though it were the gate of some great majestic football ground where the teams of the two worlds were fighting. . . . "Ye who enter here. . . ." No, it wasn't that at all. And the soldiers whom we saw driving through the arch did not look like men who had "abandoned all hope." They looked like men who were hoping that the gate would be moved farther and farther west —in course of time. . . .

All along that Vyazma-Smolensk road we saw large numbers of troops; and although there were very few natural obstacles on the way, there appeared to be a variety of tank-traps and other defences, and there were numerous batteries, particularly near the woods.

Soon after passing under the wooden arch with the portraits and flags and slogans, we turned off the main road and drove bumpily along a cross-country road. The deep cart-ruts crossing a field were sometimes the only indication of where the road was going. We were getting near the front line—or fairly near it. Gunfire, at first distant, and then louder and louder, could be heard. But even here, with the guns firing close by, with bangs that made you start up, life seemed to be continuing—almost normally. We drove through fields of flax, and meagre fields of rye, with thousands of cornflowers. A few cows and horses were grazing along the roadside. And in a village, near the front line—the guns in a neighbouring wood were going hard—a girl wearing a blue beret was hanging up the washing, and there were ducks in the pond, and two little boys in sheepskin coats waved at us.

Gogol-like names of villages, like "Bibino" and "Radukino," were painted on a signpost at the crossing of two mud-paths. For all one knew, a few miles away the Germans might be in possession of one of these villages. The colonel made inquiries from a sentry, and we drove into a wood, no longer following any road, but simply winding our way among the trees. We passed a battery, and at length reached an open space. Through the trees we could see a plain, a little below us, and a few miles wide; there were wooded heights on the other side. Somebody said that the Germans were "over there." The cars stopped; and we were taken down a forest path to a large tent, which turned out to be the regimental headquarters. Then, one or two at a time, we went down to a dugout, decorated with a portrait of Stalin, and paid our respects to the colonel. He was a red-faced man, about forty, thickset, and going slightly grey. *"Polkovnik* (Colonel) *Kirilov,"* he announced his name in a loud voice, and with a hard hearty handshake that made your fingers creak. "Polkovnik Kirilov," he repeated, *"milosti prosim"* (be welcome). He asked us to lunch in the mess, which happened to be in the big tent outside. We also paid our respects to the political commissar, in the neighbouring dugout.

The lunch, of course, was no improvisation. The colonel had been warned of the visit of fourteen or fifteen strangers, and there was a great display of zakuski and vodka bottles all down the large table, and the plain-clothed female attendants served round enormous dishes of roast beef, and half-pound hunks of bread.

Colonel Kirilov, with his honest, blunt manner, was a simple, unsophisticated man to whom the army was everything. My neighbour, a young lieutenant, told me that the colonel was a man of reckless personal courage; throughout the meal I do not remember hearing him say anything about himself, but he was proud of his regiment: it was one of the Russian regiments, he said, which had always advanced and never retreated. He was a typical *voyaka,* a soldier of the old tradition which had produced Lermontov's lovable Maxim Maximich and so many of the simple, brave, unassuming men whom Tolstoy drew so well in *War and Peace,* and especially in *Sebastopol.* Toasts were, naturally, drunk to the Red Army, and to Stalin, and to Great Britain, and to the United States, and each toast meant swallowing a substantial glass of vodka, and the vodka was followed by Armenian brandy and Crimean port. There was, on that occasion, certainly no limit of one hundred grams of vodka per day—a ration which "our Stalin," as Colonel Kirilov said, "had ordered to be given to the Soviet troops." In a way, this Russian vodka dinner, so near the front lines—it just happened to be a particularly quiet sector of the front at that time—was slightly incongruous and artificial; but I am sure that Colonel Kirilov and his officers did not look at it in that light; to them, it was something of an event to treat and to show round a bunch of British and American newspaper men, and a British M.P.—a species none of them had certainly ever met before. . . . I might say in passing that some of the younger officers took a certain scientific interest in testing our capacity for absorbing vodka. . . . At least one of our party was drunk under the table. The Russians thought it rather a joke.

On our way into the tent, I had noticed a little fellow, in an army coat that was much too large for him, standing on guard with fixed bayonet. . . . As we were going out, I asked the colonel about him. "Oh, you must talk to Sasha," he said. "He's the son of our regiment. We have adopted him. You see, he lost his father and his mother in the bombing of Yartsevo, a few miles from here." He was a pale little lad, with a sad face. The cap was coming rather over his ears, and the coat was certainly too large for him. The colonel went up to him and patted his cheek. "Well, Sasha, how do you like being with the Red Army?" "Very much, Comrade Colonel," the boy said, and there was a look of affection in the boy's pale-blue eyes as he looked at Kirilov. "How old are you, Sasha?" "Just fourteen." "Well, you are too young to be a regular soldier; but we'll make a good Red Army man of you yet." "Yes, Comrade Colonel, I'll serve the Red Army all right." "That's a good boy." Sasha told me in a few simple words how he had lost his parents in the bombing, and how the regiment had picked him up and adopted him. As I was saying good-bye to Sasha, I asked the colonel if I could give him ten roubles. "No, don't give him money, but if you can give him a little souvenir, he'll be glad." I went through my pockets, but could find nothing except a fountain-pen—which I needed— and one of those unbreakable steel pocket mirrors. He was very pleased with it; he had never seen an "unbreakable" mirror before; and there was a broad grin on his little pale face as he looked into it.

From the tent we walked through a wood to a battery some distance away. Intermittent shelling was going on from both sides, but nothing serious. "It's very sad," the colonel said, "when you think of all these little towns that have been shelled, or bombed, or occupied by the Germans. These Germans are beasts. There's a little town, Dukhovstchina, not far from here, which is nothing but a heap of ruins. One morning twenty planes came over and razed it to the ground. What for, I ask you! It was off the main road, and not of the slightest military importance. You may think we are simple people, but we are cultured people—*culturnyie ludi*—but the Germans are technically efficient people—*ludi's tekhnikoi*—but savages. And cruel; I have never known such cruelty." A shell whizzed past with a faint mosquito whine. Our good pince-nez colonel got slightly agitated. He took the political commissar aside, and then turned to Colonel Kirilov: "Hadn't we better turn back? Rather too much of a crowd to take up to a front-line battery, with the enemy obviously watching. And two women among them, too." "Well, yes, I suppose so," said Kirilov, not quite convinced. "But they aren't shelling the positions here," I remarked. "No," said the pince-nez colonel, "but, you see, they might start at any moment, and if they see a lot of coming and going round the battery, it'll encourage them. I'd feel responsible if any of you got killed—and," he added as an afterthought, "if any of our soldiers got killed into the bargain." It was no use insisting.

The shelling had, meantime, got a little heavier, though I did not actually hear any German shells land anywhere near us. We were taken into a dugout, which was a sort of soldiers' club. We sat on benches among the soldiers and drank beer, and some of the soldiers sang, and others danced a Russian folk-dance, and the music was provided by a young N.C.O. playing a tinny piano. On the walls of the dugout were numerous posters, including the one of the British and Soviet airmen shaking hands over Berlin. There was something slightly incongruous and "Intouristy" about the whole setting, and the soldiers, I felt, were about as ill at ease as many of us were. However, they talked of the present operations west of Yelnya, where the Russians were still pushing forward. I asked if they had any trenches; and they said no. They stayed about in the woods, and the dugouts. The batteries were facing the German lines, enough to keep them in order. At last the shelling subsided, and we walked back to our cars.

Outside a small village some of the officers and I talked to a woman carrying a small child. Her clothes were tattered, and she looked wretched. "*Akh tyazhelo,*" she sighed. "It's a hard life for me. I've got to live on charity. Only a month ago I still had my home. And I don't know where my husband is. And I've got this little one to look after." She was living from hand to mouth in the half-deserted village, doing odd jobs, and living on scraps from the army. "And there's no milk I can get for him; only now and then." One of the officers put his hand in his pocket, and pulled out two chocolates wrapped in paper. The woman took them, and walked on.

That night we were taken to our sleeping-quarters some five miles behind the front lines. It was getting dark when we entered a large village. There were plenty of people around here, and sunflowers were growing outside all the houses. A crowd, with several soldiers among them, were having a heated discussion. A number of German airmen, who had been shot down that day, had just been brought to the village, and an officer in the centre of the group was asking questions in broken German. I went up to the crowd, and saw, in the middle of it, a pale, fox-faced German airman; but before I could see or hear anything more, a soldier ordered me away. Another crowd had gathered on the other side of the road. *"Nemtzev poimali*—they've caught some Huns," a little barefooted boy of eight or nine joyfully informed me. An elderly bearded peasant remarked, pointing to the boy: "They've got no chance round here, any airmen or parachutists; once they're down, they're caught. Our village boys are great spy-hunters and suspect-hunters. The moment they see anyone in the least suspect, they report to the army. They've caught several spies that way."

We were put up for the night in a large dormitory in a building that looked like a school. Marx and Engels and Mr. Mikoyan looked down on us from the walls. The beds were narrow iron beds, but the bedding was clean and there were plenty of blankets. The Narkomindel had certainly done everything to make us as comfortable as possible at the front, sometimes at the expense of other people's comfort, I feared. But there was no suggestion anywhere that we were intruding, and at the officers' mess, in the same building, where we had supper that night, we were welcomed with true Russian hospitality. All the officers were very interested in "what England was doing." Towards the end of the supper, the major said that there were some German airmen who had been captured that day; and would we like to have a talk with them? They were among the airmen who had bombed Vyazma that morning. Cy Sulzberger was very enthusiastic at the prospect. "Anyone who's bombed me out of my bed gets space in the *New York Times*," he said.

The table was cleared, and three Germans were brought in. As they entered, one of them saluted. They were asked to sit down at one end of the table. The major asked that we should not fire questions at them direct, but ask them through the Russian interpreter, a young corporal, with the pale-green stripes of the Soviet frontier guards. It was all rather complicated. Anurov and I had to translate the questions into Russian, and then the interpreter turned them into very indifferent German. It was all a little absurd; and Cy Sulzberger, with both elbows on the table, looked very stern, and reminded me, I don't know why, of Justice Frankfurter, of the Supreme Court, whose pictures I had seen in some paper. The three Germans looked slightly puzzled at all this English and American speech going on in a place like this. I wished I could have told them we were here to prepare billets for five thousand British bomber crews.

These three Germans were all about twenty-five, but different in other respects. Number one, the wireless operator, looked a simple-minded and rather amiable youth; his father was a tailor—*ein Herrenschneider*—at Stettin. He was the one of the three who had saluted on entering the room. He clearly tried to make a good impression, and perhaps give one the idea that he was one of the "good Germans." He had been convalescing somewhere near Munich when he heard that the war against Russia had started. "To me it was like a bolt from the blue," he said—"*wie Blitz aus heiterem Himmel.*" Was he sure it was in Germany's interests to attack Russia, somebody asked. "I have to carry out the orders of my superiors," he said; "we don't question orders." "But do you still think Germany has a chance of winning the war?" Number one smiled ingratiatingly. "Every soldier thinks he is on the winning side; we think so, and the Russians think so, and the English think so, *nicht wahr?*" Number two and number three did not look at it in that way. Number two, with one eye bandaged, was the type of the fanatical Nazi. With his remaining eye he looked at us with animal hatred. "What is your name?" He gave his name. "And your Christian name?" "Walter," he snarled, impatiently. "Do you think you are still going to win this war?" the interpreter said to number two. "*Jawohl,*" he snapped back. And what did his father do? "He's a manager of the N.S.V." "What's that?" Neither he nor the others would explain at first. "N.S. surely stands for *Nationalsozia-*

listisch," somebody said. "Yes," said number two defiantly, "and N.S.V. means *Nationalsozialistische Volkswohlfahrt*" (National Socialist People's Welfare). The fellows seemed to have the idea that if they were discovered to be Nazi Party members they might be shot there and then, just as Communist Party men are automatically shot by the Germans when they enter a town. So number three intervened. He was the pilot of the Heinkel that had been brought down. He was as much a Nazi as the other, but he had a cold, foxy face—he was the chap I had seen in the village earlier in the evening—and he explained calmly that no German on active service was allowed to belong to any political party. "So none of us are party members," he said emphatically. He went on to explain that the war against Russia had been rendered inevitable by the war against England. It was part of the same war. If the German Luftwaffe was no longer attempting day raids on England, he said, it was because these raids had been found to be too costly. And for the same reason, he added, the British day raids on Germany would soon stop. "They are losing a colossal proportion of their planes." "And you still think Germany is going to win the war?" "Yes," he said. "First we'll knock out Russia and then we'll bring England to her knees." "And what about America?" "Oh, America," he said with a faint shrug. "America—that's a long way away. *Das ist sehr weit, Amerika.*" Perhaps he was not entirely wrong. . . .

"Did any of you take part in any raids on England?" somebody asked. "Yes, several raids," said number two, who, as I watched him, was beginning to look more and more like a minor Göring, with the same mouth and jaw, and the same snarling way of speaking. "And what did you bomb?" "Lonndonn," he said, with a touch of boastfulness. "You know, of course, that you killed a lot of civilians?" "Yes, but the English started that."

We then talked about the raid on Vyazma. What was the idea? "We were given orders to bomb the aerodrome," said number three. This was too much for old Cholerton. "Aerodrome, aerodrome," he bubbled. "You bombed *me*," he cried in German, ignoring the arrangements; "me, in my bed, at my hotel. Smashed my window. Aerodrome, indeed!—centre of Vyazma, miles away from the aerodrome." The Germans had nothing to say, and number two merely shrugged his shoulders contemptuously. "And do you know," somebody else said, this time through the Russian interpreter, "that some of us saw the dead; two little girls and some old people?" I watched the three Germans carefully. Not a muscle moved. They took it with perfect indifference. "And then how were you brought down?" "Five Russian fighters attacked us all at once," said number three; "so naturally—" "Not five, but six," number two said.

They were then taken away. Numbers one and three saluted as they went out. To some of us the whole interview was a trifle distasteful, but instructive for all that. There was also number four; but he was severely injured when the plane crashed, and was now in hospital.

The next morning we drove cross-country to a large field, and there the Heinkel, riddled with bullets, lay on the ground. It had come down slickly, without much damage to the machine. Fox-faced number three must have been a good pilot. There was a clear blue sky, but a cold north wind was blowing, sweeping the cornflowers around the Heinkel. It was so cold that, for the first time, I put on my dog-coat.

That day and the next we got a good idea of Russian roads and of "General Mud." And my general conclusion is that mud is an important factor but not an overwhelmingly important one in this war. Our little four-seaters got stuck in the mud many a time, and it was a long job to drag them out; but along that incredible country road which we followed that day—and in places the mud was about a foot deep—we saw many lorries travel along, not rapidly, of course, but travel along all the same. A few we saw stuck in the mud, but never permanently; with some pushing and shoving, and, if necessary, towing, they were always extricated, sooner or later. But the most revealing thing was the tanks. We met several on our way. They seemed to slither through the mud without any difficulty at all, and almost at normal speed, and their caterpillars tackled the bumps and holes and pools in the road without serious difficulty.

It had rained heavily some days before, and it certainly was not a comfortable journey. But how lovely the Russian countryside looked! At about four miles an hour we drove through what seemed an interminable wood. The birch trees were just beginning to turn yellow. The air was filled with the perfume of grass and earth. At last we reached the end of the wood and were faced with the problem of crossing a ravine, the bottom of which was thoroughly swamped. It meant laying down a sort of bridge of planks and bundles of straw. The villagers came out and helped. It was a poor-looking village, with the ravine dividing it in two, and was not much different from any village in *Dead Souls*; and the conversation I had with one of the village women was quite Gogol-like. "Where is this road leading?" "Where do you want to go?" she said. "I don't know," I said ingenuously. "Then why do you ask?"

There were plenty of women and children in the village, most of them poorly clad, but hardly any men. They'd gone off to the war, and life, one of the women said, had become very difficult. When at last all the cars had been safely taken across the ravine, with much pushing and shouting, and the engines roaring at top gear, one of the officers, who was accompanying us, said: "Well, thank you, comrades, and good luck to you. And," he added, "do everything you can for the Red Army." There was a young woman with three children clinging to her skirt. "Yes, we'll do what we can," she said plaintively. "But what can we do? Our men are away, and we haven't got anything ourselves." What misery and hardship this war had brought to Russia—even to the parts not yet invaded by the Germans! . . .

This village was a good twenty miles away from the front, and that day we travelled from one point of the front to another in a semicircle. It was not until six in the evening that we reached the regimental headquarters for which we had been looking. Some mistake had been made about the eating arrangements; through taking the wrong road we had apparently missed our lunch, and, for once, nothing had been prepared for our arrival. Much severe fighting had gone on round here only a week or two before. We passed through a number of villages which had been completely burned to the ground, and the trees in the wood had been slashed about by shellfire. . . . The regiment whose headquarters we had now reached was a Siberian one. They were rough, hardy people, rather like some of our Canadians. We were shown many wrecked German gun-carriages and a couple of wrecked tanks. The rest of the booty had been sent away. There had been several tanks, still in good condition, and about a hundred guns. This, the major proudly said, was country reconquered from the Germans. . . . We were asked to an improvised meal, round a long table, that had been laid out under the trees, deep in the wood. "Sorry," said the major, "we've only got our ordinary soldiers' food; we didn't know you were coming today." However, he ordered a few tins of pickled fish to be opened by way of *zakuski*. But the *kasha* and the cabbage soup and the stewed beef were excellent. Just as we were in the middle of the meal, we heard the droning of a plane, flying quite low. We looked up; between the tree branches we saw a Fokker-Wolff reconnaissance plane. "Ah, the stepladder again," said the major. "That's what our people call it; it's got that queer shape." I was glad to see the last of the "stepladder"; the big white tablecloth was much too good a target. . . . Meantime, the anti-aircraft guns around us were firing like mad. . . . But they failed to bring down the "stepladder," though the moment it passed over our table it cannot have been flying at more than two thousand feet. . . . And again we drank the health of the Red Army, and they drank the health of Great Britain, and America. . . . A wolf-faced, elderly colonel, with a ruddy complexion, got very merry, and when, later, we walked across a field towards a battery emplacement, I heard him say in Russian to Mrs. Haldane: "Ah, there is something glamorous about you, something Spanish about you. May I call you Carmen?" I volunteered to interpret. "Isn't he a pet?" said Mrs. Haldane. . . .

It was quite dark now. The German lines were some four or five miles away, on the other side of the plain, the no-man's-land. They were firing star shells. These lights, across the dark plain, looked like so many lighthouses on a not very distant coast. . . . The major said the Germans were constantly lighting up the no-man's-land; they were afraid of a Russian counter-offensive; and there was nothing they hated more than being disturbed at night. . . .

The major thought we could probably be put up for the night in a field hospital some ten miles north. We drove through the dark, with only the lighthouses of the German starshells lighting up the "coast" beyond the no-man's-land. Now and then a distant gun could be heard. Poor Andrei Pavlovich was exhausted and worn out after the day's driving along these Russian country roads, and grumbled under his breath. I fully sympathized with him, and felt we could sleep perfectly well in the cars, for once. But the organizers of the trip would have thought this a fiasco, and since we were "guests" they considered it imperative to provide the best possible hospitality. This, in the circumstances, was the field hospital. Groping our way through a dark wood we arrived at the mouth of a large dugout. The hospital consisted of several such dugouts, and, since it was, fortunately, passing through one of its slack periods, our party had a dugout all to ourselves. With the use of stretchers and blankets and sacks of straw, we spent a perfectly comfortable night, and the faint smell of carbolic perhaps added to the soporific effect of sixteen hours' driving through the Russian countryside. It was better not to try to imagine what pain and suffering our dormitory had seen perhaps only a few days before.

All the nurses were pupils of the Tomsk medical school; they were all young and extraordinarily pretty, as Siberian women usually are; and the chief surgeon, who, the next morning, took me along to two of the other dugouts, and who himself was a Moscow man, said he had never known such an efficient, earnest crowd of nurses. Here, in the dark but well-heated dugouts, I caught another glimpse of some of the horrors of war—a young fellow, scarcely conscious, with both his legs amputated; another who had lost both his eyes, and whose head, a mass of bandages, was like the head of an eyeless snowman. He lay completely silent, uttering only faint groans from time to time. But there were others, only slightly injured, who were able and willing to talk. I particularly remember a young fellow who had received a flesh wound through the leg while dragging back across no-man's-land a severely wounded comrade. "I had to get him back at once," he said; "if I had waited till nightfall, he would have died from loss of blood." Only some twenty or thirty wounded were at the hospital now; but only a week or two before, it had had to handle as many as three hundred a day. There was a staff of 7 surgeons, 6 doctors and 48 nurses, besides other medical personnel. The operating dugout was well equipped, and there were X-ray and blood-transfusion outfits. As yet, the chief surgeon said, he had not been short of any medical supplies.

It had rained heavily during the night; the mossy ground among the trees was like a swamp, and the roads were worse than ever. After some hours' difficult driving—we had again gone some distance away from the front—we at last reached the *sovkhoz*, where we were supposed to have stopped for a meal the day before. It was a large, vegetable-growing State farm, with a dairy attached, and we were given a snack meal of sausage, eggs, cheese, bread and butter, and large mugs of tea. Here were two captains who were going in the same direction as ourselves, and they asked for a lift. One of them, who had been a secondary schoolteacher in civilian life, travelled in our car. Captain Lebedev's home town was Kharkov, and he had studied history and economics at Kharkov University. He had been engaged in some heavy fighting round Kiev last month, until his regiment was moved to this Smolensk sector. He was a realist. "It is no use pretending that all is well," he said to me. "The flag-waving—the hurrah-patriotism—of our press is all very well for propaganda purposes, to keep up morale; but it can be overdone—as it sometimes is. And we shall need help from abroad, and very important help, before we are finished. I know the Ukraine; and I know how immensely important it is to our whole national economy. We have lost Krivoi Rog and Dniepropetrovsk, and, without the Krivoi Rog iron ore, Kharkov and Bryansk will find it difficult to work at anything like full capacity. Leningrad also is more or less isolated; Leningrad, with its highly skilled labour. And we just don't know how much farther the Germans are going to push. If you people have got any influence with the British Government," he said, almost appealingly, "for God's sake, don't say all is splendid." I said we didn't, but that there was the censorship to cope with. "Yes," he said, "but there are ways of saying things; they don't need to be put in such a way as to offend the censors. But, seriously," he said, returning to his main point, "there is no doubt we have already been severely weakened in an industrial sense, and some other important industrial centres may be lost before we are finished. I am not altogether sure about Kharkov, for instance. The Germans are already at Poltava. We've been hearing for weeks about this Economic Conference in Moscow; when *is* it going to meet?" I said I thought Beaverbrook was already on his way, and that it would meet next week. "This is a very grim war," he said. "And you cannot imagine the hatred the Germans have stirred up among our people. We are easy-going, good-natured people, you know; but I assure you, they have turned some of our people into spiteful muzhiks. *Zlyie muzhiki* —that's what we've got in the Red Army now, men thirsting for revenge. We officers sometimes have a job in keeping our soldiers from killing German prisoners. They don't do it; but I know they want to do it—especially when they see some of those arrogant, fanatical Nazi swine. I have never known such hatred before. And there's some reason for it. Think of all those towns and villages over there," said he, pointing west; "think of all the torture and sadism and degradation—not to mention hunger—these people are made to suffer. I have seen things which I did not think were possible. I have seen the mutilated bodies of young girls—almost children; these beasts had not merely raped them, but murdered them afterwards, with all sorts of sadistic refinements. Our people have made up their minds that when the day of reckoning comes, none of these things will be forgotten. . . ." There was a flicker of mad hatred in his eyes. "And I cannot help thinking of Kharkov, of my wife and my little girl of eight. . . ." He was silent for a time, controlling himself and hammering one knee with his fingers. "Of course," he at last said, "there are the partisans; they are at least a *personal* solution to thousands of people over there. There comes a moment when people can't bear it any longer. They go off into the woods, in the hope that they may murder a German some time. Often it's like suicide; often they know that, sooner or later, they are almost sure to be caught, and put through all the beastliness that the Germans are capable of; but there's just a chance, they say to themselves, that they may live, or at least die without the indignity of seeing the Germans around them all the time."

"How important in your opinion," I asked, "is the partisan movement?" "It's very important, though not as overwhelmingly important as it might be. Sooner or later, if our troops go on retreating, the partisans are bound to lose touch with their sources of supply, I mean the supply of armaments. They can continue to carry on sabotage and various forms of passive resistance, but they may no longer constitute a serious armed force. Some are also sure to become physically exhausted; and in some cases even morale may break down. If only we had fully prepared the partisan movement. If only we had piled up thousands of arms dumps throughout western Russia! The partisan movement might have accounted for fifty per cent of our victory. Something—in fact, a great deal —was done in that direction, but not nearly enough; and in the south there are, unfortunately, no woods."

"Are you going to Dorogobuzh?" I asked. "No, not to the town, but only to the station, which is some nine miles this side of the town. But the town of Dorogobuzh—just you have a look at it! A little masterpiece of German culture." I said I had seen a few in England. "If I had control of your air force," he said, "I'd have three hundred bombers over Berlin every night." I said I thought there'd be plenty of that this winter. "Somebody in our Government said the other day that the bombing of London was child's play compared with what the Germans were going to get." "I hope so," said the captain, and smiled, for the first time.

At last, at sunset, we got to the end of the river of mud, through which, with a variety of minor delays and mishaps, we had been wading for several hours. Here, at last, was the Vyazma-Smolensk highroad. Despite a damaged spring, we travelled along it rapidly for some miles, with a purple sunset in front of us. Then we turned left, along a narrow, but still tolerable secondary road, to Dorogobuzh station, where our two captains said good-bye. The station, though battered by blast, was functioning, and munition trains were slowly moving along the rails, belching smoke into the evening sky. Again we drove through wide fields of oats and flax, and again the starlings were practising—flying above the fields like a vertical oval cloud, and suddenly turning into a round cloud, and then going oval again. While we were at the station I had got into Cholerton's car. Dear old Chol; he seemed happy to be in the Russian country; he said he so seldom managed to get out of Moscow. "What a lovely country, and what lovely, lovable people!" he kept on saying. "And there's no doubt about it," he said; "all that's best in this country is in the army now."

It was raining when we reached Dorogobuzh, and it was too dark to see anything clearly. There was a stretch of water before us, and we drove slowly through deep mud towards it. We passed a dark shape which looked like a pile of debris, with half a wall standing up. Then we stopped. We heard the voice of the colonel asking questions. "Where is that bridge you told me about?" A gruff soldier's voice replied that it must be farther up the river, but "the whole town had been smashed up, and he didn't know if there was still a bridge there." Then we saw the colonel and the other man go away somewhere and disappear in the darkness. We waited for a long time. A few faint lights were shining somewhere, dimly reflected in the river and in the surrounding mud. In the distance a gun was booming. A man on horseback, with a pointed Red Army cap, rode silently past. He looked enormous against the dark sky. "Glow-worms," said Chol. "Surely not, it's too cold for glow-worms," I said. And yet it looked as if there were little lights just beside our car. "These lights must be some distance away," I said. "Yes, I suppose so," said Chol; "I am a bit shortsighted." It wasn't that; in that strange eerie setting one was beginning to lose one's sense of perspective. We waited. At length there was some shouting ahead of us. Then the engines again began to drone, struggling with the thick mud. Again the giant on horseback rode past. Sliding, skidding, and plunging into dark pools, our little car moved on. We felt it sliding down an embankment, and then it seemed to swim gently across the river. It was actually a temporary bridge, scarcely wider than the car itself. Wherever we looked, there was water, or some of it was mud, wet deep mud. But after another hysterical scream of the engine and an upward leap, we felt we were on solid ground at last, somewhere on the other side of the river. And then we drove slowly on through a town of ghosts. On either side of us were the black shapes of houses; but through all their windows the dark sky was showing. They were not faces, but skulls with empty sockets—burned-out houses. Houses of different shapes and sizes, but always the same—the same dark, deathly sky showing through their windows. The gun was still booming in the distance. A street, and then another street, and then another; and still it was the same; burned out, burned out, dead. Was there a single house left in this town? At last we stopped, and the drivers were told to drive the cars into a yard. It was raining heavily. We were taken up a dark stairway, into a dark, empty room on the first floor. A woman came in carrying a candle. But a soldier came running after her. "The windows aren't blacked out; put out that light," he said. There was a picture of Stalin on the wall, and a bench; but nothing else. This, apparently, was once the local soviet; or perhaps still was. The light was blown out. We were taken downstairs again; and there was a long consultation between our colonel and some other men. The colonel was sounding impatient. Finally he announced: "It's going to be all right. Now, drivers, just follow my car." I got back into Chol's car. We drove through another burned-out street, and then the whole thing became more and more unreal. It looked as though we were driving along the white walls of some giant castle; and only by concentrating did I realize that the "walls" were the night sky, with the trees outlined against it. But each tuft of trees, with the white walls towering above them, looked like the entrance to a rich country manor—to a château in France. What were all these mad optical illusions?

Again we stopped, and were led, through the dark, towards a dim light. There was the scent of pine trees in the air. Groping over the roots of pine trees, and over some steps, we entered a narrow door. There were two small rooms there; and sacks of straw lay on the floor. "I'm sorry, but it's the best we can do for you," said the colonel. "But come and have some supper." We were taken from this house to another house; or was it the other end of the same one? Several officers were there. Another table was improvised for us; and a girl brought in some *zakuski* and a vodka bottle and some minced-meat cutlets. We learned that we were in an army camp a mile outside Dorogobuzh. The whole of the town on this side of the river had been destroyed in July. For an hour, in broad daylight, waves of German planes had showered incendiaries and high-explosives on it. There were no troops there at the time; the place was not of the slightest military importance. Men, women, children had been killed—nobody knew how many.

There was nothing fantastic about the place when I looked at it in the morning. There was no French château anywhere; we were in a pine wood, with a large number of little uniform bungalows among the trees. They must have been *datchas*, used in normal times by the good people of Dorogobuzh. It was seven a.m. Andrei Pavlovich, who had, as usual, slept in the car, was already busy putting on a new spring. There were several Russian A.T.S. girls doing a variety of cooking and other jobs. One of them talked to me at length about her family at Kuibyshev; I asked if her family weren't worried about her. "I suppose they are," she said. "But what am I? All of us have a far greater worry: we've got our country to worry about." She did not say it for effect; there was an earnest look on her little pale face. The style of Soviet writing is perhaps responsible for having created a certain uniformity and even pompousness in the expression of people's natural sentiments; Russian speech is not as colourful as it used to be.

But stock phrases, like the phrase this girl used, are the simple expression of genuine feelings. It is not true in Russia today that "*le style, c'est l'homme*"; stock phrases are only too widely used; but what matters is the intonation. When some time ago I went to a hospital in Moscow, I saw there a wounded little Mongol. There was a determined look in his little black eyes; he said he would go back to the front as soon as he got well again; and then he added, to show his determination to go on fighting: "*Pobeda budet za nami*"—"Victory will be ours." The slogan was the simplest and easiest way for him to express his feelings.

In one of the little *datchas* was a canteen attached to the camp, and run by the Russian equivalent of the Navy, Army, Air Force Institute (N.A.A.F.I.); they sold pencils there, and packets of notepaper, and sweets, and little packets of chocolate powder, and tins of fish. The place was fairly well stocked.

That day, we were going on to Yelnya, of which so much had been written in the press. The town had been recaptured from the Germans some ten days before, after a battle that had lasted a month; it was through this battleground that we were going to travel.

We drove through Dorogobuzh, and it no longer looked as grim as the night before. It was, in fact, no different from so many parts of Stepney and Poplar. Practically the whole of the town on one side of the river had been smashed up or burned out. It had been a town of some ten thousand people; a small trading centre, probably half-Jewish, as most towns are in the Smolensk area. But the Jews had probably all fled farther inland, and only a few hundred people had remained in the town. About a hundred of these we saw lining up for food in front of an army canteen, in one of the few only half-demolished houses. There were many women among them, and a few pale-looking children. On the other side of the river, which was the Upper Dnieper, many of the houses were still intact. The raiders seem to have concentrated on the left bank. The bridge we had crossed the night before was a temporary wooden structure; some distance away was the other bridge, half of it collapsed. We drove through a large wood, and then through miles of fields. Much of this country south of Smolensk was easy country for tank warfare. Fields of overripe oats and barley were swept by the cold autumn wind; we were in the war zone now. There was nobody there to gather in the harvest. We passed through half-deserted villages, with the thatch on many roofs untidily torn away by blast, and along the road there were many bomb craters. Many young trees were broken and crippled, though the older trees had all stood up to bombing better than anybody or anything. This road, with fields of uncut oats on either side, must have been fiercely dive-bombed and machine-gunned.

The signs of devastation became more numerous and more concentrated. A Red Army major, who had come with us from Dorogobuzh, said that we were nearing the scene of the great battle of Ushakovo. "Ushakovo itself is—I mean, was—over there." A few shattered trees was all we could see. We got out of the cars and walked. So here was once a village, razed to the ground. This was no longer a figure of speech; it was quite literally so. There wasn't a house standing; not a fragment of a house, not a single plank standing. An old tin samovar, lying on the ground, was the only remnant of the actual village. From the bare patches along the road one could roughly imagine where the houses had stood. It was in and around this village that the Germans had dug themselves in for over a month, and the Russians had shelled them, first from one, then from two, then from three directions—from that semicircle of woods a mile away east. The village was on an advantageous height, from which most of the country around was visible. The Germans had dug solid-looking trenches along the west side of a large pond, and a good five hundred yards beyond, along the ridge of the hillock. We walked along the German trenches; and then, crossing a no-man's-land of some three hundred yards, we came to the Russian trenches. But the no-man's-land was not entirely "no-man's." In it, along the slope, were deep indentations: it showed where the Russians had advanced at night, trying to capture the German trenches. They never actually occupied the German trenches; the pressure from three sides became so heavy and, farther west, the Germans were in such serious danger of being surrounded, that they escaped through the Yelnya bottleneck one night. They retired after a night of fierce Russian shelling and some hand-to-hand fighting, and they left many of their dead behind. These fields round the non-existent village of Ushakovo were like a lunar landscape; they were a mass of shell-holes, and nothing grew on the wet yellow clay. What a strange rubbish-heap! Here were scattered German tin hats, some with bullet-holes; right across a path running south from the village lay the carcass of a dead horse; beside the trenches, in the puddles, there lay about pieces of the *Münchener Illustrierte* and of the *Frankfurter Zeitung*, with an editorial on the "Rout of the Budyenny Army," and even a letter in smudged faded ink beginning: *"Lieber Rudolf! Wie geht es dir? . . ."* Off the road lay a smashed German gun-carriage. And then, on the other side of what was the village, we came to a large grave with a primitive fence round it, painted purple. The tumulus was partly covered with fir branches; and some kind of weeds, with little purple flowers, were planted on top. And a rough tin plate said: "Soldiers of the Red Army who died at Ushakovo fighting for Country, Honour, and Freedom. July 28th to September 1st." There were hundreds and hundreds of Russian men buried there, in what in Russian is so well called *bratskaya mogila*—brotherly grave. The political commissar, who was with us, broke a branch off a little fir tree and threw it furtively on the grave; he looked self-conscious in the presence of strangers. The Germans had been buried in shell-holes.

A mile or two north was a small river, and on the other side of it a small hill. The Germans had turned it into an observation post. Galleries, passages, dugouts, had been built inside the hill, and there were gun emplacements on top of it. The little river in front of the hill was the Germans' first line of defence. On the river bank was a deep, wide hole in the ground; a tank had been dug in here, acting as a pillbox. In their hasty retreat the Germans had been unable to remove it, and the Russians had captured it. The observation post, with its dugouts and galleries, had been built with German thoroughness, and every wall had been solidly propped up and sandbagged. Much equipment had been left behind, and some of it was still there: cases of machine-gun ammunition, cases of hand-grenades; even the wooden cases were pieces of tidy, efficient workmanship. The insides of the dugouts had been furnished with beds and tables and chairs stolen from the neighbouring villages. A large oil-stove suggested that the Germans were already making preparations for winter conditions. Here again many German tin hats were lying about, and biscuit cartons, and empty vodka bottles, and German illustrated newspapers only two or three weeks old.

Ustinovka was the name of the neighbouring village. Most of the thatched roofs had been torn away by bomb blast, and on one hut there had been a direct hit. Where the hut had stood there was now only a large crater, with a bit of roof protruding from the wet clay. The people of the village had fled; but now there were some faint signs of life again. An old peasant and two little boys had returned since the Russians had recaptured the village. The boys were already working in the deserted fields, digging up potatoes—potatoes that had been planted long before the Germans had come here. But there was nobody else in the village except—an old woman. A blind old woman. I saw her wandering about the road, carrying a few dirty rags, a rusty pail, and a tattered sheepskin. She would go from one spot to another, laying down her possessions for a few minutes—her only possessions—and stare with her white, blind eyes. Then she would pick up her belongings again and wander on. She was here when the village was shelled, and she went mad. *"Babushka!"* (grandmother), one of the officers with us called to her, but she paid no attention and only clutched her possessions closer to her stooping, wretched body, and wandered on, her bare muddy feet wading through the mud. One of the boys who came up to us said she slept in her shattered hut, and they gave her potatoes, and sometimes soldiers who passed through the village would give her something, though she never asked for anything. She never uttered any articulate words, except the word *"Cherti"* (the devils).

We drove on to Yelnya, through more miles of uncut fields. Once we drove off the road into a wood, because there were German planes overhead—three or four; perhaps only reconnaissance planes, but our colonel wasn't sure. There were batteries and other signs of military activity in the wood. Yelnya was as mournful a sight as one might have expected. On both sides of the long road that led to the centre of the town, all the houses—mostly wooden houses—had been burned, and all that was left was piles of ashes and chimney-stacks, with one or two fireplaces some way down. It was the same in the centre of this town of some fifteen thousand inhabitants. The only building still intact was the large stone church. Even the civilians who had been here during the German occupation had now gone except just a few. A young woman in a blue jersey was carrying a bag of vegetables across the street, apparently to an army canteen. The story of Yelnya gave one an idea of life under German occupation. The town had been captured by the Germans almost by surprise, and very few civilians had had time to escape. Almost all the able-bodied men and women were formed into forced labour battalions and driven to the German rear. A few hundred elderly people and children had been allowed to stay on in the town. The night the Germans decided to evacuate Yelnya—for farther west the Russians were closing in, threatening to encircle the town—the remaining people of Yelnya were ordered to assemble inside the large stone church. Huddled together, they spent there a night of terror. Through the high windows of the church black smoke was pouring in, and they could see the flames. For after locking up the inhabitants in the church, the Germans had gone round the houses, picking up what few valuables they could still find, and then they systematically set fire to every house in the town. The Russians drove into Yelnya through the burning wreckage, and were able to release the now homeless prisoners.

Ushakovo, Ustinovka, Yelnya—perhaps the first villages, the first town recaptured from the monstrous German war machine on the continent of Europe . . . and all that was left of them was rubble and ashes. And what did it matter to Adolf Hitler and his eighty million people how many families were left homeless, how many children starved, or how many old women went mad? When would the hideous sum-total be added up? *Garçon, l'addition!* Platitudes. . . . But it was platitudes like these that ran through my head as we drove out of Yelnya that evening, among the rubble and the chimney-stacks. . . .

Sulzberger and some of the others were clamouring to go back to Moscow. Beaverbrook might arrive at any moment; Yelnya would be stale news. So it was our last night at the front. No, it wasn't really the front. The Russians were pursuing their counter-offensive some ten miles west of Yelnya. Except for a few shells that had whizzed over our heads, and that quite unexpected raid on Vyazma, we hadn't seen much of the war itself—I mean, of the actual fighting. Newspapermen are seldom taken into an actual battle, least of all foreign journalists in Russia. But it didn't matter. In this one week I had seen more Russian men and women, I had seen more courage and fine human character, and also more human hardship than I had seen in nearly three months in Moscow.

It was our last night, and this called for a special "do." We were taken for the night to an old country house, with an old overgrown park round it, and a green, slimy pond at the other end. It might have been the scene of a Turgeniev novel. We were now far away from the front—twenty or thirty miles. We had a lot to eat and a lot to drink. I was called upon to make, in Russian, a speech of thanks to the organizers of the trip. I said all I wanted to say about the Russian Army and the Russian people. I went on for twenty minutes and never thought I could roll off such Russian perorations. The Russians were very pleased, and one of the political commissars— of all people—said I had a *russkaya dusha*—a Russian soul— and insisted on my having another drink with him on the strength of it. He was an amusing little fellow; and so was the whole party. However, the next morning both we and the Russians started out on the return journey to Moscow in a subdued mood. The commissar who had drunk to my "Russian soul" no longer said anything more to me. After six or seven days' exceptionally hard driving over Russian country roads some of the cars were no longer at their best, some of the springs were sagging, and two of the cars had to stop and re-tire, thus holding up the rest. We did not get to Vyazma until two p.m., and had a quick lunch in the little Gogol hotel. They had had no more air-raids since our last visit, and the man in the *french* said there were many people in Vyazma who believed the Germans had specially come over to bomb us! It was raining when we left Vyazma; I wished I had had a chance to talk again to some of the local people; but there was no time. We drove along the main road towards Moscow. In the woods through which we passed the trees seemed a shade yellower than a week before. It was a dreary journey, especially after we had passed Mozhaisk and it had grown dark. The headlights were very dim, and Andrei Pavlovich kept muttering that it would have been much more sensible to stay the night at Vyazma. Bartlett and Jordan and I tried to pass the time composing clerihews, chiefly about the other members of the party. It was well after midnight when we reached Moscow. Vernon had some difficulty in getting into his hotel, as it had already been commandeered for the British and American Economic Missions, who were expected to arrive any day. Andrei Pavlovich looked very worn out; I said I hoped he would get a few days off; couldn't he go and see his family? "No," he said, "I'll go home now and get a few hours' sleep, and then I must get the car into decent working order, and no doubt I'll be on a new job again in a day or two."

PART V

AUTUMN

September 25

Back in Moscow; and the news is bad. Leningrad, which was causing the greatest anxiety the day we left for the front, is holding out well; but the fall of Kiev is announced. This was not entirely unexpected since the Germans managed to push south along the left bank of the Dnieper, and so threatened to cut off Kiev altogether; but the news has had a depressing effect, none the less. Partly because it's *Kiev,* and partly because this "Tobruk" no longer stands in the way of a further German advance in the central Ukraine. The Germans— though the ordinary Russians here naturally don't know about this—claim to have taken 300,000 or 400,000 or even 600,000 prisoners. This is nonsense: the indications are that the Russian defenders of Kiev have been skilful in getting away across the Dnieper, and that, in fact, the defence had been a good job of work. The Germans claim that they have "encircled" hundreds of thousands of Russians round Poltava; but the "encirclement" is on such a scale that it doesn't necessarily mean anything at all; and the news about the actual capture of 600,000 men is a piece of wishful thinking. (The encirclement and the "capture" apparently refer to the same people.) But it seems a ghastly business, none the less, and Kharkov is seriously threatened. What Kiev looks like is hard to imagine; the Germans say that the Russians have "barbarously" set on fire both sides of the Krestchatik, the main street, before clear-

238

ing out; the Russians, without specifying to what extent exactly the "scorched-earth" policy has been applied, say that nothing of any value to the Germans has been left behind in Kiev, and that about one-half of the population—that is, 300,000 people—have been evacuated. The figure is probably an over-estimate, and what is going to happen to those left behind is terrible to imagine.

There are rumours that the Germans have already set up a Ukrainian quisling government in Kiev; but I doubt it. There is no evidence that the Germans have had any success, so far, in recruiting any "Ukrainian nationalists."

Nevertheless, the fall of Kiev has had a bad moral effect in Moscow. Hence the mild defeatist crack: "Just as well we've occupied Iran, we shall now know where to go when the Germans take over the whole of Russia."

For the third time I have been asked to write an article for the Soviet press, this time for the weekly paper *Sovietskoie Iskusstvo* (*Soviet Art*), which has a circulation of about 100,000. I went to discuss the matter with the musical editor (why musical, I don't know), Comrade Rabinovich, in the paper's editorial office—a queer, dark, old-fashioned place which you enter from the balcony of the Petrovka Arcade. I believe this Arcade, like the famous Passazh in St. Petersburg, used to be one of the whoring centres of Moscow in the old days. I remember the famous story in St. Petersburg about the attempt made by the police to keep the whores out of the Passazh. They started going to the place, carrying portfolios with "*Musique*" written on them, and pretending to be pupils of the Conservatoire. Comrade Rabinovich, an amiable little man with an artistic mop of hair—he was, or perhaps still is, a professional pianist—said his paper was very keen on the closest cultural co-operation with England, and they had all "much admired" my two earlier articles on war-time London, and would I write a 1,500-word article on my impressions of

Moscow's cultural life in war-time. One of the remarks I had made in that *Izvestia* article had "immortalized" me, he said, for my "famous euphemism" had entered the current language of Moscow. When anybody was described today as having had "a piece of bad luck"—*ne povezlo*—it meant that he had been blown to bits by an H.E. Rabinovich then talked about Shostakovich who, he said, had just come from Leningrad and would shortly conduct his wonderful new Seventh Symphony. He had been very reluctant to leave Leningrad, which he adored. For a long time nothing could persuade him to go to Moscow. He had spent his time between composing his new symphony and fire-watching, and the grim romance of the Leningrad blitz had been a source of artistic inspiration to him; so also was the deep tenderness he felt for the great and lovely city in its hour of peril. Rabinovich thought that Shostakovich was by far the greatest of Russia's composers: "Give him another five years, and he will out-rank Tchaikovsky and Rimsky-Korsakov; at thirty-five, he is already the greatest artistic phenomenon this country has produced in the last forty years." Rabinovich said he had heard some extracts of the Seventh, and he believed it was an even greater work than the First, Fifth, and Sixth. All together, he said, this war was producing great art on a large scale; had I heard Victor Belyi's latest choral work, *The Song of Anger*? I confessed I had not. I asked if Shostakovich had brought any news of bomb damage to Leningrad. "The damage," Rabinovich said, "hasn't been very serious so far, though one bomb dropped on the Pioneer Palace, formerly the Anichkov Palace. But all the portable art treasures of Leningrad have been moved to safety." He promised to arrange for me a meeting with Shostakovich, and also to send me a ticket for the first performance of the Seventh, as soon as it is announced. All being well (but will it be?), I should have an interesting winter in Moscow. More interesting than Malcolm Muggeridge's!

I saw *The Three Sisters* at the Moscow Art Theatre. Never have I seen a play performed with such *sustained* perfection. It was a wonderful, "all-star" cast—though "star" is the last word in the world one can apply to the Moscow Art Theatre. Every movement, every gesture, every word, every pause, were full of revealing significance. The actors were not playing, they were, I believe, genuinely *living* their parts; and when the women had tears in their eyes, I am sure they were genuine tears. How well these Soviet actors understood all the human *tendresse* of Chekhov! There wasn't, in all the four hours, one single false note in the whole play. Irina was played by a young and apparently quite new actress, Gosheva; but she was very lovely. Elanskaya (whom I had already seen as Anna Karenina) played Olga, and Androvskaya, Masha. Andrei, the brother, was played by Stanitzyn, Vershinin by Bolduman (perhaps the least perfect of the cast), Levanov made an unaccountably terrifying Solenyi; the old doctor—what a sweet old boy!—was played by Gribov, and that jarring Natasha by Georgievskaya. Four hours at the Moscow Art Theatre make up for a lot of things in Moscow. Khmelev alone as Baron Tusenbach was a little disappointing, though through no fault of his; it is a colourless role, and, besides, I had seen him in his unforgettable performance of Karenin, and it seemed all the time as though Karenin had dressed up as Tusenbach.

Just my bad luck. There was an empty seat beside me, and two young girls, real theatre enthusiasts, squeezed into it. But, at the last moment, before the doors were closed, the legitimate owner of the seat arrived, and turned out to be one of our British majors. The poor man didn't know a word of Russian, and was bored to death. He kept on asking me what the *action* of the play was; and that, frankly, is not easy to explain. However, I did my best, whereupon he said: "I see, much ado about nothing." However, he got quite excited at the beginning of the third act, when the glow of the great fire in the town is seen from the windows: "What, a fire? Ah, well, I suppose something is going to happen now." However, no firemen appeared on the stage, and there were no hairbreadth escapes, and my poor major sank back into his former state of boredom. In the end he confessed he didn't care much for "this kind of play," and preferred the ballet every time.

MONDAY, *September* 29

The great Economic Conference opened this morning. They've all arrived: Beaverbrook, Harriman, and a variety of British and American experts. Cars are dashing about in large numbers between the Kremlin and the National Hotel and the British and American Embassies. I cannot help wondering how much really vital assistance to Russia it is going to produce. The atmosphere is very business-like, both the Russians (Molotov) and the Anglo-Americans emphasizing the urgency of the business and the *preciseness* of its nature. The main questions are (1) how much Britain can give, out of her own resources; (2) how much she can spare out of the stuff she gets from America; (3) how much America can give direct to Russia; and (4), above all, how the stuff is to be sent, and how quickly. It doesn't look, though, as if the Americans were going to give the Russians anything on a Lend-Lease basis. Beaverbrook has been saying that the conference will take only a few days, and that he hopes to leave for England again in less than a week. Cripps and the Mission have been working hard in preparing the conference; so perhaps the main points have already been settled. A cold rainy autumn day in Moscow.

The bulk of the American Mission were the first to arrive last Wednesday, and Steinhardt gave a very interesting cocktail party at the Embassy in their honour. The cocktails were, later, followed by a very sumptuous "cold" buffet, including hot dogs and canned American beer, etc. I like the pillared hall of the "Spasa House." With its Empire chandeliers and white pillars it would do well as the setting for a ballroom scene in *War and Peace*. I wonder who the Moscow magnate was to whom the place belonged before the Revolution.

I had a long talk with one of the experts; and although he seemed a very intelligent person who knew his job (I gathered that he was one of the shipping experts), I am not quite satisfied yet that the Americans are taking this war sufficiently seriously. He himself was, clearly, a Roosevelt man, but what he dwelt on chiefly was the great difficulty the President was having in dealing with "a hopelessly divided opinion." And the problem of Russia was a particularly difficult one, in view of so many old prejudices, and with all the noise the isolationists were now making on the religious issue, using it as a first-class political weapon against the Soviets. "And, anyway," he said, using a phrase I had already heard from somebody else quite recently (I forget who): "In 1917 a college boy didn't feel a decent member of society unless he went to fight in France; there's no such feeling in America now. Only fifty per cent of American opinion is *in* the war." He gave me some figures of the proposed deliveries to Russia "within the next two or three months"—the tanks from Britain, the planes from America, and the copper and aluminium ("aluminum," he called it), and certain other raw materials. The Russians, he thought, were asking a little too much of certain of these raw materials. It was very, *very* unfortunate, he said, that the Russians had lost so much of their own aluminium output. The figures he quoted sounded moderately good to me, but not overwhelmingly so; a few spoonfuls for the gigantic Russian war bucket. And there were certain metals which the Russians were needing urgently; and I wasn't sure that they were going to get them. "But transportation," the American said, "is the real problem." He did not think much of the Archangel route, which is frozen for five months in the year; nor was the Iranian route—though better in some ways—very satisfactory; about 3,000 tons a day was all it could carry. Much more important was the Vladivostok route, despite the appalling distance; but much depended on whether the Russians would be able to double its present capacity—increase it to 10,000 tons; did they have the rolling-stock? "And then, of course," he said, "there may be complications with Japan, and we mayn't be able to use Vladivostok at all." "What, not even with convoys?" "Well, I don't know. It may all be very complicated." "But, surely," I said, "you could fly the bombers direct to Russia?" "Yes, probably we could," he said, "but it will require a certain amount of organization—airfields in northern Siberia and all that—and flying conditions in the far north aren't too hot in winter. And the Russians need a lot of things other than bombers." He also suggested that the diversion to Russia of any stuff originally earmarked for England might meet with some opposition among the British, who might say it was upsetting their strategic plans for the winter. "*That* difficulty, at any rate, ought to be overcome," I said.

I wonder if foodstuffs are also going to be supplied to the Soviet Union. What about sugar, "the nerve of war"? It's running short in Moscow (though we, as privileged foreigners, don't suffer from any serious shortage yet); but it is sure to get hopelessly short when the present supplies run out—and with no more to come from Vinnitza, Poltava, etc. And will there not be an appalling tobacco shortage if the Crimea is cut off? It's already bad enough in Moscow.

On Sunday, Cripps had a tea-party, at which we were to meet Beaverbrook. I had never seen Beaverbrook before, and thought Low's little imp rather a pretty piece of flattery. He appeared only at the very end of the reception, bursting in like a hurricane and with so much vitality that the Embassy flunkeys got all nervous about the teacups. He swept past us and made a bee-line for Jordan, who has been acting as the

Express correspondent. He talked to a few people for five minutes or so, and then swept out again as quickly as he had appeared.

This morning, before starting out for the conference, Beaverbrook saw the British Press (which means five people, all in all). I liked him much better this second time. But I can't quite make up my mind yet whether he really intends (as his whole manner suggests) to do his very damnedest for the Russians. I hope he does; I am told he was rather half-hearted about the Russians at first, but for some weeks past he has been more and more impressed by their resistance, and is now favouring an all-out Pro-Russian policy. He and Eden are said to be the most whole-hearted Pro-Russians in the Cabinet now. The Cabinet will need somebody to live down the Moore-Brabazon utterances. These were, naturally, not published in the Soviet press, but they have been duly noted in the Kremlin. Beaverbrook, of course, also knows that the British people are, as somebody said, "madly in love with Russia," and are feeling a bit guilty about not having done more during these three critical months; and a Pro-Russian policy is very popular in England now.

The Russians have, naturally, been hoping for a great big British landing somewhere on the Continent to draw off German troops and planes from here. It doesn't look as if we were going to do anything like that—least of all now that autumn has come; so the next-best thing to keep the Russians reasonably satisfied will be "all-out aid." *Can* Beaverbrook give it—taking account of the transport difficulties?

Last night Lozovsky was very reassuring about Leningrad; he said the Germans were losing tens of thousands of dead; and that, however many more tens of thousands they lost, they wouldn't get Leningrad; that communications with Leningrad were still being maintained and that although there were, of course, ration-cards in Leningrad, there was no food shortage.

It looks as if Leningrad was going to become one of the great heroic episodes of this war. As regards actual communications, at least one thing is certain; and that is that the Germans are no longer claiming Schlüsselburg. If they haven't got it, then it's just possible that supplies are still reaching Leningrad along the Vologda railway. The German lines must, in many places, be a good long way away from the actual city. The Germans claimed the other day to have shelled Kronstadt and Oranienbaum (which is over twenty miles west of Leningrad), in which case their earlier claim to have entered Peterhof and even Strelna is just nonsense. Or perhaps they were driven back? The mention of Oranienbaum reminded me so clearly of the dirty-white stucco building of the railway station, with its buffet, where we used to have glasses of lemon tea and *pirozhki* on cold winter evenings before getting into the Petrograd train; and also of the shops in the main street of Oranienbaum, particularly the photographer's, who used to sell me Kodak films, and whose window displayed "studio portraits" of his more distinguished-looking customers, and wedding groups. I still remember his name, which was Yakovlev. But that by the way.

Lozovsky also said that there was very heavy fighting "for the Crimea." He added that the fighting was still going on outside the Crimea itself, and even "outside the Perekop isthmus." He denied the foreign broadcast story, attributed to "an official Moscow spokesman," that the Germans had been landing, or trying to land, thousands of parachutists in the Crimea. "I didn't say it, now, did I? And what other official Moscow spokesman is there?" he said.

As regards the German claims to have captured three or four or six hundred thousand Russians, he was more vague on the subject; the battle in the central Ukraine, he said, was going on day and night, it was not ended yet, and he did not think it was in the Russians' interest to give out any informa-

tion prematurely. But he added a somewhat sinister phrase:
"The farther east the Germans push, the nearer they will get
to the tomb of Nazi Germany." I could not help wondering
if he was preparing us for new big territorial losses—Kharkov,
the Donbass . . . ?

The name of Budyenny is no longer in great evidence in the
Soviet papers. I shouldn't be surprised if he has been superseded or moved to a less responsible post. Many people here
have been shaking their heads about Budyenny, whose *brav'
général* presence they admired, but whose qualifications in a
war of this description they doubted. He was said to have had,
since the start, a good chief of staff; that may be so, but it isn't
enough; especially if, as seems only too obvious, the Ukrainian
front has suffered from a constant shortage of equipment. He
ranks as one of the heroes of the Revolution; and his appointment was, in a way, a political one. Timoshenko, on the other
hand, is first and foremost a soldier. I am even told he is not
a party member; but I don't know about that. In the last two
or three years people have been received into the party regard-
less of their social origins; also many non-party men are holding high positions.

I am getting more and more worked up about this Reuter
business. This job of "supplying the whole British press with
copy from Russia"—as it was described to me before I started
out—is extremely important; but the other day I received
letters from three different people in England; all three
praised my *Sunday Times* pieces, "they give us a clearer idea
of Moscow than anything we've read," etc., etc., but equally,
all three wondered where my Reuter messages were appearing.
According to them, there seems little trace of my "specials,"
not merely in the London papers, but even in the better-known
provincials. No doubt my specials go to South America and
all sorts of places whose reactions to Russia, one way or an-

other, don't matter much; but the reactions of Britain are supremely important, and if my copy is not being used I'm largely wasting my time here. The whole question needs going into. The Embassy cuttings include nearly all my *Sunday Times* stuff but do not contain a single one of my Reuter specials except one completely silly and pointless "rewrite" about a Moscow kolkhoz (God knows who rewrote it), which appeared under my name in the provincial press. I got so worked up about the whole thing that I wired to find out if at least my five specials from the front had been used. I now hear that a few little bits ("rewrites" again?) were used on Tuesday and Wednesday by some of the provincials, and that's about all. If this "special correspondent" venture is a new thing in the case of Reuter's, then it doesn't seem to have been a success. I shouldn't think it was the fault of my copy —allowing, of course, for the limitations of the work here. Perhaps some organizational question,[1] which I just don't understand, but which is important because it affects the general problem of British news from Russia. I am going to cable suggesting I go to London for a short time to discuss the matter.

The deportation of the Volga Germans has had a sequel—as far as this house is concerned. Bertha, our little maid, has not been ordered out of Moscow; apparently she was saved from that by her father's good record. But there is some other old spinster who was sent east, and she left her dog behind, and somebody brought the brute along, and, appealing to Maurice's feelings of humanity, managed to inflict it upon him. Maurice is tenderhearted, and is being as friendly to the animal as is humanly possible, which is not easy in the circumstances. Only a German spinster would have a dog like

---

1 This was written before the Commons debate and the reorganization of Reuter's. Improvements in the work of the great National agency are to be hoped for.

that. She's a cross between a dachshund and a setter, with long black setter hair, flapping ears, a sloppy expression, no legs worth speaking of, and no vitality at all. A real case for Thurber. Maurice was, of course, told that the dog was well behaved, and house-trained, and—she just isn't. As a result little Bertha threatens to give notice; twice a day she tells me her tale of woe: "I took her out for two hours, and she wouldn't do anything—*nu nitchevo, nitchevo*—and the moment we got home—" The bitch is called Bella. Bertha, to punish us for Bella's misdeeds, has now got into the habit of announcing in her pidgin Russian, at the beginning of a meal: "There'll be no soup today . . ." or "There'll be no third course today. . . ." So, rather than see Bella poisoned by the vet, we meekly submit to Bertha's little vendetta.

OCTOBER 4

The conference is over, and is being acclaimed on all sides as a huge success. Impressed by the remarkable speed with which the conference got through its work, people are perhaps apt to forget the limited scope of the talks and the limited possibilities of delivering the stuff to Russia, even if, as the communiqué said, "practically everything the Russians asked for" has been agreed to. Have they asked for anything in excess of what can in actual practice be delivered? The question has been worrying me. The Russian papers today are making a big display of the success of the conference, of the "united anti-Hitler front" by three of the greatest industrial powers in the world, and all that. People reading the papers in tram-cars appear to be very pleased; though I don't think they are overwhelmed. They know that a fearfully hard winter is ahead of them, and while, politically, the agreement is of the greatest importance, they rather take the view that time alone will show to what extent it is going to speed up a successful end of the war.

Beaverbrook has been very much in the centre of things, and has pretty well eclipsed everybody, including Harriman, who, I must confess, struck me as rather a colourless person. Cripps, also, was somewhat pushed into the background. This may be a little unfair; for Cripps and the Military Mission certainly did a lot of the preparatory work for the conference, and without that work it might not have been over so quickly. Even so, Beaverbrook's "dynamics" have unquestionably contributed to the success of the conference; and his nightly talks with Stalin seem to have been of decisive value in smoothing away the rough edges, and in giving the Russians the maximum satisfaction possible at present. Beaverbrook seems to have met with good grace some of the more difficult Russian demands for certain raw materials. Whether, as regards actual war material—that is, tanks and planes—Beaverbrook has gone much beyond what Harriman's shipping expert told me the other day I just don't know. But probably he did. It looks as though Beaverbrook has fully realized that the Russians are the only people in the world who are seriously *weakening* Germany, and that it is in Britain's interest to do without certain things and give them to Russia.

At the little press conference yesterday he was bursting with exuberance. Slapping his knees, he was saying that the Russians were pleased with Beaverbrook, and the Americans were pleased with Beaverbrook—"Now aren't they, Harriman?" To which Harriman replied: "Sure, you bet."

I wasn't asked to the Kremlin banquet. None of the press was, and if Vernon and Quentin Reynolds got in, it was only because they have been acting as "press attachés" during this conference—with rather vague functions, it is true. Banquets are a bore, but I wish I had seen Stalin, and the whole Kremlin set-up. Beaverbrook is praising Stalin up to the skies. It would be easy to be funny about it; but I imagine Beaverbrook has been genuinely impressed by Stalin's practical mind, his organizing ability, and his qualities as a national leader. Cold, sceptical Molotov made an unusually warm speech.

At the ballet yesterday there was another performance of the *Swan Lake,* but this time with Ulanova as the *prima ballerina.* She is very young, and has the loveliest and most expressive arms. She was dreamy and lyrical, with none of Lepeshinskaya's vivaciousness. Her dancing harmonizes more perfectly, I think, with the Tchaikovsky music. Of course, everybody was at the ballet. Beaverbrook sat in the front row, sandwiched between a strangely assorted pair—Vishinsky on one side (what a mild little man the terrible Public Prosecutor of the Trials looks, with his well-groomed white hair and his little white moustache!) and Litvinov on the other. Litvinov, who hadn't changed much since I last saw him at Geneva, is at last really coming into his own again, though his official function at the conference was at first stated to be merely that of "interpreter."

That last evening in Moscow, Beaverbrook had an amusing little party in his rooms at the National, to which he asked only the members of the British press, two British generals, who had come with him, and M. Oumansky, the Soviet Ambassador to Washington. A lavish buffet was laid out and, to add a Beaverish touch of fantasy to the whole affair, he had ordered a band of three down-at-heel musicians with some kind of Caucasian banjos, and a dark lady singer, to perform for the party. The dark lady bawled *Volga-Volga,* and the *Volga Boat Song,* and *Allah-verdy* and other well-worn Caucasian favourites, which, for a moment, made me feel as if I were in some White Russian bar in the rue Pigalle. Beaverbrook was still in high spirits, though he looked tired and, judging from his expression, he seemed to think the dark lady was overdoing her stuff.

On Wednesday I got a cable from Reuter's agreeing to my London visit "if I thought it was in Reuter's interest." Of

course, I think it's in their interest that their Russian news
service should be put on a sounder and more productive basis.
Yesterday I got my exit visa from the Russians, together with
a return visa. I tried to get permission to travel with the
Beaverbrook party, but got, right up to my knees, into a quag-
mire of official stickiness and decided to wait for the next
opportunity. So the "Beaver" party have gone off without me;
which is damned annoying, for it's a devil of a job to get to
London from here, especially if one wants to do it quickly.

OCTOBER 5

Rather disquieting news from the front. It looks as
if another big German offensive had started, after all. The
Russians are not saying anything yet; but the B.B.C. is full
of German reports of this big offensive, which Hitler announced in his speech on Friday. Well, we shall just have to
wait and see. We had the feeling, this last week or two, that
the Germans had had about enough of it for this year, and that
in Moscow, at any rate, we could look forward confidently to
a moderately quiet winter—apart from possible air-raids, of
course. Today the season of symphony concerts opened in
Moscow; both at the Tchaikovsky Hall and in the other place
—I forget its name—not a seat could be got after twelve
o'clock. Musical programs for the whole winter season have
been announced!

I wish I had gone to one of today's concerts. Instead, I took
Wally Caroll to the Moscow Art Theatre—to a play which
he could more or less follow: *The School for Scandal*. It was
admirable as a "period piece"; the Moscow Art Theatre had
certainly studied the English eighteenth century with all their
usual thoroughness. Costumes, furniture, musical instru-
ments, everything was perfectly correct. Andronskaya, as
Lady Teazle, was bursting with fun and vitality; the actor
who played Charles Surface was most *sympathique* as the

good-natured rake, but the high spot in the play was Lady Teazle and Sir Peter playing their harp-flute duet; it was a little masterpiece of musical comedy, with the music as good as the comedy. Still, there is not much room in *The School for Scandal* for the finer shades of acting, and even the Moscow Art Theatre couldn't squeeze much more out of it than meets the eye.

Lucien has been ill for a week and is feeling very sorry for himself. I don't think he's in good health generally, and he is homesick for France—though he loves Russia in his own way. He is a brilliant journalist, and must suffer from the lack of a proper full-time job. Maurice and I went to see him this evening, and whom should we meet there but Jean-Richard Bloch! Bloch left Paris as late as April of this year. I had met him only once in Paris, in the company of old Charles Rappoport, the veteran French Communist (wonder where the poor old boy is; he was going to celebrate his seventy-fifth birthday on the very day the Germans marched into Paris). I rather dropped a brick mentioning Rappoport to Bloch; I had quite forgotten that old Charles had quarrelled with Moscow at the time of the Bukharin trial. I had, of course, read Bloch's books, and was interested to see someone who had been in Paris so recently. Bloch said he had spent months in Paris writing and editing clandestine leaflets; and he had never slept in the same house for more than three nights in succession. One day he discovered that things had really got too hot for him, and he went off to Russia—he didn't tell me, though, by what route, and I didn't like to ask. He said that since the sacking of Langeron and the appointment of Admiral Bara to the job of Préfet de Police there had been a terrific purge in the Paris police force. The Santé Prison was crowded with policemen, and Langeron himself had spent two months there. Bloch said that, at least until the spring, the majority of the Paris police were absolutely opposed to co-operation with the Germans; in the streets they continually cracked jokes at the Germans' expense, jokes which the Germans were too stupid to understand; and when they were sent to search the houses of "suspects"—whether alleged Communists or de Gaullists—it often happened that incriminating documents were destroyed there and then by the very *flics* who had discovered them. But Bloch thought things might be less pleasant now, since the purge at the Préfecture, and also at the Sûreté Générale, and there were, he thought, some dangerous elements among the *garde mobile* who might well form the nucleus of a French Gestapo. Even so, he didn't think that any large and solidly pro-German body could be assembled in France for any purpose. There would always be "traitors." He thought the shooting of Laval a very promising sign. Bloch is doing a lot of writing here.

MONDAY, *October* 6

I hear a convoy is expected to leave Archangel early next week, and I have been promised a seat on the plane on Thursday or Friday. Wonder if it'll fall through again. I saw X this morning. He seemed remarkably calm and unperturbed about the new offensive, and didn't think it amounted to very much. The point that was worrying him most was Bryansk; the Germans, he said, were getting dangerously near it. (Well, they've done that before and have been turned back.) On the other hand, he considered the situation round Leningrad definitely more hopeful; whereas in the south the Germans seemed to have been held up since their capture of Poltava. Kharkov was no longer in immediate danger. He thought the Germans were preparing feverishly for a winter campaign, commandeering and confiscating winter clothes on a vast scale in Norway, Denmark, and Finland; but their plans seemed to have gone wrong, for they had confidently expected a decisive victory over the Russians, and started much too late with their winter preparations.

TUESDAY, *October* 7

It isn't looking so pretty after all. Damn these Huns. The latest offensive promises to be the biggest and bloodiest yet. And there was some chap on the B.B.C. who smugly declared today that "on the eve of this winter he had a glorious feeling of spring in his heart"; this was the third winter of war, he said in effect, and London was not being blitzed, and the Russians were such grand chaps. Grand chaps, quite. But what new sufferings and bloodiness are they going to face this week—if they are not facing it already? X was incomparably gloomier today than yesterday. He talked of a great big German pincer movement ultimately directed at Moscow, one pincer coming from somewhere north of Smolensk, and the other striking at Bryansk. In the central sector Timoshenko's troops had been advancing for some time now, and it was possible that they had been caught on the hop, before they had had time to consolidate their positions. It was the worst moment for facing a counter-offensive. According to all the rules of the game, it was much too late in the year for a big offensive in this part of Russia, but the Germans had often disregarded rules with impunity. The last Hitler speech did not sound like a mere piece of bluff; he was clearly out for very big, perhaps decisive results. It looked as though the Germans were throwing in a tremendous amount of armour despite all the losses they had suffered; there was the danger of a serious Russian inferiority in tanks just at this stage.

This morning I had a visit from Comrade Weber, the assistant editor of that excellent monthly, *Znamie*. He asked me for a 2,000-word article about my impressions at the front. It gives me a juvenile kick to write for Russian papers—especially for so highbrow a paper as *Znamie*. To see myself in print in Russian is as exciting as it was to see my first editorial in the Glasgow *Bulletin* seventeen years ago. It was on the centenary of Byron's death—of all things! I spent most of the afternoon writing the *Znamie* story—in English, though, for it takes me much longer to write in Russian, and Weber said he would have it translated, and let me look over the translation. He wants the full text by tomorrow. I asked Weber what he thought of the military situation and he said, a little gloomily, that it looked as though there might be a few nasty moments ahead, but he wasn't expecting anything very serious to happen. "Timoshenko knows what he's doing," he said.

By the way, my article in *Soviet Art* was given over the Moscow radio in full the other day.

Later in the afternoon I went to Lozovsky's conference—which was, of course, particularly important today. These conferences are now held in another *osobniak*, in a small side-street in the Arbat district. The former Greek Legation place has been abandoned for lack of adequate heating arrangements, and the last time the conference met there we all shivered with cold. The new place is a pretty little house, with portraits of Stalin, Molotov, and Kalinin, and a few remnants of the past—a couple of rather doubtful eighteenth-century landscapes, and a marble nude in a niche on the stair.

Curious how little notice I had taken of Hitler's speech last Friday. He had pretty well suggested that the great "final" offensive against Russia was about to start and said that the Russians had, in fact, already been defeated. It may be because the Russian papers didn't, as far as I know, publish a single line of it. Lozovsky looked a little worried, but not very. He said Hitler's speech showed that the man was getting desperate. He knew he wasn't going to win the war, but he had to keep the Germans more or less contented during the winter, and he would certainly attempt to achieve some major success, which would suggest that a certain *stage* of the war had been closed. (What "major success" of far-reaching moral importance, I wondered, could there be, short of the capture of

Moscow? Clearly, Hitler would try for it.) The second reason why it was essential for Hitler to do something big was, Lozovsky said, because the Anglo-American-Soviet agreement had caused a feeling of despondency in Germany. They could *à la rigueur* swallow a "Bolshevik" agreement with Britain, but a "Bolshevik" agreement with America was more than they had expected. Anyway, the capture of this or that town, Lozovsky said, didn't affect the final outcome of the war. (Was he trying to prepare us for a possible loss of Moscow? I wondered.) "But all our forces are mobilized to meet worthily this new offensive," he concluded. "And," he added acidly, "if the Germans want to see a few hundred thousand more of their people killed, they'll certainly succeed in that, if in nothing else!" The old boy was full of punch, and not unduly depressing. Asked if the great German offensive had already begun, he said: "It's beginning."

By the way, he was rather snooty about the news "from" Russia which came from Stockholm and Bern—doubtful news centres, he said, which were being largely spoon-fed by German propaganda.

OCTOBER 8

The German offensive is even more serious than we expected yesterday. Last night Maurice and I were playing two-handed bridge in the sitting-room—that's what one is often reduced to in Moscow in black-out hours, for the A.R.P. people in the street are so fussy that there's hardly enough light for reading—when, at eleven o'clock, he rang up the Nark to get the night communiqué. Palgunov himself answered the phone. I could hear Maurice saying: "Oh, really, that's very interesting, very interesting indeed." He looked a trifle upset as he laid down the receiver. "What's so interesting?" I asked. "Well," said Maurice, speaking a little more quickly than usual, "the night communiqué says that there is fighting all along the front, but particularly fierce fighting in the direction of Bryansk and Vyazma." Vyazma! So, after all, it wasn't the pincer movement that X had described to me yesterday morning. They weren't striking from somewhere north of Smolensk, with the other pincer aiming at Bryansk. It was a direct break-through—a break-through across that very part of the front where we had been only a little over a fortnight before. "Nasty," I said. "Well, yes—a bit surprising," said Maurice. For a few minutes I had that hollow feeling inside me—that feeling I had known so well during those last days in Paris; especially on that night when we learned from Colonel Thomas that the Germans had crossed the Meuse at Sedan.

But no, surely, it wasn't the same, it couldn't be the same. The Russians would stop them; all the country between Vyazma and Moscow was, as I well knew, heavily fortified. It was clear the Russians would concentrate an immense number of troops to save Moscow, or hold it as long as was humanly possible. But what had happened? Had not that Yelnya victory proved something of a boomerang? Had not the Russians been over-confident in their advance? Had they not gone too far ahead, and failed to consolidate their new positions, thus exposing themselves to a successful German counter-attack? I could see the Germans back at Yelnya; I could see their tanks and lorries driving through the burned-out streets of Dorogobuzh; I could see the Nazi swine desecrating the "brotherly grave" of the Russians who fell in the Battle of Ushakovo. And, with a pang, I thought of Colonel Kirilov and his men, and of little pale-faced Sasha in the coat that was much too large for him, and of the red-faced colonel who had paid those compliments to Mrs. Haldane. Where were they? Had they been surrounded? How many of them were still alive? Was little Sasha still alive to look into the unbreakable "lucky" mirror I had given him that day? They were so confident and so cheerful—only a fortnight ago. And Vyazma? That little

blitz that blew us out of our beds must be child's play compared with what Vyazma is getting now. I spent a bad night
thinking about these people, and feeling for Moscow a strange
tenderness I had never felt before.

This morning, after breakfast, I put some finishing touches
to my *Znamie* article. It was difficult to conclude it on an
appropriately optimistic note. Natalia Petrovna, Maurice's
secretary, arrived, looking rather upset. "What's the matter?"
I said. "Oh, nothing; except that my husband is somewhere
near Smolensk, and I am just wondering."

I then went out to the Nark, where I had arranged to meet
Weber. At the tram-stop in the Pokrovka, people were reading
Pravda and *Izvestia* in their glass frames. The *Pravda* editorial was on "The Work of Women in War-time"—not in the
least ominous. The communiqué was given no more prominence
than usual. In the tram there was the same impenetrable, non-
committal expression on people's faces, with no visible signs of
worry. At the Nark, I picked up a copy of the *Red Star*; it
was much more outspoken than *Izvestia* or *Pravda*, and much
grimmer, particularly the appeal in large letters addressed
to "Every Man of the Red Army." It said that "the very existence of the Soviet State was in danger," and that every man
of the Red Army must "stand firm and fight to the last drop of
blood." And the editorial was revealing. It described the German offensive as a last desperate fling; Hitler, it said, had
thrown into it everything he had got; every old, out-of-date
tank, every *tanketka* (baby tank) that the Germans had managed to collect in Holland, France, or Belgium, had been
thrown into this battle. The Russian soldiers, it said, must at
any price destroy these tanks, old or new, large or small. All
the riff-raff armour of ruined Europe was being hurled against
the Soviet Union.

In the little press room Cassidy was indulging in macabre
humour. Others were saying that Moscow would now become

a super-Madrid; Weber, to whom I gave my *Znamie* article, looked rather *distrait*, and thought it might be somewhat out of date by the time the paper appeared. I couldn't help being amused by Palgunov. "What's your impression?" I said. "Well," he said, and quoted a line of verse about the changing fortunes of war, or something. "It's Pushkin, isn't it?" he asked, as though I were a great authority. I said I hadn't the vaguest idea.

I had lunch at the Caucasian restaurant with Rabinovich of *Soviet Art*; Maurice also was there. The little man again talked exuberantly of Shostakovich; asked if I was going to England soon, and if I did, would I find out what was being done there about performing the modern Soviet composers. "It would be so nice if we could send our opera or one of our symphony orchestras to London, and get some of your theatrical companies to visit Moscow; but, of course, the question of transport is a bit difficult at the moment." "You're telling me!" I said. I said I would find out this afternoon about my travelling arrangements, if any, and would let him know later. We had the usual Aragvi menu—caviar, and *shashlyk*, and green onions, and some white Caucasian wine. We then talked about Maurice's flat, and I remarked jokingly that Maurice's predecessors had left there a most demoralizing assortment of books—for instance, the complete works of Trotsky. Rabinovich looked frankly scandalized. "Why, I call that pornographic literature!" he said, and laughed a little uneasily. Several young officers were sitting at the next table; among them was a very handsome youth—with only one leg; he had come in on crutches.

In the afternoon I went to see M., who said that the plane he had told me about some days ago would leave on Friday morning, and if I wanted a seat on it I should make arrangements at once. It was a plane belonging to the Russian Naval Department, and the Narkomindel would fix me up, if possible. M. added that there would be a fairly fast ship leaving Arch-

angel in a few days for England. So I went to see Palgunov,
who, after phoning a number of people, told me that it would
be O.K. He would let me know about the final arrangements
tomorrow. "You'll be back here in a few weeks, won't you?"
"Of course," I said; "and in Moscow, I hope." "Yes, you may
be sure of that," he said. "By the way, the news from the front
is very much better this afternoon. And," he added, "I know
you are a little fed-up with not having seen Leningrad; but I
think there'll be a pretty good chance of your seeing it when
you come back. And, when you are in England, remember this:
there may be some black days; but this country is a damned
sight tougher than a lot of people imagine." I hate to leave
Moscow just now; but if I am to carry on with newspaper
work from Russia, I may as well have it put on a proper basis.
And there mayn't be another chance for some time to get to
London, especially if we are moved east.

OCTOBER 13

I am writing this in my cabin on board H.M.S. I
have been here since yesterday. Last night the captain asked
me to dinner, and was greatly interested in all I had to say
about Russia. Eggs and bacon for breakfast this morning, and
real marmalade and real Players at 1s. 3d. for fifty! Everybody is extremely friendly. Strange, this little British oasis in
the middle of the White Sea. I have just been up on deck. A
glorious evening, with a starry, dark sky, and a calm, dark
sea. It is almost mild, with a gentle breeze blowing. A mile
away, on the starboard side, is a little island with a few small
houses, and a slightly larger one among them, perhaps a customs house. And far away, on each side, is a thin slender line
of forest; desolate, endless forests of northern Russia. The
lines of forest stretch southward along the narrowing bay of
Archangel. Archangel itself is a good many miles away from
here; but during the day one can distinguish the smoke rising

from it—a few factories, or maybe ships in the harbour. And looking north, I saw a glow in the sky, a glow of the Northern Lights—they call it that here, not the *aurora borealis*. It was like a fan of dim searchlights, of no particular colour. Russia —how little of it is to be seen from here! Just those two slender lines of forest, that forest stretching right on to Vologda and beyond, and on to the Pacific, and, in the west, on to Leningrad. It makes me sad to think I didn't see Leningrad; perhaps when I come back, but now it's too late.

What an odd adventure it was to get here! Life is full of unexpected things. Could anything be more unforeseen than shaking hands at Vologda with Frederick the Great?

But, first of all, about that last day in Moscow.

It was a succession of good-byes and see-you-soons. I went to the Stoleshnikov Lane again, and bought my daughter a *zaichik* coat made of fluffy white hare. "No children's sizes," the assistant said; "but take the smallest ladies' size. She'll grow up in time; or you could get it altered." To my male mind it seemed reasonable enough. Everything in the town looked normal. I walked down Gorki Street, the pride of Soviet Moscow; then along the Kuznetsky Mosst, past the modest apple-green wooden building of the Moscow Art Theatre. The bills outside announced *The Three Sisters* for October 12th. The stalls outside the second-hand bookshops were still doing a brisk trade. I bought for five roubles a novel by Valentin Katayev which I hadn't yet read. At the Nark I was given instructions about the next morning.

I dropped in at the National Café in the afternoon. There were many officers there, all looking very calm. I went to telephone, but was forestalled by a bearded old gentleman—very European-looking and whose face looked vaguely familiar to me. As he rang off, he said he had noticed me waiting, and apologized profusely for having taken the phone out of turn. Later, sitting with an army man at the table next to mine, I heard him ask the waitress for cigarettes, but as she had none I offered him one of mine, which he accepted after some protesting. From the conversation that followed I realized that he was the great Nemirovich-Danchenko, the head of the Moscow Art Theatre, whose bust and portraits I had seen in the foyer. At the National I also ran into that Portuguese or Brazilian or whatever he is. "Oh, please," he said, "when you get to London please find out something I've been trying to find out for months—*who won the Derby this year?* You remember I asked you last time, and you said you didn't know. But it shouldn't be difficult to find out in London. And—just another request—when you come back, would you bring me a box of cigars? And also, they make in England those *lovely* little badges of Scotch terriers or fox-terriers you can wear on your lapel. Could you bring me one of those?" "You mean on *your* lapel," I said, and promised to do my best.

No, decidedly, everything was strangely calm and normal in Moscow; though the battle was still raging round Vyazma and the Germans were crashing ahead, Moscow was not in that state of jitters—or anything like it—that I had seen in Paris for a whole month. The calm confidence on the faces of the soldiers and officers was the most striking thing of all.

There was no air-raid warning at night—the infernal German planes were much too busy at the front (poor Vyazma!). Maurice and I did the accounts, which I was to take with me to London. He also gave me a note to his old father and mother in London; he hadn't seen them for three years. Would I go and see them at Pinner and give them news of him? His wife and child were in America, and he hadn't seen them for over a year. I often wonder how much credit they really get from our public, these anonymous agency men who, year in, year out, do good, indispensable, but often uninteresting and certainly very tiring work, and who are often for years separated from their children, from the woman they love, from their parents and their friends at home? How often do they ever get any credit at all from the newspaper-readers, who imagine that all they read comes from "our own famous brilliant special correspondent," when half his story, or more, was sent by an agency man?[1]

"What do you think about Moscow, Maurice?" He reflected for a while. "I think it'll be all right. But—as I already told you in July—I think we are going to spend this winter on the Volga. Moscow will not be surrendered, but *we*, the foreign press, will be sent to Kazan, or maybe even farther away. But we'll be back here in the spring. I have a vague idea that arrangements are already being made to move the Nark's press department." "There'll be damn' all to do at Kazan," I said. "Yes, it'll be a bore. I think you are right to go to London just now."

The white hare coat filled up a good half of my suitcase, and, as I was flying, I wasn't going to take more than one suitcase. I decided to leave most of my things in Moscow. Then I went to bed, but gloomy, pessimistic thoughts kept me awake. What if Moscow were to fall, after all? What if the Germans were really to get away with it? Dietrich and Goebbels and the whole foul gang were boasting as they had never boasted before. Again I thought of Captain Dodonov and his Siberian soldiers, and the nurses in that field hospital; and of Colonel Kirilov and little Sasha. I could see him lying there, dead, with my "lucky" mirror still in the pocket of his greatcoat— till the Germans decided that so warm a coat was too good to be wasted on a corpse. The sufferings of the Russian people are equalled only by their bravery. I felt it would be all right in the end—but at what a price in Russian blood!

It was strange to spend that last night in that room—with

[1] This incorporation of agency copy in "own correspondent" copy is a practice from which, it must be said, a number of papers still refrain, notably the *Manchester Guardian.* This, I think, is only fair to the agency and sometimes, also, to the "own correspondent," for agencies, who have to work at top speed, are not always infallible.

those nondescript rows of books (including "pornographic" Trotsky), the three ikons, the lampshade of blue and yellow crepe paper, and the other lamp with the dragon-like stand—what an absurd collection of junk the dynasty of Reuter correspondents had assembled here!—and that insipid seascape in the large black frame; and the straight-backed wooden dining-room chairs, with their bogus "Russian peasant art" designs! Yet the thought that these absurd objects *might*—however unlikely that seemed—be sent as loot to Lotte (who would think them artistic) made me feel almost affectionate towards them. There was an uncanny stillness outside, except for the A.R.P. woman walking, from time to time, past the window. Perhaps it was the same rather morose, elderly woman with the black shawl to whom I had talked a few nights before, when I took Bella out for a walk, in the hope that I might be luckier than Bertha. "What do you call her," said the A.R.P. woman. "Bella? Belka? I've never seen anything look less like a *belka* (a squirrel)," she said, looking at the Thurber specimen. "Perhaps you've got squirrels like that abroad; you wouldn't find any like that in this country!" I remarked on Bella's large appetite and thought it was unfortunate at a time when it was getting hard to buy food. "Oh, there's still plenty of food in our country for everybody," she said, obviously disapproving of my remark. She was, I felt, rather on her guard when talking to a foreigner—and she knew from my passport that I was one (for she was on the House Committee).

That night, after talking to the woman, I had walked down the Khokhlovsky Lane; there was a full moon and the modern concrete houses and the dilapidated old church looked fantastic and beautiful in the moonlight. I had walked on, down several other old lanes, and reached a square with some old stucco buildings on one side, and a forest of church towers and domes on the other. Probably some old monastery. It also was floodlit by the moon and looked almost pale-blue. The streets were deserted except for the *dejurnye* (watchman), the A.R.P. people, and the fire-watchers.

At eight thirty the next morning the car came to fetch me, and after farewells to Lovell and Bertha, the little maid, I drove to the Embassy on the embankment opposite the Kremlin. The British members of the party, mostly naval men, were to start out from here. It was a cold, foggy morning, and the domes of the Kremlin were half-hidden in a greyish-white mist. I thought of Stalin, inside that Kremlin, and wondered what was in his mind at that moment. We then drove up the still fairly empty Gorki Street and up to the aerodrome. The visibility was very poor; but our Soviet airmen, after a brief consultation, decided to chance it. When would I see Moscow again? I wondered. In two or three months—if all went well; much later if it didn't go so well. But I knew I would see it again within a year. . . .

> Moskvá, kak mnógo v' étom zvúke
> Dla sértsa rússkovo slilós' . . .

"Moscow! how much that word means to every Russian heart!" I remembered how, in his *Patriotic Medley*, Yakovlev had recited these Pushkin lines on that sunny summer day in the Ermitage gardens; Moscow looked so cheerful then, with the young soldiers, and the girls in their white summer clothes, sitting in the sun. But now, as one looked back from the plane, Moscow was hidden in a mist. The men at the aerodrome looked tiny. For a while we flew over the suburbs of Moscow, and then over some of the *datchnye mesta*, with the now uninhabited bungalows standing there among their pine trees, deserted for the winter. In the spring—but next spring seemed so infinitely far away. And then we flew over several villages. The trees were red and yellow, but the grass was still almost green. As we crossed the Volga, near Rybinsk, the weather seemed to improve. We were now flying over the great forest belt of northern Russia. As far as the eye could see, the earth was like an ocean of thousands and thousands of dark-green fir trees, with, here and there, a few bright yellow patches—these were the birch trees in their autumn colours. Gradually the colour of the landscape changed. Below us was no longer a dark-green ocean, but a vast white fluffy expanse of snow-covered fir trees, though again, here and there, with patches of brown and yellow. Sometimes we flew high above this white space, sometimes we almost skimmed the tree-tops. For a time we followed a railway line—the Archangel-Vologda railway, one of the few Russian channels for British aid. We crossed one or two wide rivers, still dark-blue between the snow-covered banks, and a timber camp, with narrow-gauge lines running deep into the endless forests. We were now within an hour of Archangel. And then, suddenly, we ran into a violent blizzard. From time to time the outline of the tree-tops could be seen leaping up and down, and then for several minutes we saw nothing but the whirling clouds of snow. The more experienced passengers on the plane were, I thought, beginning to look a little fidgety; and then one of the Russian crew came along and said that the weather had made it impossible to go on; a wireless message had just been received from Archangel saying that we were to turn back to Vologda. So we turned south again and, with remarkable skill, our Soviet pilot brought us down on Vologda aerodrome, after two more hours' flying.

I knew, of course, that Vologda was an important strategic point, the junction of the Archangel line and the Leningrad branch of the Trans-Siberian; that it was the most important town in this almost uninhabited part of Russia, and a former *gubernsky gorod*, the capital of a province. But I had no idea of what it actually looked like. This opportunity of spending a day in a provincial backwater in Soviet Russia made up for the delay in reaching Archangel. A day—if the weather improved; or perhaps longer. The party, composed of several

British naval men and a number of Red Army officers, and myself, waited at the aerodrome for some time. The snowstorm had not ceased. Eventually a dilapidated old bus came to collect us; the luggage was locked up in the plane, which made matters easier, for the bus was a very small one. We drove along a muddy, bumpy road. It was narrow, and several times we were held up by horse-carts which had got stuck in the mud. We passed the Kremlin of Vologda—a cluster of churches and Government buildings, surrounded by a high stone wall, with strange red and green circles painted on it. The place, somebody said, had been built by Ivan the Terrible. The people in the road were wearing all sorts of padded and fur coats, and the slashing snowstorm had given red cheeks to everybody.

We then drove down a long avenue lined with rather uniform wooden cottages, and rows of yellow-leaved birch trees. This was apparently the main street of Vologda—Chernyshevsky Street. The side-streets presented the same air of provincial, almost rural calm, though their names were all revolutionary: Herzen Street, and Marx Street, and so on. At length we reached the Vologda River, with quite an impressive embankment of well-built pretty little houses, and several Government buildings, and two churches, both with their crosses intact. There were steamers and barges on the river. We crossed one of the bridges and arrived in an old-fashioned square, in front of an old stucco building. It must have been the Governor's headquarters before the Revolution; now it was the local soviet. In front of it was a garden, with yellow birch trees and a statue of Lenin. We were conducted into a large refectory. Here we were given lunch—a very late lunch—by a pretty young waitress—a cheerful young thing, rustic and bonny, and with just a touch of carefully applied lipstick. There was, to all appearances, no food shortage at Vologda. Here were large hunks of black rye bread, and plenty of butter, and the salad was made of Vologda-grown tomatoes and cucumbers, and then came a partridge shot in the Vologda woods, and as a special delicacy we were served tinned walnuts floating in syrup. The Vologda beer was disappointing, though. Next to me sat a young Russian major, with a slightly English, rabbity mouth. He was a great sportsman, and had no end of stories to tell of how he would spend weeks in the forests round Vologda shooting not merely partridges and hares but big game—wolves and foxes. A Russian sees no disgrace in shooting foxes; but a real Russian sportsman, such as our major, would think it unsportsmanlike to shoot a bear. You attack a bear with a dagger; and the major gave us many details of how it is done. "Wait till the bear stands up on his hind legs and tries to hug you—that is the time. . . ." I forget how many bears he said he had killed.

After lunch we were conducted to our sleeping-quarters in another building, not far away. The place was comfortable, well-heated, and the lavatory alone was on the primitive side. I went for a stroll through the town. It was getting dark, and they were as strict about the black-out at Vologda as in Moscow. I did not want to lose my way in this strange town, and went back. From the river came the sound of ship sirens. The weather had improved, and there was a starry sky. When I got back, I learned that our party had been invited by the management of the local theatre to the evening performance. We learned that, in honour of the Allied guests, the management had decided to change their program and to perform an all-cast play instead of the play previously announced, with only five or six characters. At 7.30 we drove to the theatre, which turned out to be a large wooden building with seven hundred hard wooden seats. The proscenium was decorated with patriotic slogans, and to the right of the stage stood a large cannon. The play was called *The Keys of Berlin*, and was a historical play dealing with the entry of the Russian troops into Berlin in the Seven Years' War. There was something slightly grim and ironical about it all, with the Germans so close to Moscow; but nobody at the theatre seemed in the least worried about that. It was an enjoyable play; for it was acted with all the old tricks of melodrama. Here was Frederick the Great, with an enormous cardboard nose, strutting up and down the stage and bellowing cynical and villainous machiavellianisms in true Hitler fashion. Here was the dark French countess, Frederick's secret agent, who uttered sinister threats, and went off into peals of fiendish laughter. The hero was a young lieutenant of the Russian Army with a yellow moustache and wearing a moth-eaten Tsarist uniform. It was this Lieutenant Kartashov who, in the end, not only defeated the Germans, but also showed up his own colonel as a Fifth Columnist. And the heroine was the unhappy young daughter of the lady with the fiendish laughter; "*Mamotchka*," she kept calling her, in a baby voice, and laying her head on the villainess's lap, and trying to look like a kitten. "*Mamotchka, mamotchka*," she went on. One could not help rejoicing for gallant Kartashov when the Fifth Column colonel, as he was being shown up, fired his pistol at the damsel and shot her dead. The Russian soldiers in the play were all good fellows, full of peasant horse-sense, while the Prussian soldiers were half-wits and cowards but with a passion for looting, if it could be done with complete impunity.

In the intermission we were asked to meet the manager and the actors. We drank to Frederick the Great, and to the prosperity of Vologda's theatre, and to the Anglo-Russian alliance. Frederick the Great was an "Artist of Merit"—though not of the U.S.S.R., but only of the Karelian Republic. The company was the permanent Vologda company. It performed thirty or forty plays a year; and, as the manager proudly told me, all the scenery and costumes were made on the spot, from designs sent from Moscow. The theatre, he said, was nearly always crowded, and the seats were very inexpensive, the back rows costing only one rouble. He was the very type of the old-fashioned Russian actor, clean-shaven, with a flowing black tie and long white hair. I remarked that he looked very like

Stanislavsky. He was visibly pleased with my remark and said: "Ah, yes, dear old Constantine Mikhailovich. . . ." And our rabbit-mouth major was busy telling Frederick the Great with the cardboard nose more of his shooting and bear-stabbing stories. Unfortunately we were not presented to the actresses —I don't know why. I gathered that the theatre, though more or less paying its way, was State-subsidized.

We spent the second intermission in the foyer. Here was, in one corner, an enormous stuffed bear, holding a brass tray. The walls were decorated with posters and patriotic drawings and prints, chiefly relating to Alexander Nevsky and to 1812. The 1812 "exhibition" included good coloured reproductions of Verestchagin's paintings of the fire of Moscow and of the grizzly retreat of the Grande Armée. The exhibition cannot have been assembled on the spot and must have come from some central propaganda organization. The foyer was crowded with young soldiers and girls. Some of the girls were in uniform and nearly all were very pretty and with fresh complexions. They were a credit to the climate of Vologda.

I wish I had had a chance to see more of Vologda; but early the next morning we were told that the weather was reasonably good and that we had better start out as long as it lasted. A piercing cold wind was blowing from the north and the ground was frozen. Again we drove down Chernyshevsky Street, and past the Kremlin, with a few soldiers outside. The aeroplane engines took some time to warm up, but eventually we took off. It was a much clearer day. Below us were again those hundreds of miles of forest, dark-green at first, then increasingly white, with patches of yellow. Again we flew into a blizzard, but, as the pilot later confessed, he decided to ignore the warning that again came from Archangel, on the ground that he had not enough petrol to turn back. And then, after three hours' flying from Vologda, we swooped down in a half-circle, through the mist, over the roofs of Archangel and over the ships in the harbour, almost touching the topmast of one of them. Rain, snow, and sleet were slashing against the windows of the plane as we glided down to the airfield. It was a filthy day. "Well, we've done it," said the pilot, and laughed. "Felt just a little nervous during this last half-hour." "Certainly a slick piece of work," said one of our R.A.F. men, "finding an airfield in weather like this." "You are lucky getting here today," said the pilot. "In October there aren't usually more than eight flying days—if that—in this part of the world. But if we'd waited another hour at Vologda, we couldn't have done it." I could now afford the luxury of trying to visualize a forced landing in the middle of the Great Forest, hundreds of miles away from anywhere. At least, there would have been no mosquitoes at this time of year.

We went in a bus to a Russian naval club in Archangel itself, on the waterfront. There were many ships in the harbour, some of them British. Russian soldiers, officers, N.C.O.'s, naval marines, and sailors were eating at the canteen. There was plenty of vodka, and the pale smoked salmon, for which Archangel is famous, was delicious. A young Russian lieutenant, to whom I was introduced, showed once more how the youth of Russia is fascinated by the vast Arctic spaces of the Soviet Union. The summer before last he had spent two months in the Kola Peninsula. "I don't like big towns," he said; "give me wide-open spaces, and as uninhabited as possible. Nothing is better than the Kola Peninsula for that. These spaces give one a sense of freedom that nothing else does. I was there with a survey party belonging to the Red Army. We would walk thirty miles a day, across almost unexplored country. Hundreds of miles of tundra and woods and lakes; it's one of the most beautiful countries in the world—if you like the Arctic. Once we walked for over a week without seeing a single human being. It's glorious in summer-time, when the sun shines almost right through the night. Nature bursts suddenly into life

with a speed you've never seen anywhere. Lovely wild flowers;
and millions of birds and hares, and all sorts of animals." "And
mosquitoes?" I said. "Yes, mosquitoes, too, plenty of them.
We wore netting over our faces and round our hands. There
are bound to be mosquitoes, with all those marshes and lakes."
"Aren't you apt to get swallowed up in a marsh?" "No, you
follow the reindeer tracks and you are all right." He told me
more about the routes they had followed, crossing the interior
of the Kola Peninsula from north to south; but I forget the
details. He also told me about some of his other adventures,
his journey to the mouth of the Yenissey River in the great
Siberian Arctic, and how he had climbed to the summit of
Mount Elbrus in the Caucasus. "It's a wonderful country, our
Soviet Union," he said; "there isn't another country in the
world where there's so much to see, so much to learn, so much
still to develop, and so much to do." The lad—and there are
thousands of lads like him in the Soviet Union—had that spirit
of adventure, combined with a love of nature, which was that
of Papanin, and Otto Schmidt, and the men of the *Cheliuskin*.
Thousands of young Russians would like to roam about the
wild north of their country, and nowhere are explorers more
popular than in Russia today.

It was growing dark when we left the canteen, and it was
too late to go in search of the shop where they sell those enormous wolf and reindeer gloves—for eighty roubles a pair.
Some of our people who had come from Archangel to Moscow
were very proud of them. The gale was blowing more fiercely
than ever as we walked along the waterfront to the British
House. The ships in the harbour were tossed about in the gale,
and sometimes the spray would splash over the embankment.
One of the ships a mile or two across the harbour was signalling with green and red rockets. The cold wind was so fierce
that it was as hard to walk against it as it was to breathe, and
it made one's eyes water. The British House, though built of

wood—there is no lack of this building material at Archangel!
—was a fairly large building, newly painted and decorated
with somewhat eccentric wall-paper, probably the best that
Archangel could provide in a hurry. There were several bedrooms in the place, for the benefit of official visitors staying at
Archangel, or passing through it, and also a modern bathroom and lavatory. The rooms were well heated by large tiled
stoves and smelt pleasantly of timber. Most of the party were
staying at Archangel; but two naval men, who had done a job
of work in Russia, and I were told that we should be ready to
leave by nine thirty at night.

We had a pleasant cold supper, of Archangel-made sausage
and hard-boiled eggs, and a Russian cheddar-like cheese
(rather mild, though); and the domestic staff were Russian
girls, which was a pleasant change from the everlasting Volga
Germans one sees in almost all foreigners' houses in Moscow.

Through the slashing gale, in complete darkness, we drove
to somewhere in the harbour. At last we reached a ship moored
on the quayside; but in the darkness it was impossible to distinguish her outline, except that she was fairly small, probably
not more than 1,500 tons. She turned out to be a small ice-
breaker, or rather ice-cutter (which is not the same thing),
and we spent a pleasant evening with its skipper, Captain
Zamshin, and his two lieutenants, Korolkov and Semionov.
Captain Zamshin, a round little man, almost bald, and with a
white toothbrush moustache, was a native of Leningrad and
a naval engineer by training, and he was working in close
contact with the British at Archangel to increase the harbour's
capacity. One of the lieutenants was dark and lanky, and very
untalkative, while the other, a tiny little man, looking like a
Japanese, was full of fun and good stories and spoke tolerably
good English. Zamshin talked a great deal of how Archangel
would be kept open in winter; the place, he said, didn't really
freeze until December, and there were adequate ice-breaking
and ice-cutting ships to keep the harbour going all winter. . . .

The Russian middle-aged matronly W.R.E.N.—not in uniform, though—brought us glasses of hot tea and bread and butter, and we then taught the Russians draw poker, and the Russians taught us some other game, the name of which I forget.

*Moroz—Frost—*was the name of the ice-cutter, and her sister ships had equally appropriate names—*Snowstorm*, and *Tempest*, and *Snow*, and *Hurricane*. We went to sleep, as well as we could, on board the ice-cutter. In the lieutenants' cabin there were a few books—among them a cheap edition of Pushkin, and a translation of *Pickwick*. During the night we sailed; and when I went on deck in the morning, Archangel could no longer be seen. We were in the middle of a wide bay, with slender lines of forest on both sides; these two lines met in the south, at the mouth of the Dvina. The weather was grey, but it had become warmer, and the gale had abated. Only the gale had been such on the previous day that the convoy that had been expected in during the night had not yet appeared.

We spent the morning waiting for news. The sea was quite calm now; trawlers went by, and once we saw a Russian submarine. One or two patrolling planes zoomed overhead. And then in the grey distance in the north they began to appear, one little dark dot, and then two, and then three, and they grew larger and larger; and the convoy of British ships appeared, bringing to Russia the sorely needed weapons of war in her great struggle against Hitler. . . . One, two, three, four, then more and more; nearly all large ships, most of them camouflaged, and all flying the Union Jack. Glasgow, Newcastle, Bristol, and other ports of registration—names that mean docks and chimneys and blitz—could be read on the lifebuoys, and men of the British Merchant Fleet could be seen on the decks, silhouetted against the sky. And with them came the escorting vessels of the Royal Navy. . . . "*Krasota!*—lovely!" Captain Zamshin exclaimed. . . .

The ships sailed on softly towards Archangel, again turning into little black dots. Only one of the escorting vessels [1] anchored quite near the *Moroz*. And so here I am, in this little British oasis, in the middle of the White Sea. Little Lieutenant Korolkov came on board with us, to discuss some naval matters concerning the convoy. But we said good-bye to Captain Zamshin and his other, silent lieutenant. . . . There are large portraits of the King and Queen in the wardroom, and no longer Stalin and Kalinin. But even at night the thin, slender lines of the Russian forests are still there, faintly visible, separating the dark sea from the dark sky, streaked with the searchlights of the aurora borealis. . . .

LONDON, *November 4*

It is strange to be back in England. Two days ago I was still on the high seas. What fine, lovable people they are, these men of the Royal Navy! Here is something with a great tradition that no other service has—a tradition that has a deep effect on the men's character. Without that tradition, without that character of the men on British ships, we might never win this war. They are deeply conscious of their great role in this war, but I have heard no word of *parvenu* boasting from anybody. If anything, there is a tendency to joke about things: "Of course, the Navy has done better than the Army," Commander Z said jokingly one night. "But it's because the Huns haven't got a navy. Even so," he said after a moment's reflection, "I liked the life in the Navy much better in the last war. Now it's becoming too damned *professional!* It's becoming almost a dangerous job, not for a chap like me, who likes a quiet life." I knew he was one of the bravest men on all the Seven Seas. He had been in Japan, and knew more about the Japs than anybody I had ever met; "tough and treacherous

---

[1] I wish I could write more freely of this gallant ship of the Royal Navy, of its remarkable war-time record, and of the officers and men in whose company I spent seventeen happy and thrilling days. But that must be left till after the war.

little bastards," he called them. In his cabin, the ship's surgeon spent his spare time painting nostalgic little watercolours of his cottage in Sussex; they were rather indifferent, but the tweeds he wove on a hand-loom were very beautiful. And Lieutenant-Commander X—a Highlander, with a dry wit but a gentle heart—spent his spare time (not that he had much) writing fairy-tales for the surgeon's two little daughters. One of the tales was called *The Jet-Black Beetle*. He typed them, and tied the margins with blue ribbon.

This ship had seen things since the war began. These men had been "at it" since September 3rd, 1939, almost without respite. Five or six months ago they had had a week's leave in Scotland, and they were still talking about those days at Greenock and Glasgow. They had spent nearly all the year in northern waters, and had seen no summer—"plenty of sun, but no heat." I didn't think their winter clothes were quite warm enough, if they were going to sail in the Arctic through the winter, as everything suggested they would. Many of the men tried on my dog-coat, and thought it was an improvement on their winter clothes.

Royal Navy, Merchant Fleet; it will be their great job, added to all their other great jobs, to keep the war supplies going to Archangel, and to fulfil the promises made to Stalin by Lord Beaverbrook.

It took a long time to get back; much longer than I had expected. For one thing, we lay anchored off Archangel for over a week before we sailed. The weather was variable; warm and sunny one day, and heavy snow the next. And then, one evening, the word went round that we were to sail at nightfall. That night the sea was calm and there were strange northern lights in the sky. It was like a gigantic white rainbow, each end of which touched the horizon. Were we to sail through this great arch? Commander Z came up on deck. "You'd better put on your lifebelt. It's the rule. It's tricky, this bottleneck of the White Sea. They torpedoed a Russian ship there, just the other night. Not that a lifebelt will do you much good, really," he laughed. "Three minutes in this water would be enough to change your sex!"

And then the days moved on, in quick succession. I got to know the officers and the men, and felt as if I had known them for years. No people like human company more than do the men in the Navy. They live an artificial life, but a noble one, without meanness and without many petty personal rivalries. And their standard of intelligence, culture, and understanding, and their human sensibility, are very high. For a week we followed a strange zigzag course. There were adventures on the way, but I cannot go into details, except that I saw these men in moments of danger. There was no false bravado in their conduct, but they took it all calmly, and often with a good deal of humour. On one of those "dangerous" nights, I went into the surgeon's cabin. "Aren't you painting or weaving?" "No," he said, "I somehow haven't got the *inspiration* tonight." He seemed a trifle depressed as he looked at one of the blue-skied watercolours of his Sussex cottage.

We sailed for a week about the Arctic. Is the Arctic monotonous? Not if you spend there a sufficiently long time. The water is not a monotonous blue; it is ever-changing—jade-green one day, and then white, and then grey, and sometimes bright blue; and there are wonderful sunsets over the Arctic, and the combinations of mist and snowstorms and sunshine are infinite in their variety. The nights are lit up by the aurora borealis. I saw the Arctic in fair weather and in a gale the like of which I had never seen. It was glorious, this tumultuous infinity of water stretching on the starboard side towards the North Pole, not so far away, and on the port side towards the South Pole, all the way down the globe, past the tormented world of 1941—a world that seemed very far away in this wild tempest, which was calm and serene and pure in comparison.

And then one afternoon I saw miles and miles of cliffs and

mountains rising out of the ocean. They were wrapped in a purple mist. The high coastline stretched as far as the eye could see. Iceland. . . .

I had imagined Iceland to look quite different, flat and green. It was like Norway; large, barren mountains forming a wild rugged coast. We spent a day in an Icelandic town on the banks of the calm clear waters of a fjord. There were British soldiers there, and a church and three shops and many corrugated-iron huts; the Icelanders were non-committal, the girls not unusually beautiful—not very different from girls in Manchester or Glasgow—and the shopkeepers were sticky and a little troublesome, and spoke perhaps deliberately poor English. They wouldn't accept pound notes, and insisted on being paid in silver for their tins of cod roe and of Lyle's Golden Syrup, and for their British-made silk stockings, and the British-made art-silk handkerchiefs with "Iceland 1941" printed on them in golden paint, which sailors bought as presents and souvenirs. They had no black-out in Iceland; it was the first unblacked-out town I had seen since September 1939. When I went on deck at eight thirty the next morning it was still as dark as though it were five o'clock, and the lights in the town were burning, reflected in the clear, still waters of the fjord. . . .

And then the homeward voyage began.

London. . . . How strange to be here again! The sky is not what it was that morning when I left for Moscow. But the buses are running down Fleet Street, and the wreckage of the Temple and of Serjeant's Inn has been turned into a tidy waste, and where the remains of houses stood there are now deep water-tanks—for blitzes that may never come.

On this first day I went for a stroll round the back of St. Paul's, and up Aldersgate. The wreckage of the burned houses has all been neatly tidied up. I was sorry to see, though, that St. Giles, Cripplegate, which had received the very first bomb that fell on the City of London, had since been almost completely destroyed by fire. I did not know it had happened. I remember how that morning, after the first bomb, Milton lay among the autumn leaves, knocked off his pedestal by the blast. And now, through the windows of the burned-out church, the evening sky was showing, as it showed that night through the burned-out houses of Dorogobuzh. . . .

PART VI

Looking Back— and Forward

In a proclamation that is little short of hysterical, Hitler has announced his decision to become Commander-in-Chief of the German Army. He called upon German soldiers to stand firm; and to be an example to "our loyal Allies"— who are, apparently, not sticking it too well. The Finns are becoming greatly alarmed at the thought that they have backed the wrong horse. To reassure them, the Germans are telling them that their troops in Finland will not be withdrawn. God Almighty and "intuition" have prompted the Führer to sack von Brauchitsch, who failed to fulfil Hitler's reckless, boastful promises of October 2nd.

Referring to his plans for surrounding and capturing Moscow, Leningrad, and the Donetz Basin, Hitler, in an order to his soldiers on the eastern front, stated that day:

"In a few weeks the three greatest industrial districts of the Bolsheviks will be completely in our hands. At last we have created the prerequisites for the final, tremendous blow which, before the onset of winter, will lead to the destruction of the enemy. All preparations, as far as it has been possible to make them effective, have already been completed. This time preparations have been made systematically, step by step, to bring the enemy to a condition in which we are now able to inflict on him the mortal blow. Today begins the final large and decisive battle of this year."

A few hours later, on October 3rd, Hitler personally told his soldiers, in a speech at the opening of the Winter Help campaign:

"Forty-eight hours ago there began new operations of gigantic dimensions. They will lead to the destruction of the enemy in the east. The enemy has already been routed and will never regain his strength."

Still more definite were the statements made on this subject by Dietrich, Hitler's Press Chief. In his speech on October 9th, 1941, he stated:

"Gentlemen, everything which must fall by the decision of the German military command will fall. The new successes of German arms indicate the final military settlement of the eastern campaign. In a military sense, Soviet Russia has been vanquished. You cannot reproach me with ever having informed you wrongly. Thus today also, with my good name, I guarantee the accuracy of this announcement."

Hitler's order to his soldiers, issued in the middle of November 1941, stated: "In view of the importance of the events which are now developing, particularly in view of the equipment of the army operating in winter conditions, I order that the capital, Moscow, be taken at all costs in the near future."

Having concentrated all their main forces in man-power, masses of arms, thousands of tanks, planes, guns, enormous quantities of ammunition, and many thousands of lorries on the eastern front, the Germans planned in a few days, at the most a week, to break through to Moscow in one desperate fling, to encircle and capture the city.

The soldiers were told: "When you take Moscow you will get your winter quarters and enormous quantities of Soviet property for yourself. You will be given leave, peace, and an end to the war."

And now Goebbels, in a desperate appeal for winter clothing, has had to declare that "millions of our soldiers, after a year of the hardest fighting, *are facing an enemy far superior in numbers and material.*"

Neither Moscow, Leningrad, nor the Donetz Basin is in German hands. The self-confident, arrogant troops of Nazi Germany are retreating from Moscow, from Tikhvin, from Taganrog—almost all along the front. It is not yet a rout comparable to that of the Grande Armée, but it is the greatest defeat Hitler's "invincible" army has yet suffered. Klin, Kalinin, and the Tula region have been evacuated. In the process the Huns, of course, destroyed Yasnaya Polyana, the home of Tolstoy, and the New Jerusalem monastery near Istra. . . .

Yet for nearly two months the fate of Moscow was in the balance. Stalin, and many others, did not believe to the last that it would fall; though there were days when the Germans already boasted of being able to see "the domes of the Kremlin through a pair of good field-glasses." So near, and yet so far.

The Russian victory of Moscow is the greatest anti-German victory in this war; *perhaps*—I say deliberately no more than *perhaps*—it is the beginning of Hitler's end. There is a note of hysteria in Hitler's proclamation appointing himself Commander-in-Chief. He is trying to reassure the Germans that Japan will greatly strengthen the Axis. But every German reading these words cannot help being reminded that the entry of Japan into the war has also brought the United States into it. Hong Kong and Malaya are all very well; but on the other side of the balance-sheet there is the infinite industrial potential of belligerent in spite of herself, but perhaps all-the-more-so-belligerent, America.

The Germans are freezing to death in the vast snowy spaces of northern and central Russia. Trainloads of Germans, with frostbitten hands and ears and toes and noses, are being transported to the hospitals at Warsaw. A pretty spectacle for the Poles to see! *Heil Hitler. . . .*

Ersatz clothing has not stood up to the Russian winter. Perhaps the Royal Navy deserves some credit for that; but for its blockade during these two years the Germans might have had plenty of wool with which to clothe their "millions of troops." And no wonder the German prisoners captured by the Russians are whining and whining about having been let down by the Führer. Gone are the days of the jolly rape and vodka orgies in the occupied towns of White Russia and the Ukraine. . . .

I can see the Russians rejoicing over the present torments of these evil animals. The Führer "appreciates the sufferings of his soldiers"; did he ever try to appreciate the sufferings of the Russian people, of the Russian soldiers, of the millions of Europeans starved and hounded by his obscene Gestapo? The people of heroic Leningrad and Sebastopol are still suffering, thanks to Herr Hitler's ambitions. The old blind woman of Ustinovka is still mad—if she hasn't died of hunger and cold since the Germans recaptured that village in October. . . . But the Germans battered for two months against the defences of Moscow, and exhausted themselves; and the Russians, in the meantime, brought up reserves of fresh, hardened troops, and the German retreat began. 1812—but with a difference. One must face realities.

When I read through the diary, the gist of which was written during those four months in Moscow, I sometimes wonder how I managed never to lose faith in Russia's ultimate victory. Was it the sight of the Russian people, and the feeling of their own profound confidence? For the news, during those first four months of the war, was—taken as a whole—almost invariably bad.

The first two months were perhaps the least alarming. The

Russians were suffering heavy losses—losses in men, equipment, and territory. In the first few weeks territory equal to the whole of France had been overrun.

Eastern Poland, Lithuania, Latvia, and parts of Estonia and White Russia were lost in no time. The surprise attack of June 22nd had cost the Russians perhaps a thousand planes. Soon after, the Germans already claimed that the Russian Air Force had been wiped out. And yet—more planes, more tanks, more pilots, more tank-crews, more guns kept turning up from somewhere; from the reserves of the Red Army— reserves the extent of which Hitler had completely miscalculated—and from the industries of the Urals, from Moscow, Bryansk, Leningrad, and the Ukraine.

During those first two months Russia suffered enormous losses in men and equipment, but not in industrial power. Not a single vital industrial centre had been captured. Hitler hoped in July to half-finish-off the Russians by seizing Moscow. On July 13th the Germans were scheduled to enter the capital. But—for the first time since the German *Blitzkrieg* had been let loose over unhappy Europe, the German armadas of tanks and dive-bombers were stopped. Stopped by Russian tanks and guns and the "Stalin Hawks" and the incomparable Russian infantry, which, unlike the German infantry, is ready to put its heart into the battle even when not screened by tanks and sheltered by dive-bombers. It was easy for the Germans in Belgium and France, where no strong stand was taken anywhere by the enemy. Smolensk was the biggest set-back the Germans had yet suffered. They had hoped to capture Moscow and "virtually" end the war, by splitting the Russian forces into three or four sections and finishing each of them off separately. For there is no doubt that the Germans had an advantage over the Russians in one important respect: mobility. Their army was more highly mechanized than the Russian, and the organization of railway transport had been worked out to the finest point. The 100,000 engineers and workers of

the Todt organization, to which must be added the forced
labour squads recruited on the spot, were the most valuable
auxiliary to the army, and increased its mobility to an alarming extent. The speed with which the German sappers changed
the gauge of the Russian railways to fit their own rolling-
stock was astonishing; and it accounts, more perhaps than
anything else, for the speed at which the Germans were able
to maintain their advance across the Ukraine in August and
September. It was these German sapper units who also gave
the German Army such invaluable help in the enormously difficult task of crossing wide rivers like the Dnieper.

August and September: Moscow was no longer in danger;
but, on the whole, the war news during those two months was
much darker than during the first six weeks. The Germans
swept across the Ukraine. They were no longer capturing
territories recently re-annexed by the Russians, but were sap-
ping the life-blood of Russia. The fall of Kiev, "the mother of
Russian towns," after a heroic resistance of six weeks, was a
bitter blow to every Russian. The Ukrainian sugar-beet country, producing sixty per cent of Russia's sugar, went. The
richest wheat-growing areas went. And then the rich industrial
areas inside the Dnieper bend were lost, and sweeping on, almost irresistibly, the Germans crossed the Dnieper, penetrated
into the Donbass, occupied the Crimea, captured the great
industrial city of Kharkov, and occupied Rostov. Like Kiev,
Odessa held out for many weeks, but was finally lost. It had
acted as a temporary "Tobruk"; its defenders had badly
mauled the wretched Rumanians; but in the end Odessa was
abandoned and many of its troops moved to Sebastopol. The
Ukrainian campaign had clearly demonstrated German superiority in equipment in that part of the front. The loss of the
Perekop isthmus was, on the face of it, the defeat of a Russian
army that held particularly favourable positions. And yet the
loss of the Crimea, which took some time, was perhaps, to the
Russians, a blessing in disguise. Had the Germans by-passed

the Crimea and pushed straight beyond Rostov into the Kuban area and the Caucasus, before the Russians were ready to prepare their brilliant counter-offensive at Rostov under a new leader, Marshal Timoshenko, the prospects in the south might be much blacker today than they are. Now Baku, with that oil which is perhaps indispensable to Hitler if he proposes another vast campaign in 1942, is very far away from the greedy German reach.

In the north, in August and September, the outlook was almost equally grim. The Germans almost reached the outskirts of Leningrad, and the Baltic Fleet was in danger of being trapped. If Leningrad fell—and yet, in Moscow, one *somehow* had a feeling that it would not—immense new German forces would have become available for the central and southern fronts. Indirectly, the super-Tobruk of Leningrad perhaps saved Moscow and the Caucasus. The defence of Leningrad, and the timely Russian counter-offensive against Rostov, prevented Hitler from doing, as he always prefers to do, "one thing at a time"; that is, concentrating virtually the whole German Army against Moscow. Russia also proved that she was capable of a respectable degree of mobility, despite appallingly difficult conditions such as the severance by German advance units of some of Russia's most vital railway communications. At one time Moscow had only three main lines left at its disposal; the lines to Leningrad were cut, and, worse still, the line from Rostov. The Russian transport system, which foreign experts prophesied would fall to pieces in no time under the strain of war, did not fall to pieces even after six months.

The loss of the greater part of the Ukraine, of the Crimea, and of the great industrial city of Bryansk are severe blows which will continue to affect Russia's war potential. It is true that, contrary to popular belief, Russia does not "depend" on the Ukraine for its food. The Ukraine produces 60 per cent of the sugar of the U.S.S.R., but only 23 per cent of its grain, and, with a population representing one-fifth of the total population of the Soviet Union, the Ukraine has only a small surplus. The great grain-producing areas have spread far east, to the Kuban, the Volga, Siberia, and Central Asia. The most severe losses in the Ukraine and the Crimea and the parts of central Russia overrun by the Germans are the industrial losses: Krivoi Rog, Dniepropetrovsk, Kharkov, Bryansk, and many other centres. The Russian claim to have moved a large number of the plants to the Urals, where, in anticipation of an invasion, the Soviet Government had already built up an enormous industry representing 30 per cent of the Soviet Union's total output, is one of the most satisfactory features of the present situation, and another tribute to the efficiency of Russia's transport system. For the transportation of one important plant necessitated, according to the Soviet press, no fewer than 7,000 railway trucks. Parts of the industry of Moscow and of other areas threatened by the "final" German drive in October and November, have also been moved east. Russian industry thus still represents a formidable factor; and it is particularly heartening to know that the production of aircraft has been affected comparatively little by the spectacular industrial "migration" of this autumn. But it will take time before Russian industry is working at full strength again; it is not likely to do so before the spring; and though Hitler's armies are today retreating through the Russian snow, frozen and demoralized, Germany's industrial capacity is far greater than Russia's and there is reason to believe that Hitler will put every remaining ounce of Germany's energy into a new attack on Russia in the spring.

Russia is fighting the most crucial battle against the only Axis partner who counts. When Germany is beaten, neither Italy nor Japan will matter for another day. Japan's greatest contribution to the German war effort was her closing of Vladivostok to American supplies. America must find other ways and means of sending tanks and planes to Russia.

Germany is Enemy Number One just as much to America as she is to Britain and Russia. Another German failure to achieve victory in Russia will mean the end of the war, maybe in six months, maybe in a year, as Stalin said, in his realistic speech of November 6th. If, in spite of everything, Russia were defeated in 1942, Hitler would still have a great chance of winning the war. The only thing that could then prevent his victory would be the landing on the Continent of a vast Anglo-American Expeditionary Force. It may save Britain and America two or three or five years of war and millions of lives if they help the Russians to win the land war against Germany in 1942. It is unhealthy to hear the Russians say, as Yaroslavsky has already said, that "the people of the Soviet Union have been fighting the German war machine for five and a half months, without any foreign aid whatsoever." . . .

It is not quite true; but it reflects a certain Russian feeling of impatience which will go on growing if we arc not careful. . . . In addition to sending direct aid to Russia on the largest possible scale, we should, at least pending an invasion of the Continent from the west, keep the German coastline in the west in a constant state of alert.

As for Japan, the Russians have, for the present, enough on their hands. They—and we, for that matter—would gain little from a Russian declaration of war on Japan, unless the valuable Siberian bases against Japan could be used, not by the relatively small Russian Far-Eastern Air Force there, but by a formidable armada of American bombers. Germany is the real enemy; and there is no point in bombing Tokyo unless it can be bombed out of existence.

Russia has made more sacrifices, in her fight against Hitler, than any other nation. She has sacrificed not only the lives of countless soldiers; in her determination to defeat Germany, she has sacrificed the lives of many civilians. The "scorched-earth" policy that Stalin proclaimed in his speech of July 3rd is a ruthlessly heroic policy. It has meant not only the destruction of things like the Dnieper Dam, the fruit of ten years of concentrated labour, and one of the proudest achievements of present-day Russia; it has also meant the destruction, as far as possible, of the existing crops and food reserves and fuel dumps, lest they fall into the enemy's hands. The population left behind are, consequently, condemned to months, possibly years, of hardship, and even famine. It was a bitter sacrifice which the Russian Government found it necessary to make. No doubt hidden stores in the villages will keep most of the rural population alive until the hour of liberation; but in the German-controlled towns the situation is tragic. The Russian Government, taking a long view of the war, also took the ruthlessly heroic measure of preventing the Ukraine from growing food next year, and so strengthening Germany's war capacity, by removing the tractors from the Ukraine. Many a time I saw hundreds of them travel down the streets of Moscow. By reverting to primitive methods of cultivation, the Ukrainian peasants may be able to grow just enough to keep themselves alive; and they will probably not be unduly disturbed by the German troops, who prefer not to depart from the well-guarded main roads of occupied Russia. But, in any case, even if they had the tractors, the Germans could scarcely afford to spend any of their precious petrol on Ukrainian agriculture.

Russia's policy of sacrifices was described by the Germans as "devilish." They have to bring almost everything from their distant bases to keep their armies alive.

How unlike France, where the newly arrived German tanks could refill at any village petrol-pump, and where the soldiers could gorge themselves on French food! But this policy also has its fearful repercussions on the local population which has remained behind.

And what fearful sacrifices are yet in store in 1942? . . .

JANUARY 7, 1942

What can I say, at this stage, of the future of Anglo-Russian relations—a subject to which, as my diary shows, I gave much thought while I was in Moscow? Perhaps it will have been noticed how, in the course of those months, the whole attitude of the Russians to Britain and to British people in Moscow changed for the better, and how the distrust that at first existed on both sides gradually vanished.

There had been years of tension between Britain and Russia; and it would be tragic if, after the present brotherhood in arms, new conflicts were to arise between the two nations, which have every reason to like each other, and to pool their energies in the post-war effort to make the world safe for constructive peace and prosperity.

There is already a serious psychological basis for fruitful Anglo-Russian co-operation after the war: and that is the mutual admiration and esteem existing between the British and the Russian people. When I returned to London I found it was perfectly true that the "common" British people (as distinct from some of the "uncommon" ones) were, as somebody put it, "madly in love with Russia." I remember one night coming home in a taxi. It was a clear, starry night. "They wouldn't have left us alone a year ago, on a night like this," I remarked. "I am *afraid*," said the taxi-driver, "that we are not going to get any blitz again. It's the Russians who are getting it. We should be busy knocking hell out of Berlin every night; and not a damned thing is being done. It's just a racket," he said angrily, "a racket from left to right!"

The old boy was unjust; but how was he to know that, on that very night, the R.A.F. were going to lose thirty-eight planes over Germany? They hadn't been over Germany for many nights. But I could understand his feelings. He knew that Rostov was getting it instead of Peckham, and Moscow instead of Bermondsey, and Leningrad instead of Liverpool.

And he felt that we ought to go on provoking the Germans till they withdrew some of their planes from the Russian front. . . .

The Russian people, for their part, also began, after a while, to realize what the people of Britain had done in those two years of the war when little or nothing was told them by their press and radio about England's war effort. In Moscow I was not merely allowed, but asked, to write in the Soviet press about Churchill England. It was something new to the Russian people. Few Britons know many Russians, and even fewer Russians know many Englishmen. There is the language bar; there were the years of mutual isolationism. And yet, as Sir Bernard Pares has so rightly pointed out in his valuable and deservedly popular little book on Russia, the British people have perhaps closer mental, intellectual, and emotional affinities with the Russian—and, I might add, Slav people generally—than with either the Germans or the Latins. As Sir Bernard shrewdly remarks, there is one extremely important point of similarity between the British and the Russian minds—their sense of humour—usually the humour of understatement. The gentle humour of Chekhov, the grim humour of Dostoevsky, the pungent and often fantastic humour of Gogol, are all supremely understandable to the British mind. My own feeling has always been that English translators of Russian books might have made them even more popular if they had tried to be more idiomatic (and Russian idiom is perfectly translatable if you have a sufficient command of English idiom), and if they had simplified those Russian names and patronymics which inevitably give an exotic air to perfectly ordinary Russian people. Russian human reactions are very like English human reactions; and Russian sensibility like English sensibility. I have always found it highly significant that Tchaikovsky, who best expressed the "ordinary" Russian emotions, should be so popular in England, and so unpopular in France and Germany. "*Stinkende*

russische Musik" was Hans von Bülow's description of Tchaikovsky's Violin Concerto.

The "mystic" Slav soul. . . . I suppose there is such a
thing. They have their introspective, "morbid" writers in
Russia as you have them in England. They have their tormented truth-hunting Dostoevsky; but they also have their
serene, Mozart-like Pushkin. They also have ordinary people,
reacting in the ordinary human way towards love, country,
and the trivialities of life. "Mysticism" is, in fact, about as
uncommon in Russia as anywhere else. I like the Russian nonsense rhyme, which, I think, has quite a profound inner meaning—

> Vy místik;
> Znáchit vy igráete v' vístik. . . .

(You're a mystic; all right, then, come and join us for a
game of whist.)

This nonsense rhyme, it seems to me, largely disposes of the
mystical-mysterious-incalculable-Slav gibberish in which so
many still believe. Just the other day I came across a new little
book by Walter Duranty, who, with the air of a conjuror
producing a rabbit out of a top-hat, wrote: "The Russian
character. . . . How marked is their difference from us, and
how otherwise their minds work! Honestly, it really is right,
this, and I really am showing you Russia, far better than if I
wrote ten thick books of facts and statistics."

It's just no use arguing with anyone who has made up his
mind that the Russians are strange animals. Has any one of
the persons I have mentioned in my diary, for instance, anything very mysterious about him? Or, to rise to a higher level,
has any character in any Russian book—I leave out Dostoevsky, who is as special a case as, say, James Joyce or D. H.
Lawrence; that is, not a realist but a symbolist—or play or
film struck you as mysterious or incomprehensible? Is the
heroism of the Russian soldiers today incomprehensible? If

in any doubt, read the Battle of Schoengraben in *War and Peace*.

What I am trying to drive at is that there is really no human, temperamental obstacle in the way of Anglo-Russian co-operation after the war. This is very important, for, all being well, Britain and Russia will inevitably be the two powers which will have a decisive role to play in the future reconstruction of Europe. Churchillian England and Stalin's Russia are determined that there shall be retribution for Germany's crimes. The whole Slav world is with them there; and there will be trouble if, at the end of the war, England were to produce a leader speaking like the gentleman in a dinner-jacket I met at the Dorchester the other night: "If the Russians and Poles and the rest of them start a vendetta against the Germans, this country will just not stand for it; and we shall find ourselves, on Germany's side, at war with the Russians and Poles and Yugoslavs and Czechs." Nathaniel Gubbins is quite right, in his *Party Conversation*: "As long as we haven't been invaded ourselves, there will always be some people here to think the Germans are really nice people."

The Germans are not nice people; the Germans are bloody people, and the Russians know it better than anyone else from direct experience, and also from intercepted letters, like that of Lotte, which I quoted in my diary. Retribution: the Russians have given an indication of what they mean by it: the extermination of the S.S. and the Gestapo, and of other Germans directly responsible for all the Nazi abominations. The crimes of *the German Army*, which are more and more identified in the Russian mind with the crimes of the Nazis, are significantly emphasized by Molotov in his note to the non-Axis Powers of January 6th. The Russian people "will not forgive," it says. And let no gentlemen from the Dorchester interfere. . . . As for Lotte, she may deem herself lucky if nothing worse happens to her than a strict and long-term application of Article 8 of the Atlantic Charter, which will teach her that, in matters of armaments, Germany is not fit to rank as the equal of other powers.

Perhaps long years of education and "conditioning" and at least a brief experience of the horrors of war on German soil will teach the Germans that it will be in their interests to be "good Germans," and not to start their Third World War....

Russia, at the end of this war, will be a tired, devastated country. She will, more than ever, be concerned with rebuilding her towns and industries, and creating real prosperity for the Russian people. It may take her twenty-five or thirty years before such prosperity is attained—prosperity greater than anything she has yet achieved. She will not be interested in world revolution; she hasn't been for years. But she will want security. And nothing should suit England better than if, after the fiasco of the French guarantee to Czechoslovakia and of the British guarantees to Poland and Rumania, Russia took care of the security of eastern Europe. With this war, the bonds of friendship have grown among all the Slav peoples. The smaller Slav peoples, while maintaining their national independence, will enter a large security bloc based on Russia. In the west, there can be another security bloc, based on England and a resurrected France, and closely co-operating with the eastern bloc. After a long period of mental convalescence, perhaps Germany also will become a reasonable member of the European community. But no premature risks must be taken, and Article 8 of the Atlantic Charter must remain in force until the Slavs are satisfied—for they know Germany better than anyone else—that a new arrangement may be reasonably made. And no one must be guided by the externals of Germany's régime—whatever régime she may adopt. The Nazi poison lies so deep in the German soul that no "fall of Hitler" can be taken at its face value. It might be nothing more than a subterfuge, engineered by the equally criminal German Army leaders, and with full Nazi approval. Even the sudden establishment of a "Soviet Germany" or a "Democratic Germany" would be no reason for abandoning caution. It might only be a screen for a subsequent revival of Hitlerism, and a trick for avoiding Retribution. Such a sudden metamorphosis may mean nothing. The German Communists can no more be trusted than the Weimar Republic to cleanse the German soul of cruelty and militarist greed. Long years of "conditioning," following the bitter lesson that war does not pay, may alone cure Germany of Hitlerism. A whole young generation of Germans is poisoned by it. Give Germany economic prosperity; but not military equality. Make a Rotterdam of Berlin the moment the first German aeroplane is manufactured. *Giving up flying* is a small penalty which the German people must pay for the unparalleled catastrophe their criminal and adored leaders have brought on millions of fellow-Europeans.

With a *rapprochement* between Russia and Britain, Russia will, I am convinced, become increasingly democratic and European—the Russian people want to be both; *nekulturnyi* (uncivilized) is already the worst term of abuse in Russia—and they will want the full application of the Stalin Constitution as soon as peace conditions permit. In England we are steadily moving, in almost all directions, towards socialism in the wider sense of the word—towards a state of affairs in which the human spirit will be free, and the human body no longer exposed to the dangers of want and war.

Mr. Morrison, Mr. Bevin, and Mr. Eden, in his famous Mansion House speech, have given us a foretaste of that post-war Britain.

As for America—it is too early yet to assess her part in this war. It depends on the extent to which the Roosevelt spirit spreads—and lasts. If, after the war, America co-operates with Europe in every way, then the next hundred years may become the golden age of civilization, of the human race. If she sinks back into isolationism and selfish capitalism, then

Europe—that is, the European bloc comprising the western and eastern federations of independent states—will have to carry on alone. It will be more difficult. But with Britain and Russia as the pillars of this new Europe, it can be done. Only, all this would not mean much if in 1942 Russia were allowed to run short of equipment.